Praise for *The Art of Trape...*
Journey of Soaring, Surrende...

The Art of Trapeze reached number 1 in 2 separate
Amazon Kindle categories within 3 days!

*"Beautifully written, charmingly funny — even hilarious — and
remarkably open, honest, and down-to-earth. Ms. McCord has gifted
us with a pure example of how life can be such a beautiful, grand
adventure..."*
~ Starfield Press

*"The Art of Trapeze had me swinging through a swirl of spirit and
sisterhood. An intensely relatable read- down to earth, charming,
humorous, poignant, and infinitely wise - for those of us on the path
of self discovery and even those who just want a good story - you will
love this book!"*

~ **Sass Jordan,** Juno Award-winning Artist, *Canadian Idol*
Judge, Broadway actress

*"An inspiring memoir about a brave go-getter who makes things
happen! Molly guides us readers into the power of reemergence as
the shining jewels we really are."*

~ **Rosemary Sneeringer**, Literary Editor, Author,
TheBookNurturer.com

*"In many ways, Molly tells you how to be brutally honest with your
own soul and get on with your own life in an extremely courageous
way."*

~ **Rick DiClemente**, Author of The Exquisite Zodiac,
Intuitive Astrologer

THE ART OF

ONE WOMAN'S JOURNEY

OF SOARING,

SURRENDERING

AND

AWAKENING

Molly McCord

Spirituality University Press

The Art of Trapeze
One Woman's Journey of Soaring, Surrendering, and Awakening
by Molly McCord
Copyright © 2014 Spirituality University Press
All rights reserved.
www.SpiritualityUniversity.com

eISBN 978-0-9896045-0-5
Paperback ISBN 978-0-9896045-1-2

Cover design and interior formatting by Starfield Press
www.StarfieldPress.com

www.ConsciousCoolChic.com

CONTENTS

AUTHOR'S NOTE

WELCOME TO THE AWAKENING CONSCIOUSNESS SERIES, an unconventional book collection designed to connect you with your soul's evolution. The adventure begins here in *The Art of Trapeze*, the only memoir in the series, continues with *The Modern Heroine's Journey of Consciousness,* a spiritual resource and guidebook, and culminates with *The Unlimited Sparks of a Bonfire.* Unlike other series, each book is a different genre; yet collectively, the guiding messages lead you to a more conscious understanding of yourself as a soul in a human body. I hope you discover great value throughout this journey of consciousness.

Memoir is a re-creation and remembrance of actual events as experienced through one's personal perspective. This story is told through my own filter with a lens that reflects my interpretations of experiences, relationships, themes, and lessons. I referenced pictures, documents, journals, and personal collections whenever possible to recall specific details and information about each place and time in my life. Some people in the story reviewed and confirmed details, as well.

This personal story is now a permanent document in the public domain. As such, I have changed the names and some identifying features of some, but not all, people in the book to respectfully preserve anonymity. Events and people not pertaining to this specific journey were omitted. There are no composite characters or events. All words, feelings, flaws, and impressions are my own.

Namaste,

Molly McCord
June 2013

THE BIGGEST LAUNCH

THE SECRET TO JUMPING OFF a ridiculously high platform starts in the toes. All ten instinctively clench desperately to the cold steel slab's edge, insisting on a temporary delay until the timing is *just right*. Toes can be demanding and dramatic like that since they spend a whole lifetime rarely being seen and feel easily taken for granted. They tighten quickly and remain that way until I remember to give them adequate love; then they relaxed just enough to be my little supportive friends, but only until my focus goes somewhere else. Like over the front of this platform and into the grand abyss that fills the air in front of me. I squint my eyes to see something, anything out there, but nothing is in sight except a vast ocean of faint possibilities and foggy movements of distant clouds. All ten toes freeze up again.

So I turned my attention up, up, up to my fingers as they firmly grasped onto this tough wood bar that suddenly felt too weak. My chalked palms were satin and sticky, the perfect combination for touching this rung with commitment and agility. I loosened my wrists a bit and remembered to just let them hang, like limp noodles dangling from a slotted spoon. I tried not to blame the fingers for being tight since it was important that *they* gripped on well. It was most likely tension sent up directly from the toes as pleas of *Don't forget we need attention, too!*

A soft flurry of air tousled my long caramel hair that was held back in a ponytail; a loose strand escaped and inconveniently stuck itself to my glossed lips. The air was cooling and created goose bumps up my arms and down my spine. I could feel the tension gathering in my buttocks, unconsciously clenching and releasing to reaffirm control. I breathed in to loosen up my stomach muscles, or, more accurately the place where stomach muscles were supposed to be. (Blame the croissants.) My head briefly swayed in all directions on my neck like a bobble-head doll, twisting and moving to release any hidden tension.

Breathe.

Here I stood, once again prepared for a life-changing jump into the unknown. Breathe.

I had never been to Paris before. I did not have previous experiences of strolling along the Seine, or recollections of a romantic night in Montmartre, or a box of sepia-toned photos of myself standing in front of the Eiffel Tower in the sun, or Notre Dame in the rain, or even a still-life photo of a glorious *cafe au lait*. But in my typical brazen fashion, I was going out into the great unknown and moving to Paris. I knew I could make this incredible dream a reality. I could feel it as it pulled at my heartstrings and opened me up to a bigger life path. I barely spoke the language, I knew no one in the country, and I had no idea where I was going to live. But the details would come together once I arrived and got some grounding. Yes, definitely. Just breathe.

Everything was going to be amazing. Or it better be. Or I hoped it would be. Or it wouldn't be and this was going to fail and I'd fall again and…

Stop it. Breathe. Think happy thoughts. I turned my focus to how I had arrived at this life platform again and made this choice with my heart. I closed my eyes as the breeze kicked up my hair and my whole face started to smile, hair still stuck in glossy lips. It was four years ago when I had an unexpected date with my destiny.

I had moved back to Seattle after a year in Portland as a personal banker *(hated it, bored, tired of the sales goals and being nice to the obnoxious public)*. The hot, rented U-haul pulled into my mom's driveway the first week of September 2001. Within weeks, the economy crashed due to the horror in New York City; my stand-by job possibilities disappeared overnight. A few weeks were spent on the couch and then I went to a job placement agency out of desperation. The wide woman in a clingy red shirt reported that she did not have any suitable job interviews to send me on at that time, and my heart sank with silent terror. But after a quick reach to another side of her desk, she opened a different colored file and said she could offer me a position as a Career Counselor due to my experience at the bank. I said yes, and obediently followed the training and protocol *(hated it, bored, tired of the sales goals and being nice to the obnoxious public)*. The office became increasingly uncomfortable as I shared a cubicle farm with five manipulative women who were always out for the most placements, the highest numbers, the top managerial recognition. I could be that intense too, I reasoned; I just didn't see that daily routine as something worth fighting for.

After four months of *really giving it my all*, I sat down with the manager in a private conference room right before lunch on a Tuesday. "There are a lot of things I am good at, but this job is not one of them. I need to move on and today is my last day. Maybe we have a job in the job binder I could interview for?" Her eyes lit up with lusty dollar signs about the commission she could earn on my job placement.

On a Tuesday morning exactly one week later, I accepted a job as a Marketing Coordinator for a small company that imported French products. It also turned out to be the same day I was meeting with a psychic lady as a gift from a family member to help me find clarity about my life direction. I was nervous and skeptical about the appointment since I had no idea what to expect or how these things worked. I was open to anything though, and if nothing else, it would be a good laugh.

I thought I had the wrong address when I pulled into the driveway of an old farmhouse, no flashing neon light in sight. I arrived an embarrassing twenty minutes late due to bumper-to-horn traffic and hoped she would not cancel the appointment. Or maybe I secretly hoped she would.

I sat down at a long wood table inside her studio office, three candles glowing away. "What's on your mind? What's coming up for you right now, kiddo?" She lifted a cup of hot tea to her lips and waited.

My instinct was to hold back a bit as I watched her with sideways eyes, waiting for a magic pouf, or magic crystal ball, or the air to fill with smoke. I moved my feet around under the table. Nope, no fog machine.

"I'm trying to figure out my career situation. What should I do with my life?"

Saying the words out loud made my stomach turn a little with dread and excitement, feeling both vulnerable and fearless in the same sentence. I was open to what I needed to do with my life; I just had no idea what that single magical thing was, like it was hidden from me but maybe accessible to her. She shook her thick wavy chocolate hair, eyes staring straight ahead, and said, "I see you in France."

I blinked. That was the most random thing ever and certainly not the career advice I was looking for. My brow started to furrow as I tried to fit the idea into my head and it had no place to go. I had never even been to Europe before, the continent of. My exotic international travel thus far included trips to the glorious shopping mecca of Edmonton Mall in Alberta, Canada (*three Club Monaco stores in one place, this IS heaven!*), a few voyages north across the border into Vancouver, B.C. (as most Seattleites do), and a trip to Mazatlan once for spring break in college with a bunch of girlfriends. Oh gosh, I completely forgot, the funny story about going out to a beach club one night and dancing on top of the dirty wood table, the waves crashing twenty feet away, the music pounding, a packed dance floor, and… *me falling off the table* in front of everyone, high heels in the air, and...

Probably different cultural values in France.

"Huh," I replied, writing *live in France????* on my notepad. Then she asked if I had any connections to France, staring at me with a knowing expression and a slight smirk. My exhausted mind tried to fit some pieces together about who I knew that was French, or exotic, or maybe once brought me a souvenir from Paris. Anything, anyone?

"Oh wait. I started a new job today and they have a business connection to France." *Welcome to the topic, Molly.*

She lifted both eyebrows to the ceiling with a knowing smile. I stared at the notepad again. Me? In France? How in the world could that even happen? It sounded bizarre and unfeasible and yet incredibly awesome. I sat up straighter with intrigue and leaned in to the table, my necklace almost touching the wood surface.

"So, how do you see this fitting together? Me in France and all of… that?"

She shared the possible connections and ways things could unfold as I wrote feverishly, my brow still furrowed and overloaded with the information.

Then she paused and said, "You know, for only being 23, you have done a lot of personal development work that most women only start to look at in their forties."

I nodded silently, humbly, and wrote *a lot of self-work,* two stars. I absorbed the validation for the evenings I had spent sitting on my apartment floor figuring out which parts of myself I wanted to improve and which parts I adored. I had made lists of what I liked experiencing in relationships:

Weekend companionship

Holding hands without thinking about it

Sharing the TV couch comfortably

Trying new restaurants and ordering unpronounceable foods

Listening to all of my random thoughts

A continual collection of inside jokes

Someone else who will eat the leftovers so I don't feel guilty about throwing them away

Big feet and a big — (TO BE CONTINUED... red hearts);

I had another list going about what I wanted to experience on a daily basis: *Creativity, self-expression, supportive network, freedom to follow my energy and inspirations, financial stability, travel.* I felt a high every time I looked at this list with its bright, big letters. A smile would spread across my whole face and my body would start rocking a little.

As my conversation with this wise woman continued, I unexpectedly felt like this woman saw the hidden parts of me. Like my artistic talent that I let slip away years ago because I didn't think it was good enough for anyone to look at. Or the brief depression I went through in North Carolina and how it felt like a secret I could never, ever, *ever* reveal. Or the dissatisfaction I felt in Portland when I thought I should stay committed to a job I hated because it demonstrated that I was a real adult, making my way in the world, and therefore, it was important.

Maybe she saw all of this, maybe not. But something within me started to both relax and open up. I slowly softened in my three-inch heels to the emerging possibility that it was okay to share those parts of me: the messy, the flaws, the insecurities, the doubts. It could be safe. It could be okay. I wrote *Open up more*, three stars, on the side of the paper. Underlined.

In only forty minutes, my life became bigger as the tiny unconscious self-imposed walls I was living within fell to the ground. *I could actually do exciting things in my life,* and dream a little bigger, and push beyond conventional options. And she reaffirmed that yes, (*yes, yes, yes*) there was definitely a plan for my life. My feet were pulsing with energy under the table.

But even more uplifting than the possibilities about the future was that I felt for the first time in my life *someone saw me*. ME. The ME I couldn't even see because I was wrapped up in confusion about my life direction and paying off my school debt and trying to figure out my career and wondering if I was missing out on something or someone. She saw more of ME than I could have ever imagined, including the spiritual talents I could develop. I didn't even realize I had never been seen like this before. My last scribbles were *Trust* and *Guided to set up what I need*, two stars each.

Afterward, I flew to my mom's house, the tires on my truck barely touching the ground. We pulled two chairs up to the kitchen table and I spilled everything about the session, diligently reviewing each line on my notepad, every single doodle, and trying to recall more tidbits. She nodded with huge smiles and excitement, putting her hand to her heart at just the right times and *getting it.*

Two years later, as desire for a new adventure grew, I went to Europe for the first time by myself. I arrived at the airport covered in black because based on all the fashion magazines I flipped through, black was obviously the standard attire of the chic French at all times, everywhere, always, no exceptions. I was going to be an instant local in my head-to-toe *noir*, no doubt about it, and blend into the French Alps region effortlessly while I was there studying French for five weeks. Except it turned out people traveling and living across the Atlantic *also* own jeans and bright cardigans and cute tunics with fun patterns and comfortable shoes. Who are these magazine writers, anyway? I looked like a one-person funeral procession walking down the gateway. I tried to maintain a too-cool-for-school vibe, but really I was terrified inside. I had no idea what life was like on another continent and my first piece of certain information was obviously wrong. I arrived in Geneva and during the shuttle ride to Annecy, France, I breathed in the invigorating mountain air and breathed out my fears. Over five short weeks, that trip opened up more of me and my life possibilities, and I loved being in France. How appropriate that I boarded the plane in funeral attire since a part of me did indeed die on that trip and a new version arrived back home. I returned to my life in America and felt uncomfortable because the environment no longer matched my heart. I needed to go back there. But I had no idea how, or when, or even why. It felt impossible and scary.

Until one random Thursday morning. I was at work, looking in the direction of my computer screen but not focused on it as my morning coffee grew colder to the right. The sun blazed warmly outside and briefly danced along the tops of my shoulders, but I felt my life force slowing, painfully leaking out of me. The energy sank down, down, down through my cushioned rolling faux leather chair, out of my three-inch heels, and into the thin gray office carpet. I slumped back, head on the chair, all zest officially gone. I looked at the calendar that said 2004. *This is how I'm spending my Thursday?* I had trained myself to feel excitement around the arrival of Fridays (*TGIF! See you at happy hour! What are your weekend plans?*), but that meant I was living life for one day a workweek and two weekend days. Less than fifty percent of a week. What would it be like to feel excited about *every* day? I picked up the mug of cold coffee and took a desperate sip to feel a jolt of life. Then I stood up and gave myself an early lunch break. I walked away from that stack of files and the marketing calendar and the red blinking voicemail light and the inbox staring back at me. I needed a new life.

In a nearby vacant park, I sat down with myself over a bright salad and remembered everything I had learned up to this point about my life choices. Making a choice and taking action on it was one thing; acting with Trust was a whole other declaration. Over the past two years, I had learned incredible wisdom from the psychic lady who became my unofficial spiritual teacher, counselor, and ongoing connection to All I Could Do In My Life. I had sessions with her a few times a year and arrived on time, even way too early, with a list of questions and an empty notepad. I learned about God, working with spiritual energy, detachment, getting out of my own way so something bigger and better could unfold. I was gifted with opportunities to apply these lessons in relationships, business, moving homes, and *getting clear about what I want*. She never told me what to do; I had to learn Trust for myself and listen to my own messages. And most of those Trust messages I let sit unanswered on the answering machine, silent blinking red lights that were available when I was ready. A true teacher will never give you the answers to the tests, but they will support you in figuring out the answers for yourself because that is how you connect with your own power. And I had learned that we were continually tested on these "things we know" as a way to demonstrate our evolving choices and intentions. So yes, I *knew* all about Trust, intentions, faith, and energy. I *knew* it was okay to dream bigger and Trust what I really wanted, but now it was time to act on it and make changes.

I never touched my salad during that "getting clear with myself" session.

I returned to the office with a click, click, click of my heels and a new strength in my posture. I pulled out the computer keyboard, and with chocolate-covered pretzels in hand, I typed "graduate schools in Paris."

The idea had been brewing for a while, but only as a safe daydream about how I could someday get on with my life and not be stuck with these commitments. It represented the day I would go for it, push the start button on my real life, go big. The *hows* had scared me for months because it felt too big, too complicated to figure out something as complex as moving to another country for a long time. How would I make money? How would I get a legal visa? How would I meet people? I had kept the possibility curbed and only thought about it when I had the emotional energy to dream.

Then that new beginning turned out to be this random Thursday. *The day* I was finally ready to Trust more. My mind was flying everywhere and the nerves were kicking in, but I exhaled and returned to Trust: in myself, in God, in the process, and in the possibilities I could not see. Now was the time to take the learning up, up, up to this higher platform of choice and do something with it even though it was incredibly exhilarating and scary in the same breath. Trust that God is right there, no matter what. Trust that it is safe to go for it, all of it. Trust that the Universe had my back.

And now that back—and fingers and heart and ten obnoxious toes—were all standing firm and strong on top of this highest of platforms. My previous trip to France was the stretch and warm up. Then I committed to this choice when I put my right foot and both hands on the bottom rungs of this ladder and applied for the student visa. And next I will soar on the moving bars and gain momentum to make this dream—this blooming part of Self—a flying declaration of Trust and the life I wanted. It was time to go for it, no holds barred. Well, except for the bar I held in my hands with my noodle wrists.

Tension began to creep slowly up my body again. *Shut up, toes. The ten of you do not have a majority vote.* Breathe.

The winds of possibility picked up even more. A breeze drifted across the right side of my body, and fifteen seconds later, I felt another breeze on my left side. I allowed both to carry away any lingering residual fears because, as I have learned through previous leaps, doubts, and uncertainties are simply too heavy to carry when the aim is to be Trust-full.

Instead, I had packed in my essence the skills and qualities I have been developing during all former soaring jumps. Solitude was strapped to my back and fortified my inner connections as a solo traveler. Endurance was molded to the bottom of both feet as a reminder to keep going, to stay focused, to follow the path as it presented itself. Strength was bound inside my core to provide comfort and security regardless of the external developments known as "life." Flexibility intermingled itself around both legs to keep them limber and poised, quick and adaptable. Style was nestled with flair in the back of my flowing hair, just out of sight from my green eyes. And Heart filled up my aura and provided a protective coating to keep me safe from my ego's desire to always, always, always lead, and reminded me to return to the present moment.

Breathe.

I did a deep knee bend to stretch all stiff leg joints, and as I was halfway down, hands still on the bar, I felt the dual urges to go forward courageously and the comfort of keeping my feet on this platform. It was normal to feel the push and pull between the Heart's openness and the ego's need to control during big change, so I had learned to expect it. But I also had a mantra readily available for these conflicting directions: Yes from the Heart and no from the Ego, but still go for it. "Yes and no, but still go."

As I straightened my spine and arched with subtle confidence, I felt adrenaline quicken in my stomach. Any minute now it would be time to go.

Ya hear that, toes? Get ready. They twitched and released in waves, up and down in rhythm.

My last intentional thought before every jump, with softly closed eyes, was to visualize angel wings. Hefty, weighted white feathers padded together so thickly they were dense with support and yet lighter than air, than dust, than the chalk on my hands. I pictured satin wings with hints of sparkles embedded deeply into every fine bristle. When the bristles blew in the wind, each one moved and flowed freely, but the feather's core remained erect and strong. They were a collection of comfort that demonstrated how soaring, jumping, and Trusting could be light and grace-filled. And these wings I envisioned reminded me that I was never alone as long as my heart was open wide and beating strong, filling my body with breath all the way down to my toes.

Time to let go, little piggies. Yes, we're doing this now. Together. My toes released and relaxed as I expanded my chest and inhaled deeply. A final flutter from unseen wings cooled off my face, my throat, my arms. And in less than a second, a force of powerful air rushed in to cover the front of my body as I jumped into the oblivion of the heavens.

Let the higher levels of Trust begin.

PURE AIR

IT HAD TO WORK THIS time. Grasping the paper with the combination code in my hand, I forcefully and slowly pressed each number into the digi-code box *again*. Honking cars were now at a standstill on this one-way Parisian street, acting as morning alarm clocks to every apartment building resident. The shuttle driver was unloading all four of my packed suitcases in a hurry, waving erratically to signal to the loud line-up that he was almost done. The street was percolating with whiffs of baguettes, underground subway rumblings, and distant children's laughter. The sun began to make its debut as shadows shrunk on the sidewalk.

Still no click of the building doors unlocking. I had verified the numbers over the phone with my hostess last week, and I desperately hoped nothing was lost in translation. I brushed my long caramel hair off my face and took another deep breathe just as the shuttle driver jumped into his getaway vehicle and drove off. My non-designer collection of baggage was lined up on the narrow sidewalk like traveling ducklings, sitting in a row behind their anxious momma. Cars slowly passed by, offering sneering stares. At least it was not raining.

I hastily entered the code again, pressing one foot against my biggest rolling suitcase so it did not ease into the street, and now tried not to lose my balance as the spectators rolled by. This was certainly not how I imagined my arrival in Paris. What if this code was wrong, what if I was stuck out here for hours, what will I –

PING! And *voila*.

I propped one suitcase in the doorway to hold the door open and began to haul my luggage ducklings inside, noticing there was another door with yet another digi-code box straight ahead of me. Crap. *Where was that second code?* Jet lag was certainly not helping my efforts. I orchestrated dragging each piece of luggage from the sidewalk into the *petite* foyer and allowed the first door to shut behind me. The entryway had thirty mailboxes stacked on the wall, and with my four suitcases on the floor, there was now very little room to move myself through to the second door. And of course, this was the moment when the building suddenly came alive as people appeared from both sides of the foyer. We were all unable to move in any direction. They stared at me, the traveling alien, with obvious curiosity and silent laughter.

Again, not how I imagined my arrival in Paris.

I offered courtesy head nods and pointed to the second door as my destination. Everyone shuffled, shuffled, shuffled as the second traffic jam I had created in less than five minutes cleared out. It was not even 9 a.m., and I completely understood why it was a good idea to have wine at lunch in this country.

On the other side of the second door, I inhaled a calming breath and summoned the elevator to take me to the fourth floor. The lobby of the apartment building was cushioned with soft red carpet, brass trim, and quietness. My body tingled with joy. I could not believe I was finally here. I fought off the exhaustion of twenty hours of travel with the voice of inner excitement.

The elevator arrived, and after looking inside the tiny vertical box, it was quickly apparent I could only fit one item of luggage inside at a time next to my size six body. I slid three traveling ducklings to the corner and pushed my first bag inside with me. The elevator door gradually closed, shoving my suitcase inside further and pushing me up against the corner of this moving sardine tin. The elevator slowly crept upwards with the speed of *un escargot*. This could be another twenty hours of travel.

Glancing at my watch, I saw that my arrival was an hour earlier than expected. I hoped my hostess Francine understood. Yet at the rate this elevator was going, I could end up arriving late.

I was staying with Francine for two weeks while I became acquainted with the City of Lights and found an apartment to rent. Francine offered a bed and breakfast service to foreign travelers looking for a spare room and home-cooked breakfast to while in Paris. I had talked to her a week ago as I was preparing to leave Seattle, and we had confirmed the door codes and my arrival details.

It was also a relief to hear a warm voice on the other side of the Atlantic. I did not know much about this new life I was starting, but at least I could speak a little English with someone when I arrived.

The elevator announced my landing on the fourth floor, and I buzzed the door on the left. It never even occurred to me until this moment that she might not be home. Being almost an hour early could be my first major *faux pas*. Then I heard movement as the door opened widely and a woman with shoulder-length brown hair, keen brown eyes, and small reading glasses stood in front of me. She was wearing a simple blue tunic with brown cotton pants, a white apron tied around her waist. Talk radio was chatting away inside the space.

"*Bonjour, Mademoiselle. Bienvenue.*" Hello, Mademoiselle. Welcome.

"*Bonjour Madame. Je m'appelle Molly...*" Hello, Madame. My name is Molly...

As if she was anticipating any other American-accent with luggage showing up today.

She smiled kindly and stepped back, allowing me to enter. I followed her in to an entry foyer with beautiful hardwood floors and a slight musty smell. She slowly led me down the main hallway, pointing out the living room on the right, the kitchen on the left. I spied coffee and a yogurt on the small kitchen table and felt a crisp breeze weave through the single window above the sink. My suitcase slowly glided over the wood floors, echoing down the hall. Paintings of all sizes hung on almost every wall. The essence of lavender soap came and went as Francine's hair swayed in front of me.

I rolled into a bedroom and Francine pushed back the closed curtains. The space held a twin bed, a desk, a rolling clothes rack, a vanity, and a nightstand. An old AM/FM radio sat on the desk. It looked like a room from my teenage years. The newly revealed window had a small balcony facing the street where I had just stopped traffic. I glanced out the window to see the sun rising higher, clearing away the cobwebs of clouds. It was still real; I was in Paris.

Francine walked back to the hall as I moved my suitcase to a corner and resisted the urge to collapse on the bed.

"*Madame, je n'ai plus de sacs dans le hall d'accueil.*" Madame, I have more bags in the foyer.

She looked at my huge bag and then back at me, nodding a hesitant *bien sûr*.

"Do you need my 'elp?" She inquired in English.

"Yes, possibly. *J'ai plus de trois valises...*" I have three more bags...

Her eyes expanded. "*Trois?*" Three?

"*Oui, Madame. Trois...*" Yes, Madame. Three...

She looked at the giant bag in front of me again and now could not hide her confusion. I walked to the door and she promptly followed. Curiosity was universal.

"*Madame, je peut aller...*" Madame, I can go...

Jet lag came on stronger when I tried to speak French. "I can go downstairs and move the bags onto the elevator myself. No problem."

"*Oui, c'est une bonne idée.*" Yes, that is a good idea.

Francine then peered over the open stairway rail to try and get a glimpse of what I would be bringing her way.

Without waiting for the escargot elevator, I bolted down the stairs to find my traveling ducklings waiting patiently for me in the foyer. But immediately there was a problem. Since they were all rather large, I could not fit the bags and myself inside the sardine tin simultaneously. I pushed and shoved various combinations around until it was obvious even two bags could not fit inside because they were either too wide or too awkward for the small space. The only solution was to put one bag in at a time, and then walk up four flights of stairs to meet the package upon arrival.

I tucked my second bag inside the vertical tin, hit the fourth floor button, and rushed up the stairs. Francine watched quietly with raised eyebrows, then shrugged and went inside. I proceeded to dash rapidly up and down the stairs two more times as each bag made the slow climb up. Every time I met the elevator on the fourth floor it had already arrived two seconds ahead of me. The escargot and the hare.

AFTER FIFTEEN MINUTES OF MOVING, running, and pushing, all of my bags were finally sitting in a corner of my room. I surveyed all of my belongings and wondered, what exactly *did* I bring?

Francine appeared in the doorway. "I must know. Why do you need so much for only two weeks of holiday?"

"Oh, actually, I am staying in Paris for much longer than two weeks. I am moving here for two years to go to graduate school, so these are my clothes, shoes, towels, and books. Everything I may need for two years of living."

Her face was stuck in an expression of disbelief, revealing that she did not understand at all the concept of owning so many things. She muttered in French something about Americans, and it was probably a good thing my mind was slowing down and did not feel compelled to translate. Note to self: don't mention the additional boxes of housewares and furniture being stored in my mom's garage. Or how I planned to eventually bring my two cats over to Paris.

Francine left me to organize, closing the door behind her. I turned to look at everything. Two years means four seasons of sweaters, skirts, pants, socks, shoes, jewelry, this, that, the other thing, and a few more options, just in case. These four suitcases were my U-haul truck. And I had no desire to touch any of it right now.

My green eyes were heavy with weariness, so I took off my tortoiseshell glasses and set them on the desk. My spine crumbled onto the thin twin mattress and I finally noticed my body: tired, sweaty, thirsty, sore. The only thing I wanted to do was kick off my shoes and curl up on the bed. It was only 9:30 a.m., but it had been the longest morning of my life. I needed to rest for just a moment...just a small minute... and when I wake up... I'll still be... in Paris... ready to meet the... Eiffel Tower... and... eat a croiss—

My eyelids slammed shut at that instant.

FOUR HOURS LATER, MY EYES popped open and I sprang up from the bed in one swift motion. I looked around the room with momentary confusion. Oh no, I was reliving my teenage years. And then my eyes focused and I remembered with excitement where I was. Everything was quiet except my stomach. I hadn't eaten in hours, so I dug through the nearest bag and crammed a granola bar into my mouth while putting on my shoes. I grabbed an envelope with cash to pay Francine for my lodging. I knew money was not a topic of open discussion in France, so I did not want to forget to pay her, make her wait, or worst of all, have her ask me for the money. Better to be upfront and pass an envelope as soon as possible.

I walked down the hallway, my feet silent on the hardwood, and heard nothing. After a moment of glancing in rooms and calling out "*Madame?*" softly, the apartment was obviously empty. I set the money on the kitchen table and took a moment to explore my temporary home.

The kitchen was small and bright with faded yellow paint and potted plants sitting on the window ledge. White tiles covered the wall behind the sink, counter, and oven, all lined up together on the right side of the room. A five-foot-tall refrigerator sat along the same wall with a small pantry in the corner. The other side of the room had a quaint table with two chairs, and an upper wall cabinet with plates, pots, and pans. There was not a lot of storage or space, but there was not a lot of stuff either. Could I easily fit this whole kitchen into one of my suitcases? I wondered if Francine had had the same thought.

I glanced up to see a rectangular wire contraption hanging from the ceiling by ropes. The ropes were connected to the wall as if it traveled up and down. It was too big for hanging pots and pans; what could the rack be used for?

Across from the kitchen was the living room with a couch, armchair, coffee table, and a small TV on a bookshelf. A dining table with two chairs sat against a sidewall. Everything rested on two square oriental rugs. A pair of huge windows framed the room with a fireplace nestled in between the natural light. It was very cozy although a bit musty. Opening the windows would do wonders.

Located off the living room was Francine's bedroom. Paintings in various stages of completion sat on the floor and hung on the walls. Brushes, tubes of acrylics, and an easel were in a corner by the bedroom window. I peered through the door further to see her bed, closet, and a chair with clothes on them. Although I had the apartment to myself, I didn't proceed any further into her room, and turned back to the shared living spaces. The other rooms felt like fair game, but her bedroom was respectfully off-limits.

The toilet was a separate room discreetly tucked away by the entryway. From my experience of living in Annecy, France, I knew a separate toilet was common in French apartments so one person in the house did not also dominate the bathtub, sink, or other bathroom essentials. A sign hung on the doorknob that flipped to say *occupé* (busy) or *libre* (open). I glanced inside and a colorful flash caught my eye: something pink was hanging from a wall dispenser. I leaned in closer and found little squares of pink toilet paper. I grabbed a few out of curiosity and they practically melted in my hands. Cotton candy toilet paper? The one thing I did not pack that might be needed the most. Note to self: investigate other toilet paper options, pronto. And maybe there were other colors.

The full bathroom was at the other end of the apartment next to my bedroom, a generous room with an elegant feel to it. A white claw-foot bathtub, a vintage freestanding vanity, wall shelves for toiletries, and a petite ceramic sink all created a nurturing feminine style. I inspected the giant tub, and noticed there was no shower curtain or shower spout on the wall. How did a person take a shower without a shower nozzle? Or did Francine only take baths? And how would I inquire about it without sounding like an idiot?

Francine had left keys for me on the kitchen table, so I grabbed them, along with my purse, and made my way down the all-too-familiar stairs. I exchanged *"Bonjours"* in the foyer with a woman checking her mail while holding a young girl's hand. I stepped outside onto the sidewalk to meet Paris for the first time, resisting the urge to open up both arms wide and grasp for the city in a hug.

Every business sign could easily be for sale in an American home décor store: *Pâtisserie, kiosque à journaux, salon de coiffure, soins du visage,* and *agence immobilière.* Street signs on the building corners confirmed this was the seventeenth *arrondissement.* The afternoon sun reflected off parked cars, some angled awkwardly to fit into any space. Businessmen and couples walked briskly, chattering away in French, as a city bus stopped up the street ahead. Riders disembarked, and then more people stepped inside, assisting a woman by pulling her stroller onboard. The bus billboard displayed the latest fashions at *Galeries Lafayette,* the city's stylish department store, and then hastily left the curb, cutting off a red Smart car.

I turned a corner and marveled at how this life adventure came together in only five months. The pieces had lined up almost effortlessly. And now that I was here, I was met with a fresh set of questions and unknowns looming on the horizon: *Will I actually enjoy living in Paris? Will I meet wonderful people I adore? Will I fall in love with a dashing, handsome Frenchman who helps me learn more of the language quickly? Can I find a place to live in only two weeks?* I smiled to myself as the energy invigorated me. Or maybe it was the delicious smells from the *boulangerie* in front of me. The dancing blend of yeast, warmth, and sweets was intoxicating. Obviously the best thing to do was eat a croissant.

After taking my place in the expanding line, I realized I didn't want a single croissant; I wanted all of them. Every bread, every pastry, every treat, every morsel of sugar, every scrap of carbohydrate, every everything. Nothing sounded better than a meal of warm, fresh-baked carbohydrates and sugar. The line crept forward as my indecision grew, overwhelmed by the beauty of every example of fluffy, rolled, exquisitely baked yumminess. My eyes were fixed on the shelves as I imagined returning to Francine's with boxes of pastries and bread. I could tell her I needed to buy another suitcase for my new patisserie collection. Or I could get rid of some clothes to make room for...

"Mademoiselle? S'il vous plaît, Mademoiselle?"

Three sets of eyes were staring at me from across the counter. How did the line move so quickly?

"Excusez-moi, Monsieur. Un croissant, s'il vous plaît." Sorry, Monsieur. A croissant, please.

Monsieur passed over a small plastic bag and then moved on to the next customer as I paid Madame. The warm bundle nested in my palm as I walked back outside to observe more of Parisian life. A few women pulled carts of groceries to their apartment buildings. A man walked quickly to the metro entrance with the daily newspaper and a well-used leather briefcase at his side. Children with backpacks chattered away in high-pitched voices, following their hurried parents. A couple ambled along smiling and kissing. I meandered through more streets until I found myself back at Francine's building on Rue Truffaut.

"Bonjour, Francine," I called out while closing the apartment door. Soft voices came from the kitchen. I passed by the room to see a calm, attractive woman with excellent posture sitting across from Francine.

"Bonjour, Molly. Entrez, s'il vous plaît." Hello, Molly. Come in, if you'd like.

Francine introduced me to her mother and we exchanged polite greetings. She explained that her mother did not speak any English and when she tried, she sounded like a monkey. Francine shared this fact while maintaining a respectful, level tone. She went on to explain that her mother has lived in Paris all of her life, and she swam three times a week in order to keep up with her younger boyfriend who was in his sixties. Francine raised an eyebrow and said the relationship was a bit scandalous for a woman in her eighties. Her mother sat with self-assured dignity and maintained a polite smile on her face as we obviously conversed about her. I'm sure they were just doing the same about me. Francine continued on, saying her mother would be leaving soon and could show me how to use the metro if I was in need of assistance. I accepted eagerly as I had never used a metro system before.

A few moments later, I followed the dignified, scandalous Madame as she strode confidently down the street, directing my attention to shops and points of interest along the way: the best place for facials, the closest supermarket, the building where the farmer's market was held twice a week, and the way to the nearby community pool. She said the *boulangerie* we were passing had the best bread and the most skilled baker in the whole neighborhood. She kindly spoke French slowly as my mind rushed to translate every sentence.

We arrived at the small metro station and descended the stairs into hallways that echoed with voices and quick feet. At the ticket counter, Madame purchased a monthly pass for herself and showed me how to do the same. She demonstrated how the little ticket worked and then pushed through the turnstile, ready to return to her normal Parisian life. With a polite smile and a graceful turn, she was gone.

I returned to the apartment to find Francine gliding around the kitchen, tongs in hand, opera music filling the air. I couldn't identify all of the spices in the air, but it smelled delicious and the whole apartment felt inviting and warm. The little table was set for two, complete with folded napkins, water, and wine. Bread was sliced in a basket. Francine moved the sizzling meat to a platter, then added warm green beans on the side. She reached to remove her white apron and gestured for me to take a seat.

How in the world did I get so lucky with this type of welcome? I had heard cultural stereotypes and other people's negative stories about their experiences in France, but I consciously decided before arriving to not believe them. Good people live all over the globe. Simple things like quality food, kindness, and a safe place to rest are parts of a universal language. As we toasted to our first dinner together, I said a silent prayer that this first day was a good omen for what was to come.

THE NEXT MORNING, A TABLE properly set with a plate, napkin, orange juice, yogurt, and a still-warm croissant awaited me in the living room. Francine had already gone to work. She left a note saying the coffee was ready and to please turn the machine off when I was finished. I rushed to complete the meal like I was trying to justify "fast" in breakfast. I couldn't wait to finally see the sights of Paris.

I walked to the metro station, trailing behind the hurried steps of morning commuters. On the crammed metro platform, signs overhead displayed when the first train and the second train would be arriving, in one minute and four minutes, respectively. The first train pulled in with a jolt, the doors sprung open, and no one got off. Every car was packed, and yet more people still managed to jam themselves inside the space. I followed the pack and tentatively stepped in to try to find room for myself, cramming in on the edge. Yet there was nowhere for my body to go in the car. Should I step out and wait for the next one? Maybe it's best if I...

A loud buzzing noise sounded overhead—what does that mean?—and bam! Every door on the train slammed shut fiercely. Except the doors right behind me. Everyone was looking at the three-inch opening, hoping the doors would close so the train could move ahead. A man said something quickly to me in French. I glanced down to see that I was the superstar who was keeping the doors open. The back of my shoe was in the crack.

Awesome.

I yanked my foot forward impulsively, amazed that I didn't feel the doors hitting me, and accidentally kicked someone in the shin. A muffled response followed. There were too many legs to know which limb belonged to whom, so I decided to act French about the whole matter: I did not offer any facial indications that I cared or even did anything wrong. The standing definition of metro *blasé*. The doors slammed shut and the train pulled ahead. I endured the bumpy ride for twenty minutes knowing the Eiffel Tower would be waiting for me on the other end of the metro tunnel.

I filled up my first days in Paris with visits to many obligatory sights and made a few phone calls back home to report my discoveries. I stared up at the *Cathédrale Notre-Dame* and walked silently through its interiors. I circled *L'Arc de Triomphe* and took unlimited photos from the rooftop. I toured *Les Invalides* and read about Napoleon's great conquests. I covered the art history basics of the unending, winding Louvre.

After playing tourist for a few days, I had important tasks to complete. I needed to settle down and *live* here. Finding a home was the top priority and touristy-fun things would have to wait. I called a few classified ads for apartments, but got nowhere quickly. I headed over to the school in Montparnasse with my fingers-crossed that someone could assist me with housing. But when I walked through the front door, I was greeted only by the sound of stillness and noticed the halls were a ghost town. I padded gingerly down the hallway until I spied a woman with short black hair, reading glasses, and a focused look sitting behind a desk. Her desk nameplate said Anne-Marie.

"Bonjour, Madame."

"Bonjour, Mademoiselle." She barely looked up.

I walked into the office, introduced myself as a new student, and asked if she may be able to assist me with housing needs. She scowled slightly.

"Finding a place to live in Paris is very difficult unless you already know someone in the city. Do you know anyone or have any contacts?" She continued tapping away on her keyboard.

"No, I only know the woman I am staying with for a few weeks. I thought the school might be able to help in some way?"

"It is not something we normally do. Each student is responsible for their own housing. It would take up a lot of time for us to be searching for apartments for every student, you understand?"

"Sure, of course…"

"And one of the main reasons why we do not help is because it can take months to find a place. It is often a long, time-consuming process."

Months? Knots started forming in my stomach. I reached into my bag to pull out a bi-monthly publication with classified ads aimed at English-speaking foreigners. Francine had recommended it to me.

"I looked in this paper for some possibilities and made a few calls already, but it has been harder to arrange an appointment than I expected."

"So you have tried calling places yourself?" she inquired, finally looking over the top of her glasses at me.

"Yes, of course, I called at least ten yesterday. But the owners either told me the apartment was no longer available, or asked me questions I could not answer. One person wanted to know why I was looking for a place in Paris and when I said I was a student, he said he was not interested in me. And then two people hung up on me for no reason."

Anne-Marie gave me a knowing look. "Students are not always desirable renters, this is true. And you have an American accent when you speak, so that tells them you are not French. Do you have forms from your parents? Will they support your rent if necessary?"

I was a grown woman who had been living on my own for years, yet as a graduate student in France, I still had to provide proof that my parents could support me if necessary. A proprietor wanted legal proof that they would not be without rent. At 28-years-old, it felt ridiculous, but I understood it was how I had to play the game.

"Yes, I have a letter from my parents. I didn't think it would be so hard to find a place to live in such a big city." Pause. "So it is because I am a student and not French?"

Anne-Marie carefully considered a response. "Parisians like to rent to people they know, or people they know they can relate to. Because it is a big city with many people, the chances of renting to a

French person are high and some owners do not want to work with foreigners. This is why it can take months for some people to find an apartment, do you understand?"

"I understand. It's just surprising." I knew the exchange rate was working against me, but I had no idea being a foreigner would be an even worse challenge. And to hear that the search could take months? I only gave myself two weeks.

Anne-Marie glanced at my stressed expression and shuffled some papers on her desk. "Well, I am typically very busy, but it is summer and things are quiet now. I may be able to assist you with a few phone calls today after lunch, if you'd like."

I sat up straighter. "Yes, please, thank you so much! That would be greatly appreciated. I understand if you are busy, but I could really use some help if it doesn't take up too much of your time."

She nodded in acceptance. "Come back at one o'clock and we will make some phone calls. Bring all of your forms and we will hope for the best." She gave a slight smile as the phone on her desk rang.

I returned after lunch, and within ten minutes it was obvious that having Anne-Marie as my advocate greatly improved my chances of finding an apartment. As a local, she knew the city well and could direct me to the decent parts of town to live in. As a French woman, she was able to converse easily and quickly without a foreign accent. And as an employee of the school, she could vouch for me as a person of good standing and support my rental application with authority. The French love people with authority. I observed how her position with the school gave the proprietor a sense of reassurance and a willingness to meet me since a Parisian school official was involved. Anne-Marie knew the questions to ask, the information to obtain, and could provide any necessary information about me that the owner on the other end of the call wanted to know. I was cautiously hopeful.

In less than an hour, she had called every ad in the circular and had secured a rendezvous with three potential apartments. One viewing was for this afternoon, and the other two were for tomorrow. There was no way I could have set up these appointments without her. I thanked her profusely, practically bowing with gratitude, and then ran off to visit my first possible apartment in the second *arrondissement*.

I arrived a few minutes early with the door code in hand. The street was pleasantly quiet, the building and entryway were beautiful, and the location was highly desirable since it was in the heart of the city. But those were the only perks I determined after viewing the apartment. It was the teeniest, tiniest room I had ever seen. Did it even qualify as an apartment? At approximately eight feet long by six feet wide, the full size bed took up most of the space so the front door could not even open all the way. The generously named "kitchenette" was a flat counter a mere two feet wide with a refrigerator underneath, a single burner, and a shelf for a microwave. The bathroom held a toilet, a sink, and the appearance of a shower, but I was not convinced a human body could actually fit in there. It must be a place to wash dolls.

After turning around three times to extend the length of the tour, I thanked the owner for her time and exited, shocked by the Parisian apartments that were in my budget. Francine's place now felt like a mansion. I shared with Francine my apartment experience when I walked in the door that evening, and she shrugged noncommittally. "*C'est normal pour Paris.*" It's normal for Paris.

"I need a home that is big enough for my suitcases." I smiled.

She laughed out loud. "*Ahh, votre valises…* I've told all my friends about your collection."

The phone rang in the living room and Francine got up to answer it. There was a very short conversation, and then she hung up and came into the kitchen, frowning and tense.

"*Francine, ca va?* Is everything okay?" I asked hesitantly.

She responded with a sigh. "*Oui, oui, oui. C'est bien.* I accidentally answered the phone."

"That's a bad thing?"

"*Oui, il était très mauvaise.*" Yes, it was very bad. She paused. "Who is that character in a popular movie, he is very smart, but a little… different?"

That is a rather broad category.

She immediately answered her own question. "Ah, I know! Forrest Gump! You know that movie, *Forrest Gump*?"

"*Bien sûr.*" Of course.

"That is who calls me every night: The Forrest Gump of Rue Truffaut. He wants to be my boyfriend and he calls me regularly to ask me to dinner. I tell him no, but it is difficult to always give him excuses." She released an exasperated sigh and shook her head, then moved into the kitchen where pans rattled as she began dinner preparation.

Francine generously cooked dinner each night, but this was not officially part of the lodging agreement. I wandered around the small neighborhood grocery stored and mentally planned a few meals for us, then found the toilet paper section by accident because it felt like I had wandered into a rainbow. A wall of purple, green, peach, pink, floral prints, and finally, white rose in front of me. Some brands were even scented to match their color, such as the peach toilet paper that smelled like peaches. *Bien sûr.*

By the end of my grocery store tour, my hand-held basket held sliced ham, fruit, yogurt, green beans, bread, cookies, cheese, and a few dinner entrees. I packaged my goods into three bags I could carry back to the apartment, realizing for the first time how convenient it had been to use a car. Thankfully, all of these bags fit in the elevator with me. When I returned to the apartment, Francine surveyed my three bags and then announced, "It looks like you're stocking up for the war."

I threw back my head in laughter, not sure if she meant it as a joke or not. I didn't feel excessive, but I silently considered her viewpoint and recognized the cultural differences. There were certainly notable variances in spaces and sizes between American and French lifestyles. I wondered what she would say about a Target or Super Wal-Mart store.

A comfortable rhythm had developed between us based on Francine's work schedule, my house-hunting efforts, and our joint free time in the evenings. She cooked dinner; I washed the dishes after we ate; and in the mornings, we each put away whatever we used. One morning, I realized what the wire rectangle thing hanging from the ceiling was. I looked up to find Francine's clothes draped across the wire bars three feet above my head. A rack for drying clothes. Release the ropes tied to the wall and it lowered down to waist level to put the clothes on; pull the ropes up slowly, and the contraption raised back up to the ceiling where it was secured and out of the way. What a great use of space. As long as a sock didn't drop into the pasta sauce.

The showering method for using the bathtub properly was also solved. Francine and I gathered ceremoniously around the bathtub as she carefully explained the showering procedures as if I was a kindergartner.

"You can take a bath easily, but to take a shower, a person sits down in the tub," she pointed to the bottom of the tub, "and holds the portable nozzle in their hand to wet their body and hair. It is not necessary to plug the tub, but you can. Then you bathe while sitting." Pause. "And it is a good idea to turn off the water when applying shampoo and using soap to not waste water." Pause. "*Voila.*"

Sit upright in a cold bathtub, hold shower nozzle in one hand, coordinate other hand to grab shampoo and scrub hair, turn water on and off (responsibly), don't forget to do the same with soap, and be quick about it so you don't get cold sitting in a tub with no water. I was grateful the idea of showering evolved to standing by the time it reached my home on the West Coast of the United States.

I easily found the second apartment to check out in the fourteenth *arrondissement* because there was a line of fifteen people at the front of the building. The proprietor arrived at exactly ten o'clock to shuffle us all in the door, military style, and gave a commanding tour to four people at a time. When I was granted permission to enter, I walked up the spiral staircase, ducking spider webs and squinting to find the stair steps in the dark hall. The apartment currently housed two college students who were leaving at the end of the month. They looked like they had just awoken and were being forced to tell us how wonderful the living accommodations were despite the peeling walls, sinking futon, and gray-stained windows.

Back in the courtyard, the proprietor asked me what I thought of her apartment. Since I wanted to keep my options open, I told her it was a great location, the apartment was fine, and it could be a possibility for me. She then fired off questions about my financial resources: "Do you have two months' rent for the deposit? And a contract from your parents? Can you move in and pay me by the first of the month?" I answered yes to all of the drill sergeant's demands, and marched away when she was finished. I hoped to find better options than military housing.

My third appointment was for an apartment located across from a beautiful park in the fifteenth *arrondissement*. I was initially excited about the location's access to green space, but upon inspection, the apartment itself was incredibly dark and depressing. On a gorgeous blue-sky day the living room felt like November at night. Compared to other places, it was generously sized, and even had a separate kitchen that I was beginning to understand was a luxury. But could I manage living in what felt like a prison cell with a single small window to the sky? If this was a beautiful day in May, how dark and gloomy could it be in the winter? A halogen floor light helped a little, but electricity in France was expensive. I could go broke trying to light up this dismal space. My gut immediately told me no, this wouldn't work. Natural light was important to my mood, my lifestyle, and my ability to stay awake in the afternoon. I recalled my experience living in North Carolina and decided this environment would not do, unless I could live at the park and come inside to cook and bathe.

I reported back to Anne-Marie about my findings. She nodded her head with understanding, familiar with the trials and realities of Parisian apartment searches.

"Remember I said it is hard to find a place to live in Paris? It can take months. Maybe you are being too picky with what you have seen?" she said sternly.

"I'm not trying to be picky. I just haven't found a place that feels comfortable or safe yet. But I will."

"Well, at least you're not looking in September with all of the other students who return after summer. We will call a few more places next week. I am not here tomorrow, so stop by on Monday and we will try again. Okay?" She shuffled papers on her desk.

"Okay, I will. Thank you so much, Anne-Marie. *Bon weekend!*" Have a good weekend!

"*Bon weekend, Mademoiselle!*" Have a good weekend, Mademoiselle!

I was grateful for her support, but becoming more nervous every day. There was only one week to go before I needed to leave Francine's. I called a few more places on my own that evening, but I was only met with the same results: "*Non*" and "*Désolé, Mademoiselle.*" Sorry, Mademoiselle.

I shared my efforts with Francine while we were sitting in the living room watching TV after dinner. After careful thought, Francine mentioned she had a friend with an apartment in the city that he only used a few weekends a month; she could ask him if he was looking for a renter. My ears and posture perked up eagerly. Glancing at the time, she left the room to make a phone call as I waited on the couch with silent prayers. Five minutes later, she returned to her chair and said he was not able to rent the apartment right now because he needs the space himself for the next few months. I thanked her for the thought and effort. Then I slumped back into the couch pillows and stared at the French television show through my glass of French wine, ignoring my internal French whine.

By the weekend, I confidently demonstrated to everyone on the metro that I could get on the train without having any parts of myself stuck in the slamming doors. I had successfully collected many croissants and tried new pastries from all over the city. I discovered how much I could successfully carry back from the grocery store without looking like I was "stocking up for the war." And I put a four-pack of two-ply peach toilet paper in the *toilette* as a step in the right direction away from cotton candy restroom standards. I was becoming more of a local now. Except for not having a local address, of course.

I made more phone calls, arranged appointments, viewed apartments and followed up with previous proprietors to see if their places were still available. After viewing five more places, a predictable theme emerged: a proprietor would not accept a new renter until they had met all possible applicants, and I realized they were only searching for the best French candidate in the group. Even when I stood in front of a proprietor with all of my documents and stated that I was willing to take the place right away, no luck; I didn't have a French passport or even a decent French accent. When I called to follow up on a unit, they had already selected someone else. Click.

My optimism was fading. By the following Friday, Anne-Marie and I had scanned every possible listing and had even called a few places twice. No more leads to follow.

Reality hit. I would take anything

I rode the metro back to Francine's mansion feeling defeated and discouraged. My time at her place officially ended on Tuesday. She had a new visitor arriving Wednesday, so I would have to go somewhere else. Hotels were expensive this time of year with summer approaching, school out, and world tourists in. But at least a hotel could buy more time.

The sky was dark, cloudy, and looming potential rain on my walk back from the metro station. I completely related to the forecast that anticipated tears dropping from above soon. The apartment was dark and filled with solitude and a note on the table said Francine had dinner plans with friends. A cup of tea and a hot bath were all I wanted for dinner. I left all the lights off, content with the comfort of darkness. Maybe I was not supposed to live here. Maybe this dream won't happen. Maybe I did not think this through enough or have enough information about the reality of Paris. Maybe I needed to change the date on my return plane ticket, try again next year, and allow myself months to find an apartment. Then my eyes broke down in the lavender-scented water under the stress of the unknowns. The lack of progress was finally getting to me and the reality of this life dream not coming together appeared highly possible. I left everything that was working in my life and everything I knew in order to reach for an amazing adventure. But maybe it was all a huge mistake.

My fears became louder. What if I could not find a decent apartment here at all? What if the frustrations and obstacles only grow bigger? What if my money runs out quicker than I planned? What if I don't make any friends? What if I made this jump foolishly, stupidly? Why did I move somewhere all by myself – again?

Sitting in watery silence, it occurred to me that maybe there was one main problem with this scenario: my perspective hadn't been big enough. I was not a single entity moving around all by myself; I was not creating this dream alone without the assistance or support from others. Maybe my energetic intentions needed to expand. What if finding my perfect home also benefited the owner of the apartment, and everyone connected to this scenario, in the highest and best possible ways. What if finding my new place was a problem-solver for someone else, too. What if renting an apartment relieved the owner of a financial issue or allowed them to move forward in some way. What if our agreement was good timing for them or removed a burden from their world. What if I was exactly the tenant they were looking for and the color of my passport with matching accent did not matter at all. *What if?*

My body began to rise up in the tub. Maybe the perfect home was ready and waiting for me, but my search was taking me in the wrong direction because it was too self-directed and small. Maybe this new intention would help speed up the process and connect me to the right person at the right time. Maybe being stuck had been an incredible gift because it showed me where my energy was not working. Maybe everything in this scenario was actually perfect. Maybe.

I stretched up out of the lukewarm water, and dove into bed. Starting tomorrow, I was not simply searching for an apartment. I was searching for a win-win solution that would bring benefits to as many people as possible. I knew without a doubt miracles could happen overnight when intentions were shifted. The energy would rise up to meet me. It had to.

EARLY APPRENTICESHIPS

PARIS IS ONE OF THOSE cities that belong to the world. I noticed quickly that everyone I spoke to before my trip had their own precious version that reflected every angle and side of the city, like a mosaic with each person adding their piece, layered in and extending the image. I had inquisitive conversations with well-traveled colleagues; curious acquaintances who heard about this adventure through word-of-mouth; friends who previously backpacked around Europe; and coffee shop strangers who commented on the guidebook I was reading. All eyes seemed to eventually fog over mid-sentence or mid-story as they remembered an idealized version of their perfect Parisian day when the lines were short, the hours were long, and the wine glasses were tall. Their voices turned into liquid butter, softened and melting about a moment in time they will recall forever because the architecture was breathtaking, the sunlight hit the Seine perfectly, and the *best meal they ever had* will be forever etched on their tongue.

At some point, I also realized people weren't only talking about their love of Montmartre or how perfect that trip last summer was; they were recalling the essence of who *they* were while in Paris. The *carpe diem* traveler immersed in one of the most beautiful cities in the world, watching as their concerns floated down the Seine and all of their grand worries were temporarily forgotten, as if Van Gogh had brushed over their life canvas with wide strokes of sunflowers and starry, starry nights. Life was *oh la la la* grand in Paris. I started to believe there were no bad days there. How could there be when the wine, the Seine, and inspiration all flowed so freely and easily? Every conversation nudged me forward and I had sent away my applications to graduate schools in the fall.

Dreaming about this new life in a new country, as a new me, sustained my spirit for months. *Would I wear high heels everywhere? Do the Paris Fashion Police check the labels you're wearing? Would I be stopped by a handsome Paris Fashion Policeman and then we would hit it off effortlessly and start dating and he would teach me French over lazy Sunday mornings? Would his mom be one of those finicky French women who pursed her lips if I wasn't chic enough for her standards? Would I discover he then had Mom Issues and couldn't stand up for himself and was a policeman because of the authority he had professionally but not personally and then...*

I could figure out that scenario if it became reality. At least I already had a heads up that it wasn't necessary to wear all black, all the time.

Discovering I was moving to Paris was memorable. I arrived home on a lonely Valentine's Day evening with a bag of frozen food for dinner in my hand, cats circling in figure eights around my legs, and an endless rain pounding on the roof. I had a massage after work to make Heart Day uplifting instead of a reminder or evaluation or judgment about whether or not I had dinner reservations that evening. I slowly put the food away since my muscles were too relaxed to exert effort, and then wobbled outside to get the mail. An envelope was sitting inside the mailbox and the return address was from a school in Paris. *This letter could make Valentine's Day either really amazing or even worse.* I stuck the paper underneath my coat, right near my heart, as the drippy-drops fell everywhere.

Back inside, I cleared off the counter and put the envelope down next to nearly burnt-up white candle and an uncorked bottle of wine, as if creating a shrine, of some sort, affected what the letter said. My stomach churned because it felt like my whole future sat inside that pouch. I couldn't open it until I had at least one glass of wine down, my bra and all hosiery off, slippers and yoga pants on. Then I circled, stared, and paced as the fancy-fancy-Paris stamp taunted me. The scenario reminded me of the highly anticipated envelopes my dad handed to my brothers and me on the last day of school when I was younger. If this envelope held exciting travel news, he would be my first phone call. I paced a bit more.

Then after two glasses of wine (no idea how that happened) and a reminder that I had a record of good travel news arriving in envelopes, I tore into the paper like a savage in pajamas and read the first line, holding my breath: *"Felicitations! We are delighted to inform you that you have been accepted into our graduate studies program..."*

My slippers did a happy dance followed by a pathetic imitation of the moonwalk. I clutched the paper firmly and picked up the phone, almost too excited to dial properly. The night was filled with dark chocolates and wine and huge smiles as I shared the news over multiple phone calls.

In the months that followed, I was off and running with everything that needed to come together by May. I gave notice at work and started cleaning out my desk two months in advance, just to be on top of things and make the process easier, or so I told myself. I had short timer's disease bad. I sold my truck exactly two months after the four-year loan was fully paid, and then exchanged some of those dollars into euros. Shock hit my face as I saw how the exchange rate worked against my currency: *I only get this much back for all of those dollars?* I decided to leave a large portion of my money in my U.S. bank account and access it as needed when I was in Paris. Sure, the exchange rate would still fluctuate and could go up even more, but it felt like I at least had some control over how I spent my money and maybe it would prevent me from being an impulsive spender once I was there. Cue laughter.

I took a class at a local community college about traveling through Paris that included how basic things worked (*this is what a metro ticket looks like*) and cultural etiquette (*always use "Monsieur" and "Madam" when addressing a stranger*) and the instructors *Top 10 Tips to Know Before You Go* (*try to stay at a hotel within five minutes of a metro station because you'll be tired from walking every day*). I filled up pages in my notepad and underlined several parts: *Watch out for gypsies by Eiffel Tower. Don't rush around, enjoy! Avoid Bois du Bologne at night. Many good parts of town are off the tourist path – explore!* Two stars for that last tip.

Everything came together, but one of the hardest parts was figuring out what to do with my two feline fuzz faces. I didn't want to leave them and their soft paws behind. Just thinking about the separation made a part of my heartache. We were a family. When I sat down on the couch - zoom! - two instant fuzzy blankets on my lap and legs. When I walked in the door, both would run up to welcome me home and we'd touch noses as I caressed their chenille fur. When I called their names, they would come running to find me and meow in greeting, devouring the affection. (Clearly the only two in their species that did this.) When I took a bath, I could see four little hollow triangles just over the top of the bathtub rim, waiting and watching for what we would do next, together, always, as a family. We were all highly co-dependent on each other's presence and connection, and I loved it. They always made me smile because they didn't care what was happening in the world; they just cared that we shared the same space (and that food was delivered to their dinner bowls on time). My mom offered to care for them, and of course I said yes right away with deep appreciation. But my plan was to bring them across the pond to join me once I was settled. We would be a little family on that continent, too.

As my departure date grew closer, I glowed with anticipation. I drove to work knowing every day was bringing me closer to Paris, and I left my desk each evening with more excitement tucked inside the high heels I was breaking in for my walks on the *Champs-Élysées*. Paris was pulling me onward, like a beacon was flashing on top of the Eiffel Tower and the light was only getting brighter. I smiled to myself for most of my daily drives home.

Until the evening when my deep fears hit. After I shared the adventure with everyone, and listened to every suggestion, and absorbed the pure excitement of this adventure, and prepared as best as I could, I froze in the kitchen one day after unpacking groceries (a bottle of Côte du Rhône, a baguette, camembert, brie de meaux, spinach, onions, mushrooms, eggs, and Cheetos). And I completely, absolutely, insanely freaked out. I lost it. My strength melted into fears around all the unknowns, all the unfamiliar, all the ways this choice could go wrong. Terribly, awfully, irrevocably wrong. I was *moving* to Paris. Not visiting, not traveling around, not hanging out for a bit and then returning home with postcards. I was *committing* to a new city that I have never been to before. My energy shifted from enthusiasm and inspiration to the muddy, sticky, doubts of being far from home, far from loved ones, far from the comforts of a stable existence. *How was I going to pull this off? Who was I to dream this big and trust that it would be supported? Who was I to follow this path with no backup plan? Who was I to move to Paris, where I knew no one, barely spoke the language, and had no clue where to live?*

My breath shortened every time these thoughts blew through my mind. I could cancel. I could postpone. I could reapply to graduate school the following term. I could wait a bit longer and save more money. I could give myself more time to figure out a concrete plan, and do more research, and go to more classes, and collect more...

Stop. Breathe. Relax.

Knock it off. There will always be a long list of reasons *not* to do something. Always. But there is only one way to do it, and that was to do it. So do it. Courage kicked in, a trait I had in spades, and I recognized the situation: the simultaneous feelings were yes and no, but my conscious choice was to still go. *Courage says go.*

Then I flipped every doubt around 180 degrees:

Who was I to withhold my life dreams? Who was I to play it small and sit on the sidelines? Who was I to doubt when I thrived on trusting? Who was I to give up on what I truly wanted? Who was I to let my dreams float away as if they weren't a part of me, as if they didn't belong to me, as if they were not my skin and bones and essence that resided in my heart?

I then trained myself to give every doubt or question, especially and most certainly the ones at 2:41 a.m., over to God, to Spirit, to my Divine Support Team. *Here, please take these fears. There is no room for them in my suitcase. I refuse them with love and replace them with Trust. Thank you kindly.*

I moved through the unknowns with greater speed as the weeks passed and my launch date got closer. And I found myself in an interesting place with friends. A big life development was underway, but it was not preceded by a bridal shower, bachelorette party, baby shower, or housewarming gifts because unlike those expected rights-of-passage, there was no customary way to celebrate this type of life decision. But I wanted to do *something* to kick-off the adventure and gather with my besties. Because truthfully, in the back of my mind, I had faint uncertainties about when I would see them again and how I would be different next time we connected and how life between us would be changed. I pushed those thoughts away and instead focused on a party.

A cliché wine-and-cheese gathering made me cringe because I would be surrounded by red wine, baguettes, and a variety of stinky cheeses soon enough. Instead I hosted a highly un-French Bon Voyage party at a trendy bowling alley with everything I would not have access to across the pond: pints of frothy craft beer, terrible-for-you-fried-food, tons of conversations in English, and new photos with our cheeks pressed up together in the terribly-lit alley. Red, blue, and green balls rolled down the wooden highways for hours as the neon lights eventually came on across all the lanes. My bowling score was the lowest because I was more focused on chatting instead of sticking my fingers in the bowling ball holes and focusing on a straight line. And every time I glanced down the bowling lane, I was reminded of an airport runway and how much packing I still had to do.

The day before departure, I froze again while organizing and packing, sorting and prioritizing. I stared at all of my *stuff* splayed out on the floor, and looked at the suitcases everything had to fit into, and glanced around the living room at the comfortable sofa with the worn green pillow, and listened to the mailman's car whiz by as he delivered English-language magazines throughout the neighborhood, and then I looked back at the empty blue suitcase with a cat now sitting in it as if she had been there all along. My eyes started blinking faster as reality hit. I was really leaving tomorrow and saying goodbye to this life for a new, unknown, uncertain life. It was finally real. A crazy mixture of pure delight and slight dread pulsed through my body. Lyrics from the band Semisonic started running through my head: *Every new beginning comes from some other beginning's end.* And in this moment, I wanted both the new and the known. I'll take an order of the fresh adventure in a new land, but with a side of comfort shopping at Target and knowing the neighborhood. This type of crossroads had become a continual part of my life: change versus stability; a favorite new place versus my favorite pillow; sitting on the couch with a cat in my lap versus sitting on a plane with a laptop.

I picked up the cat sitting in the suitcase and held her close to my chest, rocking back and forth to comfort myself as she tried to jump down. I managed to squeeze her for a split-second longer and then released her, her back claws pushing off my stomach. I couldn't focus, so I laced up my walking shoes and decided to get some fresh English-speaking air before doing anything else. A short walk always makes things better.

Then I walked back in the door twenty minutes later with more clarity and strength than ever before. A resounding *YES!* vibrated throughout my being. The other cat was now sleeping in my suitcase. I returned to packing around her with gusto.

The security line at the airport the following morning was incredibly long. My mom and I paced forward together, separated by the black elastic security band and an approaching ticket checkpoint that was our final opportunity for contact. We walked as slowly as possible, exchanging reassuring phrases back and forth. We didn't know when we would see each other again and all I could do was twirl my hair a bit while pushing my carry-on forward, trying to stay in the moment. There is a beautiful scene in the movie "Love Actually" where passengers have landed at the London Heathrow airport terminal and they embrace a loved one waiting for them in the arrival area. Hugs, kisses, smiles, tears, reunions. It is one of my favorite images of travel. A reminder of the good stuff that can happen in airports, amongst the steel surfaces and hard glances and overpriced everything. And it is also the worst possible scene to be thinking about when you're venturing to a foreign land and saying goodbye to your mom in the public, impatient airport security line. *Stop thinking about it, stop picturing it, turn off the movie.*

I handed over my ticket and identification to a stoned-faced young man. His hat was too big. He grunted and allowed me through and I turned to wave at my mom. Even at 28-years-old, I still felt an emotional wave swelling inside as I waved goodbye to her known smile. I moved through the screening area as if I was on a sushi conveyor belt. I picked up my bag and stood on my tiptoes to see if she was still there. Between the moving people, I saw her hand move across her cheek. And that was when my tears started because I was really leaving my mom and my known world behind. Just like my ten year-old self had experienced years ago.

"MOM, IS HE GOING TO be there?"

"Yes, honey, definitely. He'll be right there waiting for you."

"Are you sure? What if he isn't there and forgets? What do I do?"

"Honey, he will be there waiting for you right at the gate. You will see him first thing when you get off the plane. It's going to be okay." She smiled and nodded. I believed her every time she reassured me. I just wanted to hear the plan *one more* time.

I gripped her hand tighter and looked down at my black leggings, puffy pink skirt, and cropped jean jacket. Then I twirled my hair that was held back with a fluorescent pink scrunchy. A collection of black jelly bracelets were tangled around my right arm just like Madonna wears. What if Madonna is on this flight, too? Wow, that would be the coolest story to tell everyone back at school. Or maybe Kirk Cameron will sit next to me and smile like he does in all of those posters on my bedroom wall. He's sooo cute.

"Mom, did we pack my books?"

She reached into my little bag and pulled out one *Sweet Valley High* book and one *The Babysitter's Club* book. I nodded. "Okay, good." My books will make this really long flight better. I hoped.

We walked up to the gate and my mom shuffled all of the important adult papers around with one hand, and passed them over to the lady at the counter. I held onto her hand and glanced around the waiting area to see if there were any celebrities on this flight. Then the counter lady with big brown eyes and bouncy blond hair stepped to the side of the counter and smiled down at me.

"So you're meeting your dad in Washington, D.C.? That's pretty exciting to be ten-years-old and to fly cross-country by yourself." She gave me a smile wider than the wings on the plane. I blushed shyly but felt pride at the same time. She continued. "I'm Susan, Molly, and I am going to help you get on the plane and into your seat and make sure you are taken care of, okay? This will be fun and we'll make sure you find your dad once we land, okay?"

I nodded in response. My mom smiled and winked at Susan as she disappeared back behind the counter, only her blue shoe sticking out now. My stomach felt tight like a water balloon.

It was my dad's exciting idea to fly over and visit him while he was working near Washington, D.C. He was actually working in a place called Tyson's Corner, Virginia, but I did not know who Tyson was or why he had his own special corner. I was excited to go there even though Tyson was a boy's name and his corner probably smelled. Boys were gross like that.

Anyways, there would be so much to see and do in Washington, D.C., I told myself. All of the monuments and statues and museums and stuff. I had my own special Kodak instant camera packed in my suitcase and I would write a school report on what I see and do. We were learning in school all about the fifty American states and their capitals, so it would be totally cool to see the national capitol in person. (And that's "capitol" with an '"o," not "capital" with an "a," as every fifth grader must remember because you could make a mistake with that word during the school spelling bee if you didn't ask for it in a sentence.)

My mom and I sat down in the waiting area — no celebrities yet — and I dug into my bag to open an individual pack of Cheetos. My toes were clenching so I kept shaking them out.

"Mom, does Susan know how to call you in case she needs anything?" My feet swung back and forth on the chair, toes pointed, as my fingers turned orange.

"Yes, she has the home phone number and our address and everything. How are you feeling?"

"I'm excited. We're going to see a lot of cool stuff."

"You're going to have a great time seeing all of the monuments!"

"Yeah, I told Dad I want to see the Lincoln one and the Washington one and all the other ones. We might go to an amusement park, too." My mom handed over a napkin just as I was tempted to wipe my orange fingers on the black leather.

"Everything is going to be just fine," she said again. I nodded again. Then a loud voice came over the speakers and said my mom's name and my name. Maybe I was the celebrity on this flight!

We stood up and walked to the big square doorways that led to the plane. I peeked down the hole and saw that it turned to the left. Susan smiled down at me. "Time to get on the plane, Molly! And you're one of the first people to get on board. Ready to go?" She reached out her hand.

I nodded yes and straightened my pink skirt a bit more to prepare for my plane entrance. My stomach was nervous again and this time it felt like an orange water balloon. I hugged my mom tightly and rested my chin on her shoulder as my hands clasped behind her neck. She smelled like Ivory soap and soft flower petals. Her eyes looked a little wet, like mine felt. She said lots of comforting words and nodded and smiled. It made my wet eyes feel better.

Susan and I entered the square box of doors and after three steps forward, I stopped and turned to wave, my mom leaning into the square frame. I looked up at Susan to signal I was ready to go again, and she smiled and winked. Then we walked down the long, long, long hall until we almost turned to the left. I stopped again, right before the turn and saw my mom waving still, her other hand moving across her cheek. I waved back even though I really wanted to run back up the long, long, long hall. I held onto Susan's hand a little tighter and then we turned left around the corner and a huge plane door was right there. I knew it was going to be okay because I was strong and going on a big adventure. My dad would be there when I landed. And maybe I'll see some celebrities in Washington, D.C., too!

"CAN I OPEN IT, DAD?" A white envelope with my name on it was sitting on the kitchen counter.

"Nope, you have to wait until after school."

Ugh, that's, like, in forever.

I picked up the envelope and held it in front of the window. "But where are we going? Can you give me a hint?"

"Nope! No hints! That's the fun of it!" He smiled and sipped his coffee, then walked back to his office. Today was the last day of sixth grade and I was so excited for summer to be here. But I really, really, really wanted to know where I was going on vacation. I put the envelope down on the kitchen counter and grabbed my school bag. Maybe this will be the fastest day of school ever.

Yesterday, my dad told me and my brothers that he was starting something new for us as we graduated from elementary, junior high, and senior high schools: he would take us individually on a trip to somewhere exciting and cool to celebrate! The trip destination would always be a surprise and we would not know where he would take us until after we attended the last day of school. If we ditched school, we had to wait at least another day to find out about the trip and that would just be torture because my suitcase could be packed by then!

The final school bell rang and yellow buses swarmed the parking lot like bees. I rushed home, both of my brothers trailing behind, and we all ran down the giant hill in front of the house together. We were two years apart in school so I was the only one graduating this year. I flung my backpack in the entryway and dashed up the stairs to the envelope.

"Okay, Dad! It's time! It's time! School is over and I get to open this now!" I jumped up and down with excitement, my Aquanet-sprayed bangs not moving at all.

He rambled in and stood in the middle of the kitchen. "So, where are you going?"

"EEEE!" I tore open the envelope and pulled out three brightly colored brochures and oh my gosh! Los Angeles, Hollywood, Beverly Hills, and Disneyland! We're going to all of the places where famous people live! Oh my gosh, what if I run into Kirk Cameron! Or maybe we'll see the New Kids on the Block! EEEE!

"Thank you so much, Dad!" I was still bouncing as I ran over to hug him around the waist.

"You're very welcome. We're going to have a great time. It's important for you to get out and see more of the country."

"Yes, I can't wait! It is going to be the best summer ever!" I bounced down to my bedroom to find my suitcase and start packing even though the trip was two weeks away.

"CAN I OPEN IT NOW, Dad?"

"Nope, you know you have to wait until school is over. Same rules every time!" He smiled and sipped his coffee.

Ugh, I hated waiting. Last year my brother Jeff went to San Antonio and the previous year my brother Tim went to Florida. So I knew I was not going to either of those places. But I wanted to know. *Now.*

I rushed off to my last day of junior high with my yearbook tucked inside my otherwise empty bag. Everyone just sat around on the floor in the hallways and at cafeteria tables and wrote yearbook things like *We're outta here!!! Have a great summer and maybe I'll see you around* and *It was great being in English with you, you rock!* and *See you next year in high school when we will be sophomores and rule!!!* I tried to write original things but I couldn't be creative after a certain point. I just wanted to rush home to open that envelope.

"Okay, Dad, it's time!" I called, running up the driveway. He was washing the car in the June sunshine, white suds dripping off the back bumper. I stepped wide over the stream of water running down to the road.

"I'll be done in ten minutes. Just ten more minutes, Miss!" He smiled behind his dark sunglasses.

"Can I bring the envelope out here?" Standing with a slight attitude in my legs, impatience in my voice.

"Nope, ten more minutes, you can do it! And then the best summer ever will begin!"

I went into the cool house and reread some of my yearbook messages, hovering right over the envelope the whole time. Twelve minutes later, my dad walked inside and took off his sunglasses.

"So where are you going?"

I eagerly tore open the envelope and stared at the brochure, slight confusion crossing over my face. What is West Edmonton Mall? I flipped the brochure over and oh my gosh—it was the biggest mall in the *whole* world?!

"Thank you so much, Dad!" I hugged his waist. "Wow, this place looks cool. They have an amusement park and a water park and an ice skating rink? In a mall?" My eyes were big, trying to see further into each image on the brochure.

"Yeah, I thought you would like that. You can wander around the biggest mall in the world by yourself a bit and not be embarrassed by your ol' dad." He smiled. "Plus, it would be good for you to spend some time in Canada and see how things are different in other countries." I nodded while flipping the brochure around. I had heard the money was different up there and that the numbers on the road signs were really big. People can drive really fast, like up to 110 in some places! I should get my driver's license there next year instead of here.

I ran down to my room to start packing. I was used to packing often now because my parents had been divorced for a few years and my brothers and I went back and forth between their two houses every three weeks. They lived in the same neighborhood, only five minutes apart, and we had bedrooms at each place. I stared into my closet and threw potential clothes onto the bed. I have never been on an international flight before!

SOLITUDE

THE PARIS SUNLIGHT BEAT INTO my eyes as I exited the metro station, slightly disoriented and confused about where I was in the city. A tangled intersection split off in five different directions and there was no time to take a wrong turn. I needed to be at this apartment viewing within five minutes. Streams of people glided towards the busiest street. I followed along, and we all turned down Rue Saint Charles, exactly where I needed to be. My legs sped up as I dodged slow dogs and gaggles of school kids on the sidewalk.

Earlier today, Anne-Marie had called a few more potential rentals I found over the weekend. She spoke to the proprietor of this apartment a few hours ago and the woman was willing to meet me right away. Anne-Marie hung up with a pseudo-smile, saying this was a very good area of town to live in. I thanked her in my over-the-top American style and dashed out the door as quickly as possible. This apartment could be a wonderful solution for both the proprietor and myself; I could feel it. Maybe the energy around this apartment hunt had changed overnight like I had intended.

More good news had arrived this morning when Francine shared that I could stay until Friday instead of Tuesday because the traveler who was supposed to arrive changed their plans. Francine's willingness to extend my stay was generous, especially at the last minute since even though she was accustomed to having houseguests, it would certainly be desirable to have your home back to yourself after a while.

I arrived at lucky number 153, barely two minutes late, and no one was waiting at the door nor anywhere in the vicinity. But this was France: being on time was not relative to a clock; it was relative to personal convenience. I took a step back to stand on the edge of the curb and relaxed into the energy of the fifteenth *arrondissement*:

To the left of the apartment building door was a bustling fruit and vegetable store. A worker unloaded pallets and boxes of seasonal fruit fresh from the outskirts of Paris while another employee stacked nectarines that resembled plump little balls of sunrise. A woman reached for handfuls of round, firm tomatoes, dismantling the precarious pyramid arrangement, which brought the owner over swiftly to start a new pile. A young boy looked up at his distracted mother before quickly sampling from the overflowing *paquettes* of raspberries and blueberries.

Next to the fruit stand was an optometrist's office with a flashing pair of neon eyeglasses in the window, and beyond that was a Franprix grocery store. These little shopping markets were all around the city, and it would be ideal to live so close to one. I could run to the market on a whim for dinner inspiration or when I had an immediate craving for *mousse au chocolat*.

Looking to the right of the apartment building door was a dark, I saw a dark and dated Chinese restaurant. I stepped back further on the sidewalk to see a quaint little *boulangerie* on the other side of the *restaurant au chinois*. A middle-aged woman stood behind the counter, sipping an Orangina, and then greeted a slender man with a discreet smile. She reached for a fresh baguette from the pile stacked lengthwise in a wicker basket. He handed her a coin and tipped his hat in gratitude. She blushed as he walked outside and checked his watch.

I spun around to see what the other side of the street offered. Directly across from me was a bookstore with tables of untouched printed stacks sitting quietly in the shade. A boutique clothing store, a one-window shoe store, and a small Greek restaurant were all within view. Farther down the street, through moving silhouettes of people, I spied a laundry mat and a store selling household odds and ends. Everything I needed and wanted for my basic lifestyle was right here. It was almost too perfect, too picturesque. I was hesitant to fall completely in love until I saw the apartment, but it was certainly possible to imagine this *arrondissement* as my new neighborhood. *Très charmant.*

A car door slammed right in front of the building and I came back to reality. A woman with curly brown hair and friendly doe-eyes walked up to the building's entrance and stalled, glanced at her watch, and looked down the street.

"*Excusez-moi, Madame? Je m'appelle Molly et je suis interessante en l'appartement.*" Excuse me, Madame? My name is Molly and I am interested in the apartment.

Her brown eyes lit up in response. "*Bonjour, Mademoiselle. Bienvenue.*" Hello, Mademoiselle. Welcome.

Madame punched in the digi-code and invited me to follow her through the entrance flanked with stained-glass panels. The street noise quickly fell away. We passed a spiral staircase in the lobby before proceeding through the quiet hall and then outside into a small courtyard. She led the way through another building and then a second courtyard. I looked up just in time to see a cloud coasting between the building towers. We proceeded to the final building marked "C." I had no idea there would be three buildings behind the unassuming entrance. It was like the clown car of apartment buildings.

Madame walked up the spiral wood staircase to the second floor and stopped at the only door on the landing. A funky brass handlebar was in the center of it. After a slight jingle of the keys, she pressed the center handlebar and flung the door open with a smile, allowing the apartment to reveal itself. Then she politely gestured for me to step in first.

A blue futon sat as the main attraction in the living space. A small table nestled up to the left side and a wall mirror hung above it. I inspected a compact wall closet hidden discreetly in the corner with narrow hanging space. Another door hid a sparkling bright bathroom with a window that opened onto the courtyard.

My body slowly started to spin around the studio as I looked up, down, around, and behind me. She pulled back the dramatic blue curtain covering the single floor-to-ceiling window and the space started to dance as sunlight streamed in from the courtyard and stretched all the way to the back kitchen wall. A wood countertop with two bar stools separated the kitchen and living area. A stunning wood beam over the kitchen counter added character and rustic charm to the quaint space. The three-foot-wide kitchen was a corridor composed of a small sink, two electric burners, and a giant shelving wall unit stocked with cooking essentials. A small refrigerator sat in the living room, as it appeared to be just a smidge too big to fit in its intended space under kitchen counter. No oven, no microwave, and certainly no dishwasher.

After completing two slow turns to take it all in, I had one simple thought:

I love it. I absolutely love it.

Everything was clean, comfortable, and cute. Fresh sunlight hit the mirror, the bathroom tiles, and all of the kitchen cabinets. I would need to buy some kitchen essentials, but at least there were linens, pots, pans, utensils, and plates. I could easily live here.

I love it. I absolutely love it.

Madame showed me that everything in the space worked. She was pleasant, kind, and patient, especially with my foreign accent. I would have no problem talking with her if there was a problem of any kind. She lived close by and said that I could always leave her a note in her mailbox if I needed anything. Madame then shared that the apartment had been empty for a few months because she was saving it for a relative who did not have the money. She had not found a suitable renter in the past few days and she had been losing money each month since the relative never paid her. The apartment was ready now if I wanted to move in right away. Chills went down my body and I started to smile big like an American. This was a beautiful solution for both of us.

"Oui. Je pense que c'est parfait pour moi, Madame." It is perfect for me, Madame.

"Très bien, Mademoiselle." Very good, Mademoiselle.

She reached into her bag for the rental documents and we meticulously reviewed every line on the agreement. She only requested a month's deposit instead of the typical two months' deposit. I could only pay her in cash since I did not have a bank account yet, and thankfully, she was okay with that arrangement, too. Many proprietors required a monthly check as proof of payment for their taxes.

She inquired about my *carte de sejour,* the legal document that proved I could live in France long-term. I told her I was in the process of obtaining it, but I had fortunately been pre-approved before leaving the United States and I would send her a copy as soon as possible.

We signed two copies of everything and she handed me the keys so I could move in that weekend. Gratitude spilled out all over my face. I could leave Francine's place on Friday. I had a place to call home in Paris. I could stay in France. I couldn't stop smiling.

Madame closed the big blue curtain since the show was now over. She asked if I needed anything else, elegantly bringing her hands together in front of her stomach.

"*Je suis heureuse, Madame.*" I am happy, Madame.

She smiled in return. "*Je suis heureuse aussi, Mademoiselle.*" I am happy also, Mademoiselle.

On the way out, Madame pointed to the trash and recycle receptacles, my mailbox, and officially gave me the door code to the building. We parted ways with a slight handshake and genteel smiles.

Relief was now present in my body, so I slowed down to take in more of my new neighborhood on the walk back to the metro: Dogs strolled without leashes next to their owners. Old men stood on the curb chatting about the weather, hands waving in the air. Corner *patisseries* had lines forming for after-work baguettes. A produce shop owner yelled prices down the street, talking up today's featured selections. The cheese shop accumulated a crowd of dedicated followers and a few women walked swiftly with bunches of fresh cut flowers tucked under their arms. Children lumbered obediently next to their mothers, holding on to the strollers of their younger siblings. A new surge of energy began each time a bus halted to release travelers, or a metro train arrived and more people flooded onto the sidewalks.

And then I finally glanced up to see the Eiffel Tower looming straight ahead.

I stopped in the middle of the sidewalk, dumbfounded. My attention had been captured by the street-level activity for the past ten minutes, and in all of my confusion and focus on finding the apartment, I had lost my sense of direction about where I was in the city. I had no idea I was this close to the iconic monument. Every day, any possible hour, every season, and twelve months a year, the Eiffel Tower would be present as a constant reminder of where I was in the world. I shook my head in amazed wonder.

Ten minutes later, I practically galloped into Anne-Marie's office. She was on the phone, so I shifted awkwardly in the doorway while she finished the call. Just as she began to say a proper "au revoir," I spilled my excitement all over her desk.

"I got it! I got this apartment! I signed the documents and everything! Thank you so much for all of your help! I could not have done it without you!" Hand on my heart, trying to refrain from hugging her.

"Congratulations! That is wonderful news. And very unusual! You found a home quickly."

"I am very grateful. You were so helpful, thank you again. I greatly appreciate it."

"You're welcome. It was no problem at all." She smiled and looked down to shuffle papers on her desk.

"It is a perfect little place, very bright and cozy. The neighborhood is wonderful and has everything I need."

"Yes, that part of town is very nice, very comfortable. I'm sure you will enjoy it."

"Yes, definitely." Trying my best not to do twirls and spins in her office. "Well, I must get ready to move my things. I will see you soon during orientation. You were a lifesaver, Anne-Marie! *Merci beaucoup!*"

"I am glad I could help. See you soon, Molly." She smiled kindly and reached for the phone as I glided out the door.

By the time I arrived at Francine's, I had already decorated my new home at least five different ways. She was in the hallway putting on a light coat and getting ready to leave for her painting class.

"Is there enough room for your luggage in your new home?" She asked with raised eyebrows. Glad this joke never dies.

"Yes, but there won't be enough space for them in a cab. I'll make a few trips on the metro to move two bags tomorrow." I had already mentally sorted out the moving logistics since how my suitcases went up is how they needed to come down. And this time I was prepared.

"*Bonne idée.*" She tied a soft cotton scarf around her neck and grabbed her purse, then her lavender scent wafted out the door.

Friday morning arrived quickly. Francine and I had both been busy the past few days, passing each other between errands and priorities, so we said our farewells on the sidewalk and exchanged *bisous* on each cheek. She had been a temporary landing place and now it was time to leave her nest and fly off to my own. It was interesting to live with someone, share their personal space and every day moments, and yet realize you would probably never see them again. Her waving figure gradually shrank behind the taxi as her familiar scent lingered somewhere in my coat.

The taxi driver eyed me with curiosity in the rearview mirror. After weaving through the city streets for a few moments, he kindly asked where I was from and what I was doing in Paris. I responded in stumbling French that I had just arrived to pursue some high-level studies, and today I was moving to my first apartment. He raised his eyebrows and nodded along. I rambled on; openly sharing that I was learning a lot about Paris, but it was hard at times to be a foreigner. It was a beautiful place and I was sure I would enjoy it once I was settled, once my new life was known. He listened thoughtfully, looking in the rearview mirror from time to time, then slammed on the brakes and waved his fist at other cabs. I finally fell silent. Why was I sharing so much with this taxi driver? Maybe because it was nice to speak anonymously and allow my mind to decompress. We crossed over the Seine and the Eiffel Tower grew bigger.

We pulled up to the curb five minutes later as he squeezed in between parked cars and delivery vans. He jumped out of the cab immediately and carried my two heavy bags to the front of the building. I dug in my purse for the right change, and handed him the fare.

But before taking it, he put both his hands on my shoulders, looked right into my shocked eyes, and said, *"Bon courage, Mademoiselle! Bon courage!"* Have courage, Mademoiselle! Have courage!

Then he leaned in to give me a brief shoulder hug, took the cab fare, and jumped back in his getaway car. I stood stunned on the sidewalk.

Did a Parisian taxi driver really just hug me? And it was a nice, caring gesture with no creepiness intended. He was simply cheering me on and giving me strength for this new life. People can be amazing in unexpected ways.

I awkwardly and slowly scooted my hefty bags through the two courtyards and into the back building. A man approached and offered to hold the door open.

"Merci, Monsieur."

He nodded in return. And before I knew it, he grabbed the first bag and ran up the stairs with it, and then yelled down to ask which level I lived on.

"Au premier étage!" The first level. I blurted out as his footsteps echoed up the stairwell.

Thirty seconds later, he came back down, panting, and grabbed the handles of my second bag. He pulled that one up the stairs with more ease than I could have ever mustered. Then he ran back down and dashed out the door.

"Bonne journée, Mademoiselle!" His words flew up into the clouds.

I just found where Superman lived in Paris.

I shut my apartment door quietly behind me and turned to see every item in the room sitting in stillness. I was here. I was home. This is it. Silence surrounded everything. I rested my back against the door, and it dawned on me that I was now completely by myself. Completely. Not only was I alone in this apartment or in this city; I was all alone in this country and on this continent. Everyone I knew and loved was on the other side of an ocean, thousands of miles away. There were no familiar faces here; no known connections. All of the movements, anxieties, and thoughts around getting settled had now halted, leaving me alone with the opportunity to be free, to breathe in the purity of a space without distractions, and to appreciate the grand beauty of silence. Solitude was regularly part of the re-adjusting phase after a jump. Again it was my faithful friend that I knew so well.

A NEVER-ENDING EXPANSE OF highway filled the windshield view as I leaned over to turn up Coolio's latest hit, "Fantastic Voyage." It was totally the best song on the radio right now. All four windows were cracked open, filling the car with innocent June air, as our drive south to Monterey, California from Seattle was officially underway. My brother Tim was in the passenger seat and I could see my dad and youngest brother, Jeff, in the second vehicle behind us. One car would stay with me in Monterey and the other would be their return ticket home.

I just graduated from high school last week (*Class of '95, wooo hooo!*) and I was so ready to be out in the world. I didn't want to sit in classes anymore; I wanted to move! I decided not to go to college right away since I had not found a university that interested me and I wasn't sure what I wanted to major in. And I wasn't interested in rushing back to a desk.

So I was moving to California to work at a hotel restaurant for a while. My aunt was the general manager of an inn in Monterey and I went down to check everything out a few months ago during spring break. She interviewed me, gave me a tour, and hired me to be a server at the Crazy Horse Restaurant. I had only worked in retail stores so far, and being a server seemed like a pretty cool job to try. And even better, I would be in California! It felt like a movie plot: moving to California to work at a hotel for a summer. Life was going to be so awesome! This was so much better than getting ready for college.

But there was one big problem: I was leaving behind my boyfriend Trevor. We decided to stay together as a couple even though we would be miles apart. I was already committed to this job when we started dating and there was no changing plan now. We figured we would have high phone bills every month and know each other's addresses by heart because we would send letters and postcards every week. Maybe my new job would keep me from missing him all the time? Hopefully.

Trevor stopped by this morning to say goodbye. After three seat belts clicked, the engines started, and radio station songs began humming out of the windows, we finally separated from our embrace to go our different directions. He waved longer, but I held more Kleenexes. Maybe it was harder to be the person left behind than the person leaving. I wiped a slow-moving tear off my cheek as Candlebox's "Far Behind" started to come over the airwaves. We were about to cross the state line into Oregon and all I wanted to do was turn around.

Two days later, our cars pulled up to a charming ranch house in the discomfort of a Central California afternoon. The air was agonizingly still. I fell out of the car, eager to stretch my legs, and looked at my temporary accommodations. I would be living in my aunt and uncle's unfinished one-car garage.

I saw the garage space during my spring break visit, so I knew what awaited me upon arrival. For $100 a month, I would enjoy drywall-covered siding, the backside of a brick fireplace, and an operating garage door that may or may not open as I was pulling a t-shirt over my head. Two blinding fluorescent lights hung down the middle of the open ceiling, and the floor was cement, hard, and grey. No insulation existed between the vertical wall beams, but one big window provided sunlight and fresh air. A workbench stood alone against the back wall. The "before" picture had been in my head for months.

Now, I entered the space to see it magically transformed with unused furniture and carpet from the hotel's storage facility. My garage hotel room consisted of a queen size bed, two side tables, a five-drawer dresser, and a round table with two chairs. Everything sat on a huge scrap of beige carpet. My clothes would hang at the back of the garage on an old wall-mounted coat rack and a vanity mirror sat on the floor, leaning up against the brick wall. The workbench was politely covered with a white drop cloth. I came prepared with lacy white curtains to hang in the open wall beams and a few posters to make the space more my own. I cracked open the window to get some fresh air circulating as we started to unpack the vehicles. Welcome home.

I began my new job: eager, excited, and naïve. Learning to

balance a tray full of eight glasses took time; I walked slowly, staring at the beverages as they taunted me. The drink names were bizarre and the bartender had to lean in for clarity while I repeated the order for a "gay goose under his rocks." Figuring out the chef's timing on food orders was an important strategy as I started to learn the individual styles of each cook. And making sure the cash register added up properly at the end of the night was not as easy as you'd think. How could it be off by forty-three cents? Where does that change go?

I quickly became acquainted with having sore feet and always being in motion, but it was my days off that really stumped me. There were no people my age in the neighborhood. All of my co-workers were at least seven years older and had busy lives of their own. Trevor and I talked a few times a week, but the bill became expensive quickly so I was cautious of clinging to the phone too much.

I had never felt so alone. I tried to force each day to pass faster by doing my laundry, running errands, taking care of my nails, and trying to sleep late or go to bed early. This was not the fun, easy, California-livin' lifestyle I thought I would have. It certainly was no movie plot, unless it was the slowest and most boring movie ever made.

The table fan churned away as I lay on the bed, staring up at the ceiling. I felt like I was playing a card game where I had held a great assortment before: Senior, Cheerleader Captain, Boyfriend, Busy, Fun, and Friends. Now I was holding: Bored, Alone, Lame, Work, Unfinished Garage, and Long-Distance Boyfriend. This hand sucked. Why did I decide to shuffle the deck? I did not expect this type of loneliness. It was only one o'clock on a beautiful California afternoon and I did not know what to do. Was I not trying hard enough? Was I being lazy? Was I missing something obvious? Was I... oh no... was I... (gasp!) BORING?

NO!

No way! Deny, deny, deny! I was NOT boring! I was active and full of life! I loved to do all kinds of things, and to be outside, and to learn! I was exciting! I was happening! I was just in a lull, and figuring out what I wanted to do next, and "exploring my recreational options." I have never been dull. I will not allow this description to stick to me! No, I was not *boring*.

Hmmm. Unless. Maybe, it is a little true right now.

But it was ONLY because of the situation and the changes I made, by choice, in my life. I was simply adjusting and becoming acquainted with my new lifestyle. I was considering my options, reviewing possible things to do, evaluating what would be enjoyable.

Okay, fine. I was totally lying to myself. I was horizontal on a bed staring at the dry wall of a garage on a beautiful day. I was the definition of Boring. I had three days off in a row to prove how Not Boring I was. I put my wedge sandals back down onto the floor and decided to go the theater. Right now. Gone. Not boring.

A movie called "Clueless" was just released, so I went over to the local theater. Three kids my age paced behind the popcorn counter in the empty lobby. No one else was in sight since the theater was completely empty on a Tuesday afternoon. I had never been to a movie by myself before, so it felt slightly awkward. As the previews ran, I nestled lower into the chair and put both feet up on the seats in front of me. Trevor would not be interested in this movie, anyway.

The next day, I set out to prove how Not Boring I was again by going to another movie. The difference this time was that Trevor wanted to see this movie, so it was hard to be here without him. I started to recall how cute he was, and then missed his face. I sank into the chair pushed down by a little sadness on my shoulders.

My third day off from work arrived and now there were no more movies I wanted to see. It was another beautiful July day in Central California and I was all alone with twelve full hours of sunlight to kill. I showered, dressed, and headed out to the car. I had no idea where I was going, but I was determined to be Not Boring somewhere else. I felt alone in more ways than I had anticipated and parts of my previous life were sometimes all I could see. This solitude thing was hard.

I drove west towards Monterey and then south on Highway 101, passing the Pebble Beach Golf Course as it sat on a precarious perch over the Pacific Ocean. The greenways stretched out to the water, daring the waves to take a swing at the eighteen holes. I could only imagine how many golf balls had made it into the water. I could probably start a Save the Golf Balls Foundation with my extra time.

The idyllic one-square-mile town of Carmel-By-the-Sea seemed like a good place to spend an afternoon being Not Boring. Giant trees and blooming flowers protected the town from the world's demands. I strolled lazily around the small cottage houses, walked the white sand beach, and enjoyed lemonade at a small café. I drove back to Salinas just before rush hour blocked the two lane highways. It was the first time I had so many hours to myself without conversations or interactions. The lack of social interaction was my greatest distraction.

The time before me was the longest never-ending road. My brain was starting to feel different.

After three days by myself, I was so excited to go back to work and talk – talk! - with people: co-workers, customers, managers, strangers, all of them, for longer than was needed, just to make up for the empty spaces. I couldn't wait to pick up my timecard and clock into my apron.

As the summer dragged on, a heavier loneliness crept in through the garage door cracks and started to weigh on my shoulders. I missed Trevor. I missed my family. I missed home. I didn't want to be here by myself anymore. Enough of this lame long-distance stuff and being alone. I didn't want to do it. I wanted to go home. What were the rewards of this solitude, anyways?

CHILDREN'S LAUGHTER SPIRALLED UP THROUGH the courtyard as I continued the dance of unpacking. Clothes were randomly strewn on the futon, floor, and bar chairs. The two biggest suitcases were openly bare after the victories of hanging, folding, sorting, and stacking. Another suitcase contained my favorite traveling décor items: small posters, framed photos, and soft pieces of fabric that could be used for pillow covers, window accents, or wall art. I had learned that an important part of making a home for myself quickly and easily was to arrive with personalized essentials that could be used in any space. And I was betting on one thing when I moved to Paris: at least I would not have to live in a garage again.

It was ten years ago this summer that I had been unpacking clothes in a garage over twice this size. My 18-year-old self had no idea how a summer of solitude would support my future adventures in North Carolina, Portland, and Paris. Instead of remembering it as months of quiet torture, I now referenced it as an era of growth in confidence, independence, and inner equilibrium. If I could find peace within at the loneliest and most uncertain points along the way, surely that prepared me for more solitary days ahead. I saw how the silence in my mind was an opportunity for self-discovery and the lack of social interaction encouraged deeper levels of personal knowledge. The open hours of each day allowed for new routines, new events, and new options to discover and to be comfortable with myself. To trust my inner decision-making abilities and emerging instincts. Trevor and I had broken up two years later when I was away at college. Going out into the world was the right thing to do even if I missed someone else. *Don't give up your dreams for a boy.*

I tossed the remaining random items back into a suitcase and kicked it into a corner, adding another dent to the well-used bag. I peeked outside the window to see a woman directly across from my apartment leaning out to fix her potted flowers. Now it was time to explore my *arrondissement*.

Outside on bustling Rue Saint Charles, I nearly tripped over two small dogs toddling along behind their female owner. "*Arrêter, mes petits, arrêtez!*" Stop, my little ones, stop! She sang down to them.

I turned left out of the front door. The street became quieter a few blocks away as a cemetery with high stonewalls and grand trees created urban tranquility. From just above the treetops, something that resembled a giant hot air balloon appeared to be slowly lifting off for flight. I picked up my pace with curious excitement.

Yelling children ran around a basketball court in bright streaks as I entered the magnificence of Parc André Citroën. Trees lined up in orderly rows and fountains skyrocketed water into the air. Two mammoth greenhouses sat on one end of the park, as a giant lawn of green grass appeared to my right and disappeared farther out toward the Seine. A shallow waterway surrounded the huge lawn; ducklings quacked away in the water. A long diagonal walkway moved pedestrians through the main lawn. And there was the hot air balloon, rising and landing from the middle of the park, offering incredible views of the city. Now it was descending and cast a giant globe shadow across the grass. Most heads in the park turned to watch its gentle landing.

I walked around the park and discovered a collection of small gardens along the sides, each privately hosting different types of plants, walkways, and benches. The rolling Seine came into view under an above-ground train track, and a few boats were docked on the boardwalk. Another secluded garden revealed itself on the other side of the park, with a cascading wall of water, overflowing bunches of lavender, and walkways curving between trees, plants, and well-manicured bushes. The whole space had a feeling of introspection and whispers, quite thoughts and self-discovery. The gorgeous gardens and movements of nature reminded me that being alone does not mean being lonely. Being still does not mean being boring. Being quiet does not mean being unexciting. Being single does not mean being singled-out.

I strolled around the perimeter twice and inhaled the sweet scents of silence and clarity. Connection was always present in everything. What a beautiful luxury to simply be and inhale the beauty of a new choice.

THE LADDER

STAMPEDING FEET ROUSED ME EVERY morning by seven o'clock if I dared to sleep that late. Sounds of life filled the hollow staircase and swirled out into the courtyard as children dragged their school bags on the walkways, giggling and shuffling. Then abruptly the noises ended with the building doors smacking shut, and everything returned to a temporary state of calm until window shutters began peeling open for the day.

After three weeks of settling into my place, my neighbors' routines were my new descriptions of home as I became acclimated to this daily soundtrack. Superman, the Monsieur who carried my luggage up the stairs when I moved in, was the father to two kids in my building. We exchanged *bonjours* and head nods at the mailbox or while passing in the hallways. A Madame who lived in the middle building swept the public floors and hallways, and then turned to stack recyclable wine bottles with the diligence of a daily maid, quietly swearing as she pulled out the non-recyclable corks. Another Madame directed her two unleashed dogs through the building complex, their nails tap-tap-tapping on the cold linoleum. And as the June sun squinted through the cotton balls in the sky, directly across from my window, an arm appeared from behind a shrouded window covered with white lace curtains. The arm extended around the glass to water budding flower stems sitting in a balcony display. Then it disappeared back inside, leaving a flurry of curtains in its wake.

With summer classes now underway, every day had structure amidst my unending desire to explore the city. I rushed out the door each morning to grab Bus 88 to Montparnasse and arrived at school:

high on coffee, *pain au chocolat,* and occasionally a fresh-from-the-vine nectarine. When classes were complete, I leisurely sauntered back to Rue Saint Charles with the intention of finding something new along the way: an interesting side street to follow, a different way to get to class tomorrow, or a newly discovered collection of shops nestled around one of the city's many petite parks. There was no wrong way to walk around Paris. A right turn led somewhere worth visiting while a left turn pointed somewhere worthy of wasting an afternoon. My eyes were now trained to stay alert and be inquiring so as not to miss any potential discoveries. An intersection near Metro Cambronne had the perfect combination of a *brasserie* for an afternoon *café creme*, a newspaper stand with the latest international news, and a sweet floral shop to pick up individual pink, yellow, and orange Gerber daisies to brighten my kitchen counter. I never hurried home, even with the responsibilities of reading, due dates, and writing lingering on my shoulders.

The mid-June tourists clustered around the expected places—the Eiffel Tower, Notre Dame, *Champs-Élysées,* every café in the Latin Quarter—and they bogged down the metro lines with their heavy accents and loud voices. Yet I noticed that I was no longer one of those intruders because of how my posture had changed. Gone from my spine was the eagerness and hustle of a tourist leaning forward, looking for the major sites and best cafes to cross off their vacation list. Absent was the need to stay with a crowd and follow the arrows to not get lost.

Now I possessed the confidence of an almost-local who knew the natural rhythms of the city and how to navigate strategically amongst those returning to hotel pillows every night. As gaggles of tourists stood on the street corner, waiting obediently for the sign to grant them permission to walk, I glanced left and right, then briskly crossed the street as Parisians did with no care in the world, especially for oncoming traffic. I took side streets through busy neighborhoods and walked two steps faster to grab a seat on the metro. I learned to not respond in English to the gypsies walking along the Seine, claiming to have lost their wallets or a ring. I discovered the value of keeping a mental map of the best bathrooms around town so I could plan my day around these pit stops and not get stuck in long museum lines. My purse contained both sunglasses and an umbrella to deal with moody Parisian weather. My most reliable source of information was the tiny *Paris Circulation* book with maps and transportation modes all over the city so I could figure out how to get anywhere from anywhere.

I had moved from casually dating Paris as a tourist to establishing a more committed relationship built on a deeper knowingness about its true inner workings. The romance phase of our relationship was still alive, but we had matured to a more intimate connection revealing each other's vulnerabilities and authenticity. I relaxed into the pace of life and worked with the flows of the city, focusing on it strengths and forgiving its vulnerabilities. If our relationship was to last, we must choose to see the good in one another above all else. Moving away from an idealistic view of Paris freed me up to be surprised and amazed about what it would reveal next.

But our relationship was still new enough to have those unexpected awkward moments. One morning, a woman in my little neighborhood grocery store stopped me and asked if I knew where the powdered milk was located. A look of incomprehension came across my face for a split second while pondering her question. She spoke incredibly fast to my ears and I missed the first part of her sentence. During my pause, a questioning look furrowed her brow. When my mouth opened to say, *"Désolé, Madame, je ne sais pas,"* Sorry, *Madame, I don't know,* the ruse was over. I revealed myself as un-French. A look of bewilderment and betrayal crossed her face as she took a step backwards from the foreign alien and apologized for bothering me. She then turned swiftly to ask Monsieur standing in the aisle for his assistance. He pointed her in the right direction, and she walked passed me, the Great Imposter, flinging her scarf across her left shoulder. Monsieur winked and smiled, then returned to selecting a pasta sauce. Paris and I were still getting to know each other, and it appeared that I must be the one doing most of the work at this stage. I purchased my grocery store essentials, and returned home to make room for everything somewhere in the tiny fridge and limited cabinet space. Then I fell onto the futon and called my new American friend from school, Trisha. She picked up on the second ring as I leaned back, sunlight pouring over my face.

"Trish, do you ever feel like being a foreigner is a constant dance of one step forward, two steps back?"

"Yep, always. That must mean something happened today. What was it?"

I shared my morning encounter about powdered milk as she bustled around her apartment, the sounds of glasses touching and the fridge door closing coming through the phone.

"My morning was even more exciting as a foreigner. I needed eggs for breakfast, so I put on a pair of shorts, a tank top, and some sandals, and went to the store around the corner. As I was walking down the street, people were staring at me. As I was walking down the store aisles, people were staring at me. I kept looking down at myself and could not figure out why, or what, people were looking at. It started to make me paranoid. Like, was there something on my shorts? Was my shirt inside out? WHAT?" She laughed and continued. "So I'm standing in line to pay, and notice that people keep turning to look at my legs. So I look at my legs…" Trisha said.

"To see if there's something on them?"

"Right, exactly. And nope, nothing on my legs. Until I realize — "

"Oh my gosh, I know what it is!" I blurted out impulsively.

"Everyone was staring at my shorts!" she said.

"Yes!"

"They were staring at them like I was wearing the most scandalous outfit! Especially some older women and men, they were giving me "the eye," like I was about to offer sexual services in aisle two or something."

"Oh, I forgot about this. Because French women don't wear short shorts. I remember learning that same lesson when I was in Annecy a few years ago."

"Oh, you've been to France before?" Trisha inquired, pans clinging in the background.

"Yeah, I lived in the French Alps for five weeks for an intense language study program a few years ago. I'll tell you more about it later. So did people stare at you and your daisy dukes all the way home?"

"Yeah! I tried to cover myself with the plastic grocery bags I was carrying, but a few more people were staring as I walked down the street! Maybe I was a bit paranoid, but I'm not wearing those shorts again."

"Skirts are essential here in the summer. I packed a ton of them."

"Yeah, I'm glad I could go home and change into a skirt."

"So what are you doing today?"

"I'm not sure yet. Come over and let's go walk around the Marais. I want to try a falafel sandwich."

"Love it. I'll be over in twenty!" I hung up, grabbed my purse, and immediately left to catch Bus 70. The metro may be a faster ride to the sixth *arrondissement*, but rays of glorious Parisian sunshine coming through the bus windows offered better scenery than the shady, stale subway light.

Trisha was temporarily staying in a gorgeous historic Parisian apartment just one block from the Seine. The space was huge, by Parisian standards, with beautiful exposed wood beam ceilings and a modern bathroom and kitchen that contradicted the appearance of the 18th century building. A family friend was letting her live at his apartment for a few months while he was out of town, relieving her of hunting for an apartment immediately. She knew she should start looking soon since the horrors of Parisian house hunting spread like fire at school daily.

Trisha and I met during our graduate school program orientation. We hit it off like two long-distance sisters meeting after a lengthy separation, and we almost immediately relaxed into the knowingness of a comfortable friendship. Except for knowing each other's name. After orientation ended, we each needed a cell phone, so we went to the store together to get our new Paris phone numbers. While programming my number into her phone, she asked, "Wait, what's your name again?"

"Molly. What's yours?"

"Trisha."

"Cool. Let's call each other and make sure these digits work."

Then we went to lunch in Montparnasse and talked effortlessly over a shared plate of *carpaccio*, two salads, and two Diet Cokes. We divulged personal stories with each bite and I felt myself relax as our time together kept expanding. Trisha grew up in Los Angeles and recently moved to Europe to be closer to her family in Germany and Switzerland. I felt grateful to have found someone who easily understood all of the cultural differences between life on the West Coast, in America, and in France. Instant friendship, just add wine.

I rang her apartment from the street and waited a moment for her to come downstairs. She flew out the front door in a swirly cotton blue skirt and white tank top, her shoulder-length black hair flowing as a taxi zoomed past us. Trisha was an effortless Filipino beauty with warm olive skin, a sweet dimpled smile, and oversized sunglasses pulled down on her face. We didn't even need to speak as she pointed towards the Seine and intuition guided us through the side alleys.

The sun crept in and out of the clouds as we strolled across Pont Saint Michel to the city's busiest island, Île de la Cité. We veered right to pass in front of Notre Dame and its long winding snake of summer visitors. I walked pass the famous cathedral as often as possible to appreciate the towers, arches, gargoyles, and all of the intricate details signifying centuries of stories. Trisha and I paused to stand in front of the immense architecture. While glancing up at its timeless beauty, I tried to hear the voices and activities of life from previous centuries: fishermen and merchants yelling and shouting to each other along the Seine as they unloaded boats filled with deliveries from other lands. *Citoyens* strolling arm in arm while sharing the latest societal gossip. Parishioners lining up obediently to pray in the sacred space. The trees in the square stood tall and stable now, yet would have offered less shade back then. I imagined the air was filled with a confusing mixture of hot bread and slippery fish, fresh sewage and rich lavender perfumes. In my mind, it was a Paris in motion, thriving, as it became a mecca for merchants and the world.

Then when I came back to present-day life, I inhaled air filled with the unpredictable summer breeze, numerous languages, and clicking cameras. Smarmy vendors tottered around selling plastic trinkets of various shapes and sizes. Tour guides with handheld paddles led busloads of people around all sides of the cathedral, always under the watchful eyes of the gargoyles. All the while, the Seine steadily flowed along, oblivious to the changes above the water line. Before we moved on, I looked above these modern-day activities to capture in my mind's eye the eternal essence of a place where millions have brought their sacred prayers. Then we dodged the latest tour bus passengers by strolling to the calm of the other island, Île Saint-Louis.

Trisha and I crossed over the Seine again to the fourth *arrondissement* and wound through the quieter streets of the Marais. We eventually arrived on Rue des Rosiers, a lively street known for its delicious kosher bakeries, stylish shops, and the best places to grab an authentic falafel sandwich. The vibrant energy of the Marais could be felt through the art galleries, fashionable boutiques, neighborhood cafes, and a growing gay population. The area was dense with apartment buildings and historic landmarks, but there were some quiet, hidden squares with benches to lounge on. Trisha and I gravitated towards an open bench in a petite park, falafels in hand, ingredients spilling out over the warm pita. Holding a fresh roll in your hands instantly removed all other distracting scents. We reclined and watched people stroll along, noticing that no women were wearing shorts on this warm day. They probably all knew where the powdered milk was located, too.

"Have you gone to the Prefecture yet to get your *carte de sejour*?"

I asked, moving a piece of hair out of my eyes. A *carte de sejour* was the legal visa needed to stay in the country long-term.

"Nope," she replied a bit sheepishly, "I actually don't have to get one. I was born in Europe so I have citizenship here."

"Wow, you're lucky. I guess that made your decision to come to Paris easier."

"Yeah, it really did. How 'bout you? Was your decision to move here easy?" Trisha asked.

I finished chewing before responding. "The decision was the easiest part. What I had to do after that was the bigger commitment. Have you heard how difficult it is to stay in France long-term as a foreigner?"

"I've heard a little about it, but not the specifics. What was your experience?"

"Well, I received my acceptance papers from the school, but school acceptance does not mean that the French government allows you to stay in the country long-term. I needed to obtain authorization to be in the country longer than the typical ninety-day tourist visa."

"Okay." She replied, nodding.

"So, after investigating the process, I found out that I had to visit the French Consulate for visa approval prior to arriving in Paris. And as a resident of Washington State, the French Consulate I needed to visit was in San Francisco because that office covered all issues related to French immigration for the West Coast states."

"You had to go to San Francisco?"

"Yep. They had to look at my passport and verify all of my documents first. And, I had to purchase my round-trip ticket to France and bring the ticket with me to prove I was really going to Paris."

"Wait, you had to buy your round-trip ticket to Paris before even knowing if you could stay in the country long-term for school?" Trisha said, her face scrunching up.

"Yeah. That was the first of many catch-22s. I had to buy a plane ticket to Paris to prove I was actually coming here, but that was *before* I was legally allowed to stay here for longer than ninety days. So what if they did not authorize my visa and I was stuck with an international plane ticket? I had to make the commitment to arrive here before anything was solidly confirmed, and go to San Francisco to start the visa process."

"Wow, a risk with no guarantees. But what if you came to Paris first and didn't go to the French Consulate in San Francisco beforehand? Then your student visa could be denied once you were already here and you would have to return to the States and come back later with new papers?"

"Exactly. So I flew to San Francisco and followed their procedures. After all of my paperwork was examined, it was explained to me that once I arrived in France I would have to go to the local Prefecture to continue the process of acceptance into the country and then they would give me my *carte de sejour*. And I asked, why did I have to come here first for these forms when I needed to go to a different office for more forms once I arrived in Paris? Can't I complete this whole process here now?"

"What did they say?" Trisha asked. Our sandwiches were almost gone with used napkins remaining, and we were reclining lower on the bench. The tree behind us was keeping the spot cool in the growing afternoon sun. The park was now filling up with more falafel sandwiches.

"They said that if these steps here at the French Consulate were not completed prior to arrival in France, they could send me back home. No country has to allow you to stay long-term. Then they passed over my passport with a shiny new green temporary visa. It felt like a victory to see that sticker in my passport, but I had no idea the hardest part was still to come. Yet I was already committed to the choice, and sometimes, the best way to proceed is by *not* knowing the hardest part is ahead."

"And you only find out about this kind of stuff as you go. I have heard some really awful stories about going to the Prefecture and how complicated it can be." Trisha said, pulling sunglasses down to cover her eyes. "Let's go get coffee and a pastry. I want to hear how you got through the hardest part."

We departed from our shady bench as three people swarmed in to sit down.

Our quest for *café cremes* and *pain au chocolats* became a longer expedition as we wandered into B.H.V., the big department store across from *Hotel de Ville*. We strolled through handbags, scarves, jewelry, and hosiery under the watchful eyes of stern sales people looking to protect their cherished valuables. Every counter was shining with elegance and even the air felt luxurious and polished.

Trisha and I strolled back outside, then darted in and out of the shops along Rue de Rivoli. *Les soldes*, the bi-annual sales that offered big discounts, would be commencing in a few weeks so we held back on any purchases until the countrywide sales started.

An hour later, we were nestled strategically at a corner café in Saint-Michel. Our table and chairs faced *Place Saint-Michel* with the *Fontaine Saint-Michel* spouting to the left and the Seine flowing lazily to our right. Crowds ebbed and flowed with the arriving and departing buses, subway lines, and suburban trains. I stared into the moving heads in front of us, getting lost in the rhythm of a lazy summer day. *Un café au lait* sat in front of each of us on our tiny little table with a million euro view. I had discovered that Parisian wicker chairs were more comfortable than I imagined as they allowed you to sink just enough into their tightly woven seat to be accommodating while still requiring proper French posture. And it seemed the various wicker chair patterns at each café were intentionally chosen to match the décor. Nothing that could possible make a style statement was left to chance in Paris.

For all of the action in Paris, very little wind actually moved through and rustled the leaves or pushed around napkins. Sometimes along the Seine the branches would sway a little or a woman would grab her dramatic sun hat, but not usually. It was a solid city built on traditional ways of living that didn't include the complexities and uncertainties of wind. Nature must fit into the rhythms and ways of the city; not the other way around.

We lounged further into our temporary real estate and forgot to talk for a while as we took in all of the street action. Then we decided to play a game: the first person to find a woman wearing shorts did not have to pay for her coffee. Trisha brought us back to the visa conversation.

"So tell me how it went going to the Prefecture to get your *carte de sejour*. People have mentioned how time consuming it is and that multiple trips are usually required. You did get yours, right?"

"Yeah, I got it, but it was stressful. And the anticipation of getting something you've only heard bad things about makes it worse."

She nodded. "And the school can't help with the process, so you're on your own. Did you have to make an appointment?"

"Yeah, luckily I knew from Ann-Marie to go to the Prefecture for Foreign Students not the regular Prefecture. And I knew to bring at least three copies of every document I brought to the French Consulate, plus my rental agreement from my landlord, my electricity bill, the source of my living expenses, and documents from my bank. If I was missing anything, they could turn me away. If I did not have enough copies, they could turn me away. If I was late for the appointment, they could turn me away."

"If you were wearing shorts they could turn you away," Trisha said.

"If I arrived with too much luggage they could turn me away."

We sipped our coffees, glancing around for anyone committing a fashion crime. All was safe in *Place Saint-Michel* so far.

I continued. "I presented my precious pieces of paper at the counter and the woman went through her checklist, shuffling and making piles of different copies. I told her my documents were already approved by the French Consulate in San Francisco, and she nodded eagerly, like this was a really good thing. She looked at my loan documents that verified my source of money but didn't understand what it was. I tried to describe 'loan' in French, but it is, literally, a foreign concept because student loans are not used in the French education system."

"Hey, do you want another drink? I'll get the waiter's eye." Trisha said.

"I'm sure you've already got his eye." Smile. "I would like *un citron pressé*. And now the stakes are raised higher: the bet is to find two pairs of shorts and loser pays for all drinks."

"I'm in. It's not possible I'm the only one in Paris who wore shorts today," said Trisha, looking for our waiter. And just then we heard loud shrills from the right.

A gaggle of five teenage girls passed by each wearing short shorts with one-inch inseams. They were talking loudly in English while smacking gum and tossing hair. Their attention span appeared to be as brief as their shorts because they were flicking their heads around everywhere, oblivious to other people in the area. I sensed instantly that they were American because three out of five had Coach purses slung over their shoulders. We witnessed other café onlookers observe the girls with raised eyebrows. The air became quieter as the group passed on and their laughter dissipated across the open pavement.

"Okay, the bet is off. Neither of us won. Where were we before the shorts invasion?" I asked. We sipped our drinks and I didn't want to put mine down, even as I was telling this story. There was something about sitting in an outdoor Parisian café and holding a cold drink in the blazing sun that made life better in immeasurable ways.

"She was going through your papers."

"Right. And there was one more thing missing. She asked if I had a French bank account. Nope, I didn't. She left the counter."

"They require a French bank account? I was going to just keep using my American one."

"Yeah, me too. But for some reason the French bank account is a must. And of course, there's another catch-22: a *carte de sejour* is required first before opening a bank account!"

"Wait, how!"

"Exactly! How do you open a bank account, or get a *carte de sejour,* when both require the other before proceeding? How was I supposed to prove I lived here when it was so difficult to actually live here?"

"It's allll a test of your determination to live the Parisian life...." Trisha shook her head.

"Luckily, she temporarily approved me for a *carte de sejour* until I opened my bank account. And then she said I needed to bring back my signed medical release form from the doctor."

"What doctor?" Trisha scrunched up her forehead.

"Exactly what I thought. What medical release from? What doctor? The prefecture woman stared at me blankly for a second, and then asked if I signed up for a medical exam on my way into the building this morning. I told her "No, there was no sign-up or any information about a medical exam. She handed me a piece of paper with a day and time and then put a red star on it."

"You were singled out with a red star?"

"I considered it a superstar. Then she switched her board to the next number in line and I was dismissed. Over. Done. Buh-bye."

A woman sat down next to us with a petite dog winding its way around the small table. The pup curled up at the base of the table and the woman rested her purse on the chair in between us. Her scarf was the perfect azure blue for the coloring of her skin. She pulled her dark sunglasses over her eyes and opened an issue of Vogue. Sometimes you couldn't help but watch a person who was silently mesmerizing.

"So..." Trisha continued, "did you visit a doctor? What was that about?"

"I had to have a full medical physical, complete with white robe, x-rays and a conversation with the doctor about my health. Maybe the French government wanted to know my health status before allowing me to stay in the country legally in case I had health issues and I could be a liability? I don't know, but I just wanted to get it all taken care of."

"What if you didn't do all of this *carte de sejour* stuff? What would happen if you just stayed in the country? Do they check your status somehow?"

"I guess it's possible to 'just stay,' and there are always ways to get around rules. But I realized that it was just easier to follow the full process because getting an apartment required legal papers, the school required legal papers, and then it snowballs from there. I'm sure some people stay here without doing all of this, but that would stress me out if I was caught and had to leave the country without finishing my degree. The whole experience would turn into a waste of time and money. I'd rather do this and jump through all of the hoops so I could rest assured that I was in the country legally."

Trisha nodded yes. Her eyes were a little sleepy in the bright sunshine.

"Okay, enough of this. You understand now how relieved I am to be here legally. Completely worth it in the end and I'm glad I made this choice. It was worth the commitment. I feel this is the beginning of a very important part of my life."

"Definitely. And it's been worth it."

"Yep." Big inhale. Big exhale. "I always thought, oh moving to Paris, what a dream! It will be amazing, sophisticated, inspiring, breezy. I had no idea it would be such an ordeal with so many steps."

"Because it's all the stuff you can't plan for or know in advance. You only learn as you go. I am even more thankful for my European passport now."

Our glasses were now empty. Crowds of people continued to pass by as a never-ending stream of fashion and faces. The woman sitting next to us was watching the sidewalk show as well.

"And we're together on this fabulous June day in a fabulous European city. How about we go back to your place and make dinner. I'm hungry. *Penses-tu un bon idée?*" Do you think it's a good idea?

"*Oui! Superbe.*"

"*D'accord.*"

She signaled to the waiter and we both put down more money than we planned on spending. *C'est la vie.*

With purses lazily tossed over shoulders, we walked towards the early evening sun still resting high above the Paris skyline. The summer equinox was close, so the days' sunbeams continued to stretch long into the evening, like expanding strands of gold strings. We skipped walking along the traffic-heavy Saint German Boulevard and instead enjoyed the charms of Rue Saint Andres des Arts.

Couples sauntered together arm-in-arm, zigzagging across the street to peer inside stores selling scarves, tea, cards, and books, or they stopped abruptly to review menus.

We ended up back at Trisha's apartment on Rue des Grand Augustins and made a simple dinner of grilled chicken, salad, and finished off a baguette left over from the morning. Meals were another confirmation that my relationship with Paris was maturing. The glamorous concept of dining regularly at fashionable *brasseries* crumbled away as ordinary fare became an everyday reality.

The evening covered us with weariness. We watched television until our eyes closed more often than they stayed open. I left around nine o'clock with barely enough energy to walk to the metro, while simultaneously feeling extremely content about the simple joys of a day in Paris with a new friend. It felt like the energy of this dream was expanding beyond what I could imagine. A bigger life for myself was unfolding with each step; each continual commitment I made to keep going forward with higher levels of trust.

In a short amount of time, the essentials of living in Paris had come together and I felt in my skin, in my heart, the excitement building around this life direction. *Whom will I meet next? Will I fall in love? What opportunities will unfold here because of my high-vibe intentions to make the most of everything? Am I heading down a promising direction? Or will I experience unexpected hardships like when I lived in North Carolina?*

As my lazy bones swayed with the motion of the metro, this train of thought triggered memories of having these exact same questions when I had previously started a new life in another unknown place that initially soared with adventure and fun, and then sank down into an unexpected soul-low I had no way of anticipating. My toes clenched up with the recollection.

LEARNING TO SOAR

"**D**O YOU SEE THAT TRUCK right there?" Jill leaned forward, squinting out the windshield.

"Yeah! Is he coming straight at us?" The mid-day glare on the two-lane highway made the road a glistening mirage. The front grill of a semi-truck wavered ahead as we raced downhill at 85 mph.

"Yeah, I think he's in our lane. Looks like he's going uphill and passing other vehicles against oncoming traffic."

I cautiously hit the brakes again.

Jill sat back and adjusted her sunglasses. "He has to get over. He has to. Obviously he is going the wrong direction in our lane."

"Crap, but he's not. He may not even see us in this sunlight." I glanced in the rearview mirror. "I'm trying to slow down but this guy behind us is riding our ass."

I pumped the brakes more to buy us a few more seconds. Everything was flying by quickly, like lines and dashes, and before we knew it

"Oh my god—" Jill slouched down in the passenger seat, covering her emerald eyes with both hands.

"What the fu—"

We screamed at the top of our lungs as the truck's blow horn went off. I swerved onto the shoulder just as the semi-truck and its 24 wheels veered back into his lane at the very last second. Then I honked back for a full five seconds to release my rage at that lunatic antic.

We sat in stunned silence as the starving Utah desert raced by. Our Thelma and Louise road trip freedom was dampened, but not dead.

"Are we alive?" Jill began laughing.

"I haven't breathed for at least three minutes." One hand on my heart, the other on the steering wheel. "I can't believe how fast that happened."

"Our first near-death experience on this trip! Oh my god, that was crazy." Jill began playing with her long brown hair.

"I hope we don't have a second one! Maybe we need Steven to calm our nerves."

"Got it." Jill reached over and hit play on the CD player. I relaxed my grip on the steering wheel as the air filled with Aerosmith's current hit, "I Don't Want To Miss A Thing."

Just days ago, Jill and I had reversed out of my driveway with wild arms waving out windows and the radio turned up as "Wide Open Spaces" by the Dixie Chicks blared away, the perfect send-off song for our cross-country road trip. My white Corolla was packed with everything that could possibly fit into the nooks of the trunk and the crannies of the back seat: clothes, shoes, towels, a microwave, bedding, pictures, and books. There was just enough open space to see out the back window, while the front seats contained our kicked-off sandals, water bottles, rotating CD selections, and our unwavering excitement. Ten states in ten days, Seattle to North Carolina! Woo hoo! I was going to spend part of my junior year in college at East Carolina University in Greenville, NC, and Jill was the perfect car companion because of her infectious laugh, adventurous spirit, and common   sense.

We cheered as we crossed the border from Washington into Oregon, and cheered again as we made it to Boise, Idaho to spend the first night. Our second night was in Utah at a highway hotel with stiff white sheets and moldy showers. It was easy to get on the road early the next morning and forget that stop as just another passing mile marker.

The third day was our longest, although we had no way of knowing that when the alarm went off at seven o'clock. With bluebird skies guiding us above, we made the fateful decision to venture away from Interstate 70 and take the more scenic route over the Colorado Rockies via Highway 40. We visited Dinosaur National Monument right when it opened, curious to see a place we would most likely never pass by again, and returned to the open highway by mid-morning. The oh-so-trusty map showed this route meeting up with I-70 through Denver, but we had no idea this path also meant steep, twisty climbs up two-lane highways with trucks, slower climbing speeds, and no passing lanes.

As the never-ending vertical drive stretched on, the spectacular scenery was worthy of every mile: jade trees touched the clouds; open pastures fell off cliffs; unexpected lakes danced along the highway; and mountain life peeked through the high rocky points and the low soft meadows. Late summer ice caps reflected the sun in all directions. We rode in graceful silence with open eyes and deep breaths.

After two hours of climbing, we stopped at a well-located convenience store to get gas and check the engine oil. I could practically hear my dad's words echoing through the mountain passes telling me to "take care of the car by checking and adding oil along the way." *Yes, Dad, I will.* I stepped outside the car to feel the most exhilarating fresh air met us at the gas pumps. Pure. Clean. Intense. I closed my eyes to inhale as much as possible for as long as possible and threw open all four car doors to stuff the clean air inside as an ongoing souvenir for the senses. We grabbed cold drinks and bags of unneeded calories, then Jill stuck in a fresh CD to keep ourselves jamming down the road. There were still many miles to cover before our heads hit a pillow. We stopped in Steamboat Springs for lunch and the long drive continued as road trip fatigue set in. No song could save us at that point.

Just as the air was deliciously cool and crisp going up and over the Rockies, it quickly turned into a hot stuffy ride going down the other side of the mountains' slope. We opened all four windows as the hours stretched into the early evening, feeling tired, dehydrated, hungry, and ready to be done for the day. The relentless road finally guided us to civilization at the Cherry Creek Shopping Center in Denver. And without shame, we gave ourselves washcloth baths in the sink of the mall's public restrooms to cool off and wake up. We grabbed a deliciously sinful dinner at the mall's food court and stocked up on water before getting back in the car for the final stretch. Steven Tyler serenaded us again with "I Don't Want to Miss a Thing" as we started up the car and returned to the highway. Mr. Tyler was reliably there for us each day, in every city, never wanting to miss a thing. We just loved that about him.

Our reward for the long day of driving was a spectacular sunset in the rearview mirror over the Rocky Mountains. Jill drove with one eye looking in the mirrors. I turned around to watch the splendid glory of dark ink melting down over the peaks. Vibrant pinks faded to soft lavenders and glowing purples before becoming a steady midnight blue. After the sunset spectacle was complete, we then found ourselves driving into a dark blue wonderland of bright twinkling stars on the horizon ahead. Countless pearls of light were dancing through every window. I stuck my hand outside as we cruised freely at 80 mph. The air blasted through my fingers, forcing my palm to open wide, so I tried to catch a glowing star or at least stain my hand with the sky's signature navy. It felt like we were driving off the edge of the earth and directly into an endless abyss of twinkling fireflies. Mr. Tyler sang us through the miles of swirling sparkles until we finally braked in front of a forgettable roadside motel sometime after nine o'clock. I sat in the passenger seat for an extra moment to feel stillness after a day of constant motion and fourteen hours of driving.

"I need a shower like nothing else!" Jill threw open the driver-side door and swung her tan legs out to stretch them fully. "And then I need to sleep forever."

I got out and stretched my body up to the sky. "I need to collapse and let this endless day be over. I can't believe it's still the same day we looked at dinosaur fossils, survived an almost head-on collision, drove like the Flintstones over the tallest mountains in the country, and then—" I kicked the back car door closed after grabbing my overnight bag, "—experienced the most spectacular drive into the sky. What a day."

"And we still have five more states to go!" Jill and her enthusiasm really were the perfect cross-country combination.

After a restful night of hard sleep, we took off early the next morning to meet Kansas. In contrast to the previous day of peaks, altitude changes, and mountain air, a smooth endless road with mammoth clouds and an abundance of crops guided us through each mile. The sky grew hundreds of feet taller the further we moved through the state. Humidity sat heavily on our shoulders as every minute looked like a replay of the last one. The visual monotony started to change when there appeared to be yellow blankets thrown over the tops of every field. And within a few moments, we were greeted by thousands of sunflowers on both sides of the road. Miles and miles of swaying vibrant sunflowers were pointed up to the sky, smiling and cheerful, creating a yellow highway of joy as we drove on to Missouri. I couldn't help but grin back at the dancing bright petals. And so far the same three songs rotated on every radio station in every state as the universal songs of the summer: "I Don't Want to

Miss A Thing"; LeAnn Rimes' "How Do I Live Without You" and "Slide" by the Goo Goo Dolls.

We rolled through Kansas City, Kansas right before the afternoon rush hour, and arrived in Kansas City, Missouri looking for the best barbecue we could find. Our CD selection had grown stale, the car felt more cramped, and Jill and I started to get a little punchy with each other, especially while navigating the tangled Kansas City interstate web. We did our best to shake off any residue of annoyance with a few cold beers and a deliciously messy dinner.

We turned south the next day to spend one night in Branson, Missouri. Safe to say, we brought down the average age down in Branson City by a good thirty years. After checking into the hotel, we walked along Country Music Boulevard and took in all of the Ozark Mountain offerings: twinkling lights, twanging music, gingham-clad dancing partners, and slow strollers. We decided to make the most of our night by going to a musical based on the hotel concierge's recommendation. The show started with paper decorations coming down from above the stage, a band playing not quite in unison, and stage lights blinking on and off like a distress signal. We should have escaped during the introduction, but were fueled by relentless optimism.

After five minutes, I leaned over to Jill and whispered, "Is this a high school production?"

"Shhhh. The dancing ladies are coming out."

I covered my mouth to hold in laughter. "They look like Easter eggs wearing pantyhose." The ladies started doing cartwheels and spinning batons. "Oh man. I can't sit through this torture after sitting in the car all day."

"Maybe it will get better…"

It didn't. The dancing Easter eggs eventually partnered with their male counterparts who could not lift them up to their shoulders as planned. Two wigs fell off. One dancer tripped over her heels. Another was two steps ahead during the whole dance routine. We broke free at intermission to walk outside in the silky Ozark twilight. It was only eight o'clock, but anything of potential interest to us was closing down for the night as the sun turned off. We strolled slowly through an open parking lot, sporadic parking lights sputtering on and off every fifty feet, trying to delay our arrival back at the hotel.

I stopped abruptly. "What was that? Did you see that thing in the air?"

Jill stopped next to me. "No, I didn't see anything."

We stood frozen in the darkness for a moment. Then I started walking again slowly, positive I saw movement ahead, and she veered off to the right. It was too dark to see far ahead. I felt something brush against the top of my shoulder.

"Ahhh!" I yelled at the top of lungs.

"Whaaat?!"

"Oh my god, it was on me! Do you see them? Bugs are jumping through the air!"

"Where? I don't see any—Ahhhhh!" Jill screamed. "There was one on my leg!"

"They're everywhere! Let's get out of here!"

We ran through the parking lot in our platform sandals just as a swarm of large grasshoppers started to jump and flutter all around us. They hit our heads, arms, and legs as we screamed louder and our shrills bounced throughout the Ozarks. We finally stopped to catch our breath, and noticed that the town had stopped. People on the street looked in our direction. Restaurant diners held their forks midway to their mouths. A taxi pulled over on the side of the street to see the commotion. All we could do was break out laughing.

"That was our punishment for leaving the show early," Jill said.

"Ugh, disgusting. Let's leave early tomorrow morning for Arkansas." I responded, attempting to regain some composure.

During our sixth day on the road, the only thing denser than the humidity was the traffic all the way through Little Rock as we drove east to Memphis for a night of fun. Jill and I checked into the beautiful Crowne Plaza Hotel for the night, grateful to be off the road early in the day, and then hit the scene in the cutest outfits we could find in our suitcases: skirts, loose tank tops, and clunky platform sandals that could handle dancing. We drank purple cocktails that tasted like candy, danced with our arms up in the air, and chatted with friendly bar patrons who knew the best bar to go to next.

"Mols, we need to drink water and keep an eye on the clock so we're not out too late."

"Right, right, right. So we still want to get on the road fairly early tomorrow?"

"Yeah, don't you want to stop and see that museum? Plus we have to drive to Nashville."

"Ok, true." I took a sip. "It just feels so good to be free. We're twenty-one, having a life adventure, and dancing in Memphis!" I raised my drink high in the air.

"Wooo hooo!" Jill raised her drink and threw back her head in laughter. The band returned to the stage and started strumming the familiar opening chords of "Sweet Home Alabama."

"Wooo hooo!" We screamed louder in unison. Jill shimmied to the dance floor first and I followed; the bar began to fill up with more shirts, hats, and dancers. The lights were comfortably low, the music was perfectly high, and the sweet drinks were devils in our hands. We let loose and let go, shaking off every accumulated mile and tuning out everything except the music. The tempo carried us through another round of drinks. The dance floor squeezed us together more often, requiring our arms to stay up high in the heated air. It felt amazing not to care about anything at all, also commonly referred to as buzzing. After finishing our libations, we tipped our invisible hats to the band and made our way out to the street, arms locked together, to soak up the neon flashing signs.

Beale Street continued to come alive as the night progressed. Different music pulsed from every direction: rock, country, blues, soul, R&B. We eventually let the "early morning plan" slide a bit since we decided it was obviously healthier to stretch our bodies dancing after long hours of sitting in the car. Yelling "Wooo Hooo!" became a regular release, especially when one of us found ourselves surrounded by an uninvited dancing male companion. Our research showed that a man would quickly disappear when you yelled "Wooo Hooo!" into his ear every time he asked you a question.

After hours on our feet, the cooling Memphis air hit me in the face as we slinked out the front door and left the pulsing beats behind. Unrelenting bar lights flashed up and down the street at different rhythms, reflecting off the windows and sewer tops. We linked arms and then our heels got quiet as we glanced up and down the street, trying to discern which way led back to the hotel. Jill pulled me to the right with certainty.

"Tonight rocked. We really needed an awesome night out. I'm having so much fun on this trip and I'm so happy we're sharing this together." I hugged her shoulder as we walked down the street.

"Did you see that guy in the blue shirt and cowboy hat? He was hot." Giggle. "I am loving this adventure. But I'm going to miss you while you're in North Carolina." Her bottom lip pouted and she tilted her head against mine.

"Yeah, I'm going to miss you too, doll. It will be fun to see what life at another college is like, ya know. This is the furthest I've lived from home, which is scary and exciting."

"And it's only for one semester so time will fly by. You have to tell me everything about your classes, who you meet, if there are any sexy guys on campus." She tossed her brown hair back.

"Totally! And I'll be calling when I'm lonely so you'll definitely hear from me."

We made a right turn and sailed through the hotel's automatic doors. The night ended with our heels clip-clip-clip-clipping across the lobby's tarnished floor. A janitor was gliding a mop across the far corner and turned to scold our shoes.

Six hours later, our soft flip-flops bounced off the newly polished lobby floor. Lemon sunlight reflected off every hotel surface as we shuffled, muffins and coffee in hand, to the parking garage. Sunglasses protected me from the morning's cheerfulness as we made our way to the National Civil Rights Museum before getting back on the freeway.

The early morning humidity was already stagnant and thick. The August sun did not offer any mercy as we walked up to the front entrance just in time to hear the museum doors unlock for the day. Jill and I entered with mutual silence as our eyes adjusted to the inside shadows, and then we separated to follow our individual curiosity. I moved chronologically through exhibits starting with the arrival of slaves in America in the sixteenth century and followed the trail to civil rights events in the 1950's and 1960's. With cautious steps, I boarded the bus where Rosa Parks refused to leave her seat. I was the only one inside the bus except for a sitting statue of Rosa Parks. I sat down next to her, a heaviness growing in my stomach that felt like -

"Please move to the back of the bus." A booming male voice rang overhead. I looked up towards the front windshield.

"I need that seat now. Please move back." The voice was more urgent, more irritated. I sat frozen.

"If you can sit there in other buses, suppose you get off and in one of them!" His anger began to fill up the bus as I sat silently motionless. The wax bus driver's face was in the rearview mirror, looking right at me with eyes on fire.

"If you don't move out of that seat, I'll have you arrested!" Louder, aggressive, urgent.

"Get up from there!" The intensity of his voice took over the bus and my own fight or flight response was activated. My heart was beating harder as I tried to feel into the moment and be fully present in this situation; to really feel the angry reaction coming towards me at full force. But it was still only a museum exhibit for me.

Then a narrator's balanced voice said, "In 1955, if you had not moved by this point, you would be arrested." I closed my eyes and saw in my mind's eye this dignified woman being carried off the bus. I was the only one inside the exhibit, but a few onlookers were standing outside the bus and staring inside with curiosity. After a few deep breathes, I stood up and disembarked, fighting the urge to kick the bus driver's little wax leg.

I forged ahead through the civil rights timeline and paused next to the life-size replicas of the sit-in protest that began at a Woolworth's counter in Greensboro, North Carolina after four African-American college students were denied service. I gazed at a Birmingham jail cell where Dr. King wrote a letter on tissue paper in 1963. I absorbed the picket signs and messages from the March on Washington in August 1963 that drew 250,000 people. In a side room, I picked up a phone and listened to the actual conversation between President Kennedy and Governor Barnett about James Meredith wanting to attend the University of Mississippi in 1962. Numerous other civil rights milestones followed in Little Rock, Selma, Chicago, and connected back to Memphis with the sanitation workers' strike in 1968.

I made my way slowly up the stairs to the second floor of the museum and stepped quietly into a motel room with two beds. A tray with water glasses and coffee cups sat between the beds; a newspaper rested on the foot of one bed. Everything looked like the occupant had been here only a mere ten minutes ago. Soulful music was playing from every corner of the room as if a powerful choir was standing right behind me. I glanced through the motel's curtains to see angry rain violently pounding the sidewalks. Temporary lakes covered the streets, reflecting the granite sky, with absolutely no trace of the bright, cloudless day from an hour earlier. Relentless tears dropped hard onto the balcony, the wreath, the car below the apartment. I inhaled deeply at the realization that this was Room 306 of the Lorraine Motel. The last place Martin Luther King, Jr. resided before he was assassinated on the motel's balcony.

Yet despite the unexpected violent storm outside, I felt the most comforting levels of peace inside the walls of Room 306. Love. Unity. Calm. With closed eyes, I steadied myself against a railing and felt the strong energies that surpassed this room, this hotel, this legacy. A bigger presence filled up the space. The choir sang on as I saw visions of marginalized populations and segregated cultures across humanity's timeline step forward: women suffragists; African-Americans; lesbian, gay, bisexual and transgender communities;

Japanese internment camps; the Jewish Holocaust; international genocides — united together under the colossal roof of Love. I felt a collective unity of souls pushing the boundaries of what was deemed normal, what was acceptable, what was right, and together through history they were asking humanity: how many more ways will we find to divide ourselves? How many more times will we create a hierarchy on the value of human life and experience? How many more ways will we choose to separate ourselves from each other with labels and fear? How many ways will we keep the unconscious definition of Love small and confined?

I saw the questions twirl in the air like streams of ribbons, tapping along the exhibit railings and dancing to the choir's soul music. Amongst these swirling questions, I saw a few brave souls rise up to point humanity back to connection, back to commonality, back to equality, back to Love. Souls who had volunteered to be the bridges that connected us to a bigger truth we already knew in our hearts. We yearned to remember this bigger truth because when these souls appeared, we recognized them as reminders of Love and instinctively desired to keep their messages alive on a deep level. We could not ignore their missions — and they wouldn't let us. We recognized them as us.

A man brushed passed my shoulder lightly, bringing me back to my body, as tears gently glided down each cheek. My hands were gripping onto the railings tighter, unwilling to release the spirit of the room, and my chest was filled with something stronger than air. The rain outside had turned to slow-motion droplets. The choir's low melody had paused. The room had shifted to a higher vibration that felt celebratory, joyful, whole. My skin absorbed the amazing grace of Room 306. Then I felt the energy effortlessly float up and disappear above the storm outside.

Five minutes later, Jill and I drove out of southern Memphis in silence. The humidity had returned as if the storm had never happened, except for the black cement and unexpected puddles now being soaked up by the sun.

I finally asked Jill, "What did you think of the museum?"

She paused. "It was beautiful and really moving. I felt it made some strong statements about our country and the history we forget at times. I liked that it was interesting and interactive; it was more than I expected. How about you? What did you think?" She adjusted her sunglasses and glanced in the rearview mirror as we braked in traffic, the steering wheel in her hand.

I inhaled. "I agree with everything you felt. It was more than I expected and I think it was also one of the most amazing spiritual experiences of my life." Pause. "I think this visit may stay with me for a long time." She nodded. I stared out the window as Memphis faded behind us.

A few hours later, we rolled into Nashville feeling restless and hurried. Nine days on the road had made us impatient with each other and closer to insta-crankiness than ever before. Jill steered us down Broadway, and with no plan about where to go, and no desire to drive around aimlessly, and the sticky sun relentlessly glaring down on our dry throats, we surrendered conquering the city. We bickered over how to get back on the freeway since I had authority over the map and she had control over the steering wheel. *Go right. No, straight. Just turn here. HERE.* The car circled with our tempers flaring up and the gas guzzling down. We finally stopped in stony silence at an inconvenient store for directions. Jill charmed the man behind the counter as I grabbed a few sandwiches and bags of chips. We fell back into the car with clear directions and I dove into the food immediately. The scowl on my face disappeared and a fresh smile started to appear. Maybe we just needed to pay better attention to our blood sugar levels. We forged ahead towards Knoxville, Tennessee with the hopes of getting off the road by dinner time.

Our last night on the highway was spent at an uninspiring motel outside of Knoxville. Feeling the exhaustion of 3,000 miles of cement travel, we ate an indulgent dinner at a local diner and then lay splattered across separate double beds. She flipped through the bowels of television as I stared blindly at whatever came across the screen, unattached and lacking expectation of anything grand. Perhaps just like this next phase I was starting. While a part of me was excited to arrive in this new Southern town, another part of me was kinda scared of the reality. *Will I make friends here? Will I enjoy this school? Will I fit into life in North Carolina?*

My dad and I had flown out here a few months ago so I could find a furnished apartment and have a place to live once I arrived for school. At least in California I had lived with family. It was one thing to imagine living by myself this far from home, but a whole other feeling when it actually became reality. It was no longer an idealized lifestyle to share and intellectualize about in conversations; it was now the truth of a new life in a new land far from home. Yet unlike my time in California, I would be surrounded by people my own age and be busy with new friendships, new classes, a regular daily schedule. Everything would be livelier this time around especially since I didn't have a boyfriend at home to run back to. *This is going to be a great time in your life.*

Jill and I woke up early and started the car while the air was still fresh from sunrise. We drove directly into the morning sun as it played peek-a-boo through the Smoky Mountains. Tufts of fog hid in the valleys and moved close to us, then far away, disappearing between the trees. Every smooth mountain slope appeared washed in faded denim until the sun kissed everything awake with bright bursts of yellow. By noon the land looked completely different. We cheered as we officially arrived in North Carolina and cranked up the radio to celebrate the accomplishment. Steven Tyler was right there on the radio dial and lucky him, he still didn't miss a thing.

We rolled through Raleigh and continued on the never-ending highway that had escorted us through ten states, from one ocean to another. The scenery changed from grey urban buildings crowded together to sleepy towns built on cotton and tobacco businesses. Fields and fields of prickly bushes spat out bursts of white cotton puffs. Then the land transitioned to rows of deep greens where leafy tobacco plants attempted to thrive after years of cultivation. The air felt different as the tobacco, humidity, and quiet blue breeze mingled together and created a lazy haze in my mind; like we had transitioned to a softer, simpler world. I shook the fogginess out of my eyes as the car turned into downtown Greenville.

We curved our way passed the Medical Center, churches, hotels, and schools. Brick buildings and houses lined the streets and grand oak trees provided much needed August shade. I slowed down to check out the campus of East Carolina University. Front porches of fraternity and sorority houses were covered in welcome banners for new pledges. Jill, a sorority sister, gave me the rundown of every sorority house she recognized and described their reputations at her school. It was all Greek to me.

We eventually turned onto South Elm Street where a furnished apartment was waiting for us and -

"Oh god." I slammed on the brakes hard in the middle of the empty street. Our ponytails jerked forward into our faces. "Where are the apartment keys?"

Jill's eyes grew huge. "Don't even tell me…"

I grabbed my purse from the backseat, fumbled with the zippers, and reached inside.

"Okay, we're good." Exhale. Smile.

"Not funny." Smile.

The apartment complex was composed of dual brick buildings, two stories high, and faced each other over a grass courtyard. We each hauled a suitcase up the wrought-iron stairs and stopped to look at the quiet scenery. It was late in the afternoon and no one was around; we hadn't seen any movement since arriving. Soft bug sounds whispered in the grass somewhere.

I pushed open the front door with a slight jerk and was met by groovy furniture from the 1970's covering the living room. The undesirable yellow and orange decor continued into the kitchen and the bathroom, but thankfully everything was clean and tidy. Before turning on the bedroom light, I glanced up to see glow-in-the-dark star stickers twinkling on the ceiling. I propped open the bedroom window to move the stale air out, then I did the same with the front curtains and window facing the courtyard. There was a significant lack of natural light and the space felt darker now than when I was eager to sign the rental agreement. Jill and I started unpacking the car in silence as the warm Southern air loosened up our lungs, our limbs, any remaining tensions from spending ten straight days and nights together. Each time I dropped a box onto the kitchen counter, the tired apartment started to feel a little more like home.

The following day was devoted to *getting stuff done*. After indulging in ten hours of sleep, we checked out town for a full twelve minutes and wound up at Super Wal-Mart for new living essentials. The late August heat expanded throughout the day and slowed our energy down by mid-afternoon, the heavy air suffocating and pressing into every side of my body. We donned our best summer dresses with the hopes of finding a lively Saturday night social scene for our last night together, but no such luck. Our dresses swung into a mediocre Mexican restaurant, so we made every tortilla chip count.

"Here's a toast to an incredible, awesome, scenic cross-country adventure with my favorite girl!"

Jill raised her margarita up to clink glasses. "And here's to a wonderful new beginning in Greenville! Woo hoo!"

Cowboy hats, NASCAR brims, and loose ponytails turned to stare as we woo hoo'ed. A mariachi band took our glass clinking and noise as an invitation to surround our tortillas with song. At least we got all dolled up for some type of performance.

And then the next morning, bright and fresh, our ten-day adventure together was over. I hugged Jill tight at the airport curb and promised to call her as soon as my phone was set up. She grabbed her suitcase and waved enthusiastically, brushing long strands of hair away from her face. Her wedge heels disappeared between reflecting sliding doors and only my reflection stared back to me. I envied her for getting to return to everything that was known and familiar.

As the car door slammed shut, the space filled with hollow echoes of laughter, music, and freedom. Solitude was here again and tucked itself comfortably into the passenger seat. The unstructured days of open miles and anything-goes-at-every-zip-code would now transition back to responsibility and focus as school started. I drove away from the airport, from the only person I knew in this state, and a handsome man in a white truck looked over and smiled at me. A big friendly wave followed. I smiled and waved back, attempting to smooth the shift between endings and beginnings. *Everything was going to be great. With a soaring start like this, what could go wrong?*

LEARNING TO FALL

WITHIN A FEW DAYS OF settling into my Greenville apartment, my next-door neighbor Lee wandered over to introduce himself. I suspected he was in his late sixties or so, with short white hair, intense brown eyes behind small black-rimmed glasses sliding down his nose, and a cigarette in his hand that moved when he talked, as if he was waving a Fourth of July sparkler in the air. Lee shared his stories of the neighbors in the apartment complex, along with the ways of a small town in North Carolina. He explained the "blue laws" that were in effect on Sundays and local insider knowledge, like where to buy the town's best hush puppies and catfish. Then he paused as if seriously considering his next words, and said with a concentrated stare, "It's important to know that grits are everywhere in this town. But that doesn't mean there are *good* grits everywhere."

He looked me dead in the eye, brown beads behind stiff glasses, to make sure I understood the importance of choosing good grits. "Don't waste your money on just any grits, know what I mean?"

I nodded obediently with open eyes, although I had never had grits and didn't think I'd even recognize them.

North Carolina in late August had temperatures I'd never contended with before. During the day, the oppressive air sat on my skin, heavy and suffocating, until a cool breeze blew through and released me from its grip. The evening air softened the day's heaviness into something warm, sweet, and slow, like dripping honey moving down a stick. I walked slower during sunlight hours and felt a burst of energy with each sunset. I flung open the front windows nearly every night to invite fresh air inside the stuffy apartment and move the stale air conditioning outside.

Lee sat outside most evenings, his white knees pulled up to the balcony rail, the sun a ribbon of light against the dark, cloudless night. He gestured with his cigarette where to prop open my flimsy lawn chair. We sat silently in the dusk and watched nothing happen in the courtyard. A few apartment windows were blaring television shows. Crickets dominated the front grass. Fireflies buzzed around, searching for a light, anything to gravitate towards.

"You settlin' in okay here?" He asked casually.

"Yeah, I think so. The apartment has the basics and I'm walking around the neighborhood a bit to get acquainted with it. The Tar River is lovely, I love living near water. "

"Yep, yep. Greenville is great this time of year, right before all the college kids take over again. You just missed the hottest months of summer. And dang if I didn't survive them this year, I shouldn't be living in this town."

I nodded in the dark. "How long have you lived here?"

"This area is my home. I've lived here as long as the hairs have been growing on my head. Can't imagine any other place to be." He looked at me through the dusk. "Now, may I ask why you are here? Ya know, we don't get visitors from your side of the world often…"

"Came for school mostly, but I've always wanted to check out a new part of the country. I thought this would be a good adventure. And it's the right time to make the most of college by traveling and seeing another school." I paused, inhaling. "I've never been this far from home before though. But I'm also excited and curious."

Lee eyed me in the dark while I spoke, then turned his head to look the other way. Moments passed until his cigarette, the unspoken metronome between us, stopped moving.

He inhaled deeply. "It's nice to have someone your age around here. Glad we can sit outside and talk a bit like this." Pause. "I'm happy to help you with anything ya need, so just come on over and ask, ya hear?"

I nodded silently as my lawn chair squeaked with the movement. Television noises started to turn off. The night filled with more cricket chirps. After an hour of chatting, weariness crept into my eyes. I picked up my chair to bring it inside.

"Good night, Lee. See you later."

"Night, Molly. I'll see ya around."

I closed the door and shuffled to the bedroom. Glowing ceiling stars escorted me to sleep.

After a few weeks of making Greenville my home, I was faced with the unexpected reality that trying to make new friends in this new life was difficult. Culture shock was taking hold as I tried to adjust to a school in the South, on the East coast, and with a strong sorority and fraternity presence. I had never considered all of the differences between West coast and East coast cultures; North and South lifestyles; non-Greek schools and heavily-Greek schools. And the awareness I was arriving at was that I didn't fit in. I couldn't find many people to connect to in my classes since many groups, circles, and social activities were already established like bricks in the school pathways. People were very friendly on campus, but as far as developing friends and meeting people to hang out with... no such luck so far. It was really catching me off guard. At my home university, I was a well-connected school leader; a college cheerleader accustomed to being active and involved in many activities on a weekly basis; and I had tons of connections and friends. I was constantly on the go with so many things to do. Now my schedule was open, lonely, and unstructured despite being in an environment that should be the opposite. I knew I'd be out of my comfort zone, but I hadn't expected to be out of my social zone. It felt just like my time in California a few summers ago, except without a boyfriend on the other end of the phone and no desire to watch movies.

In addition to an inactive social life, my classes were challenging in a way I had never experienced before, either. I normally excelled at school, but things weren't clicking in this area, either. There seemed to be unwritten rules and I was breaking every one of them: My reports weren't in the "right" format; my work wasn't "complete enough," my presentations lacked "expected components." All of the feedback on my work started with criticism and ended with a low grade. *What was going on?* Why was I not succeeding like I normally did? I took the initiative to make appointments with my professors so I could better understand what needed to change, but those efforts didn't help much; I seemed only to come across as an outsider. I could not get ahead or get a break. I couldn't believe I was struggling like this.

This formula of no friends, no social life, difficulty with my classes, lack of local knowledge, and a dark apartment all led to a gradual loss in my personal motivation. I started skipping classes a few times a week, which felt good. Less stress, fewer worries, who cared about creating a layout, finishing a personal logo, or writing a review for that book. I preferred not exerting any effort at all. Apathy began to set in and my desire not to do anything during the day grew stronger.

A lack of morning light in my tiny bedroom supported my preference to sleep late. I spent the day cruising through television channels, then maybe walking around town for fresh air. I drove to the mall, or went to the river, but both of those places got old fast. I returned to my dark space with a television waiting for me. I drove passed campus as fast as possible to avoid the guilt.

As my daily activities slowed down, so did my willingness to get out and move. Classes weren't worth the effort and I didn't have the energy, anyways. My eating habits faded away as my appetite slowly ceased. Nothing sounded good to eat, but I tried to force myself to chew on cereal, toast, pasta, maybe a banana. The refrigerator began to represent the state of my day: bare, dull, still.

I started staying up late, sitting in the dark, flipping through channels like a television zombie. My mind was zoned out and wanted to stay that way. Nothing else mattered. Nothing else was needed. I knew the infomercials by heart and stared at the screen until my eyes were heavy. My bed was only ten steps away. I made my way to the reliable ceiling stars and enjoyed sleeping for twelve-hour stretches, the curtains staying closed well into mid-day.

Soon TV became my regular connection to everything. I watched all of the programs I didn't like just to have something to focus on. The highlight was every Tuesday episode of Oprah because she was featuring a guy named John Gray who talked about feelings and the four main emotions: anger, pain, sadness, and grief. I had all of those feelings now, but didn't understand why. *Where did they come from and why? What's wrong with me? Shouldn't I be grateful for all that I have?* He had containers of water and demonstrated how we need to fill up our own containers before we can fill up anyone else. I felt self-empowered for a moment, but then eventually felt worse because I was totally failing at filling up my own container. I didn't know what to do about it. I didn't know what was happening. I stared at Dr. Gray's tie moving around the screen.

School started two months ago, yet I had not gone to classes for a few weeks. I didn't even want to be on campus. So one afternoon as I sat on the couch with the curtains closed on a beautiful sunny day, I decided not to go back to school at all. I couldn't focus or concentrate. I didn't care about the teachers or their feedback or the assignments. I had lost all of my motivation and discipline. And it wasn't like I had any grades to maintain at this point anyway. It was completely against my type-A personality to quit and not finish, but I just didn't have it in me. I didn't care. And it didn't matter, anyway.

I thought back on the past few months and remembered the excitement and joy I felt about starting this new adventure. Just months ago, Jill and I were dancing in Memphis with no cares in the world. The rush of a fresh start, a new place to explore, a new life to create. *Where did that go? What happened along the way? Did I do something wrong? Or did I not do something I should have done?* I was lost in my analysis because I couldn't make sense of it, any of it. I had the best of intentions and the best feelings in mind when I started my life here. Now I was at the worst and lowest point I'd ever been. Why couldn't I be stronger? This type of thing didn't happen to me in California. I was able to get up and leave the house to make the most of a day, even if it meant just going to a movie. Now I couldn't imagine going to a theater and exerting that much effort. Everything felt exhausting. Everything felt like a lot of effort; pointless effort. And it didn't matter, anyway.

When I spoke on the phone to my parents, I held back tears with my hands. I didn't know how to explain what I was dealing with or what the words would even be. I was too embarrassed and ashamed to tell them the truth. I didn't understand it myself. I felt trapped and alone and uncertain. I hung up and cried. Despair was everywhere. Kleenex was everywhere. It didn't matter, anyway.

I was splayed out on my bed for hours at a time. Tired, but not sure why. Bored, but not trying to do anything about it. Uncertain, but not willing to look for answers. I did very little to get by, completely content just lying on the soft surface as the apartment turned from dark to off-dark to light-dark and back to dark again. I did not want to leave the comfort of my bed or answer the phone or step outside for fresh air, not even to get the mail. I did nothing and I didn't care. The glow-in-the-dark ceiling stickers were always on. It didn't matter anyway.

My body clenched when Lee's feet stopped at my front door one afternoon. He knocked. I smoothed down my hair and checked my naked face in the mirror, practicing how to smile again.

"Hey Lee," I said, opening the door with forced congeniality.

"Hey, there. How you doin', girl? You doin' okay? Haven't seen ya around much lately."

"Oh, yeah, I know. Just feeling a little sick." I averted my gaze so my despair wouldn't reveal itself. He looked at me steadily for a moment, then started to nod his head gently.

"All right then. I'll let you be."

I nodded and slowly closed the door.

A few hours later, Lee knocked again. A foil-covered plate sat on my front porch with a note in scrawling black ink: "In case you're feeling better and hungry later."

I removed the foil to find a steaming plate of grilled chicken, sweet corn, green beans, and a hot roll. I started chewing without even realizing it. The chicken skin was buttery and crunchy and fell onto my fingers and the plate; the meat melted in my mouth. Then I devoured the hot roll, comforting and incredible with a hint of honey mixed inside the soft, spongy center. The bright bursts of sweet corn and steaming green beans disappeared in only a few forkfuls. Everything tasted so delicious and was completely gone in three minutes. I had no idea I was starving.

I finally returned one of my mom's daily phone calls after a week, knowing that my silence was causing her worry and concern. I just didn't know how to describe what I was feeling, or what I was going through, or even why. But if there was anyone who would understand this depression, it was my insightful and wise momma. I just had to try to get past my own embarrassment and self-judgment. The pain had become a hard tight knot, sitting in my stomach, weighing me down, grabbing at every ounce of my energy, and anchoring me to an indescribable sorrow. I was so upset with myself that I wasn't stronger.

Within a minute of hearing her voice and revealed everything: I hadn't been eating much; I stopped going to school, I've been staying inside most days. She held me over the phone as best she could, saying all the right comforting words. Just expressing myself helped move the energy and lifted the inner anchor a bit. And it felt good to finally talk with someone. I even accidentally laughed, a foreign feeling that loosened up my chest, my breathing, my heart. I inhaled a little deeper and felt a little stronger. She had sent me some money in a letter, so if nothing else, at least I'd have a personal card waiting in the little metal mailbox.

Getting the mail the next day eventually turned into short walks around the neighborhood, and the short walks turned into longer walks along the Tar River. The simple jaunts eventually turned into the bigger and more daring step of reaching out for help. Based on my mom's suggestion, I made an appointment for a physical with a doctor at the school to check my body, blood pressure, and have some tests done. I told the doctor my symptoms of low energy, lack of hunger, no motivation, and lots of sleep. He took a blood test, poked and prodded, but nothing turned up abnormal in any test. He suggested I make an appointment with a school psychologist. I stopped by the counseling center before leaving campus. Then I returned home and sat in front of the television, exhausted from the day's actions.

The next morning, the psychologist asked me a variety of questions about my family life, my relationships with my parents, my upbringing, accomplishments, and goals, then inquired about my health habits, my social life, and my exercise preferences. I answered honestly, thoughtfully, and even, dare I say, with impatience. *I know all of these things about myself already*, and none of these questions were telling me *why* I was depressed. *What has happened to me since I've been here in North Carolina? Where is the breakthrough question? When does the "a-ha, we've gotten to the bottom of this" happen?*

Yet through this inquisition, the psychologist was re-introducing me to myself. He pointed out whom I was, where I came from, what I had done, what I wanted, and what I can do. I shared with him my self-judgment about dropping out of school for the term and how it felt awful, like I failed in a big way. He provided the comforting perspective that we did not always choose how our path unfolded. It was okay not to focus on school right now. Maybe I needed a break from school? Maybe I needed to re-evaluate my life for the time being? Maybe I needed to allow myself this detour from an expected path? Maybe I needed to be easier on myself right now.

After an hour of discussion, he looked at me with compassionate eyes and said, "Molly, it is up to you of course, but I don't think you need to see me regularly. I think you are coming out of a hard transition time where your expectations were not met. You started a new life and didn't have the support you thought you'd find. And based on what we've discussed, it sounds like you are going to be okay. If you need to leave North Carolina and go home earlier than expected, then do that. It is most important that you take care of yourself right now."

My mom had said the same thing about leaving Greenville, but I discounted her words. But after this conversation with the psychologist about self-acceptance, I felt a growing sense of personal validation and compassion. Even when my mind kept trailing back to the feeling of failure, I needed to keep reminding myself that school was not the most important thing at this point. My well-being and sense of self mattered more.

I walked to town and stumbled into a restaurant for a late breakfast. I ordered grits, out of curiosity, with my eggs and bacon. The plate arrived with the bacon still sizzling and the eggs steaming, and what looked like a bowl of porridge sitting in the middle. I slowly tried a bite. The white creamy texture was comforting and not too bad. I wasn't sure if I was eating the good kind of grits or the less desirable kind though, but this would at least give me a reason to stop by and say hello to Lee. Let him know I took his advice seriously.

More light began to creep back into my world with each day. My energy was still low and I wanted to sleep late every morning and nap again later in the day, but the mild Carolina fall weather enticed me to go outside regularly. I walked over to the campus just to be near people, see faces, hear lively conversations, and feel a sense of community. I had transitioned from a world of dark to a place of grey with new shades of color slowly coming back.

One night, after the sun had disappeared under the roots of the oak trees and the crickets had made their nocturnal debut, I slowly opened my front door and pulled out my creaky lawn chair. Lee's cigarette was resting on the balcony as he reclined back into the darkness.

"I've been reserving your spot for ya, lady. Didn't want anyone else to take it."

I cracked the chair open and put my flip-flops up on the iron railing. "Thank you. I would have fought for this spot and it could have gotten ugly."

"I knew you were a fighter, Molly. Knew you had it in you to come out on top no matter what." Television noises moved back and forth in the courtyard. A car raced down the street. The crickets blasted louder as the car faded away.

"What's new out here? Did the grass grow a centimeter and I missed it?"

He chuckled. "Nope, that would be way too fast for this town." His cigarette hung below his chair and swayed lightly, carelessly, in the darkness. "Not much is new here. Just another day that ends in 'y'."

"I had some grits for the first time the other day. They weren't half-bad. Reminded me of oatmeal."

"Good then. When they're cooked up right, you finish the full serving. Did you eat 'em up?"

"Yep, every last bite. Helped wash down the bacon."

"Atta girl."

The moon peeked through the trees and illuminated the branches, the blades of grass, the walkway. A cat ran stealthily across the sidewalk and disappeared behind the building.

"Ya know, Molly, it's nice just sittin' out here with you and chattin' 'bout the day-to-day things in life. I like it." He nodded his head a few times then lowered his voice. "I 'suppose it's cause I have an estranged daughter out ther' somewher' who doesn't want anything to do with me." The cigarette darted up to his mouth in a fast swoop.

I glanced over to read his eyes, but his head was turned away. His remark sat silently on the balcony railing, teetering between fear and acceptance. I now understood his desire to cook me plates of dinner a few times last week. And why he asked if I'd called my mom and pops to say hello since he knew they'd be happy to hear from me. And why it was okay to ask him if I ever need anything, anything at all, just to knock three times and he'd be there any time of night.

I inhaled quietly. "I'm sorry to hear that, Lee." Pause. "I guess we all have a story that begins to define us, ya know. And luckily, we get to keep writing it and begin a new chapter each day." I stared at the moon curving through the courtyard. "Maybe your daughter thinks of you and doesn't know how to break the silence?" Pause. "Just a thought. It can be easy to stay in the comfort of quiet."

His head nodded in silence as the cigarette started to sway below his chair again. Fireflies buzzed around the street light. Television noises began to turn off. We sat in the night air without moving, breathing almost in unison, allowing the unexpected breeze to cool off any hot emotions and sweep away any dark thoughts. This time he was the first one to stand up and grab his chair.

"Night, Molly. Sleep well, lady."

"You too, Lee." He closed his apartment door just as the last television clicked off. I lifted my molasses bones up off the chair and got ready to start a new chapter in my own life tomorrow.

After breakfast and a walk around the block, I drove to the one place in this town where I knew there would always be action: Super Wal-Mart. I slowly strolled the aisles, touched the towels, sniffed the candles, read detergent labels, and bagged fresh fruit. I purchased my essentials and then lazily pushed the cart through the front corridor where the pharmacy, optometrist, McDonald's, and an employment agency were located. An employment agency? Seemed a bit out of place. I parked my cart next to the counter and exchanged smiles with the young man at the front desk.

"Hey there. I didn't know there was an employment agency at Wal-Mart." I leaned a bit on the counter. "What type of jobs do you have?"

"Well, we have quite a few jobs at the moment. What are you looking for?" he asked, pushing his long white sleeves further up his arms. His navy tie was slightly lopsided but his brown hair was freshly cut like the courtyard grass.

"Well, I didn't think I was looking, but I could be. I have experience with office work, managing projects, and administrative assistant positions. What do you have available?"

"Are you available during the day?"

"Yes, I am. My schedule is pretty flexible right now, but I'd need something temporary."

He grabbed some files from a side desk and shuffled paper around. As I watched him flip through his organization system, something suddenly clicked within me: I really wanted a job and a new start. I wanted a return to normal with focus and productivity. I wanted this. And I knew I could get it. He would hire me. I could feel it. I kicked into high gear with smiles and persuasion as he turned back to face me.

"So what's your name?" I said.

"Cory." He held two files.

"Cory, I would like to get a job through you today. I'm sure you have a client who would be so happy with everything I can do for them: my professionalism, my admin skills, and my office experience. I'm available now, so if they have an urgent need to fill a position, I could jump right in and get going on it soon."

"Well yes, I do have a few possibilities here -"

I kept talking. Confidence was back and all over me. "Hiring me is going to be effortless because I have quality references and I can start work next week. I've done a lot of office projects and admin work, so I would require minimal training. I'm the total package." Big smile.

He just stared back.

"So how about this idea, Cory." I shifted my weight, taking control of what needed to happen. "I'll come back with my resume in an hour, and in the meantime, you can see where I might match up with one of your employers. Then assuming you like what I have to offer, we could make a few phone calls, sign some paperwork, and get this finished today. I bet you have job placement goals you need to meet, right?"

He nodded yes. "I have weekly and monthly goals—"

"Right. Then maybe I could be an easy placement for you this week and for the month. You won't have to work hard for this one. I'll make sure and sell everything I've got." Wink. "From your files there, Cory, who would I possibly be interviewing with for a job?"

He stared at me a beat longer, then broke the spell by looking back at his desk.

"Uh... let me see." Cory pulled a piece of paper from the closest stack. "It would be Betty in Human Resources at a local government agency."

"Wonderful! Do you want to call her right now and see if she's interested in what I can do for her, and maybe has an urgent need? I could do a quick phone interview right now, too, if that's convenient for her."

He nodded excitedly. "Um, yeah, actually that's a good idea."

Cory picked up the phone to call Betty in Human Resources. After a minute of introductions and reviewing the job, he passed the phone over to me across the counter. I answered a few questions, and the call ended with Betty inviting me over to the office tomorrow for an interview. I smiled and winked at Cory while confirming the address and time. Then I passed the phone back over the counter as he grabbed some paperwork for me to fill out while he continued talking with Betty. He glanced up at me occasionally like he didn't know what had just happened. I smiled and nodded encouragingly like a bobble head doll.

In less than ten minutes, Cory and I had lined up a potential new job that would start next Monday at 9 a.m. with an orientation tomorrow morning. I congratulated Cory on his placement skills and told him I'd be back to see him shortly with my resume.

"Yeah, I'll be here still." He put a label on a new file. "This is really unusual, a placement doesn't normally happen this fast..."

"Well it sounds like it was a lucky day for you, me, and Betty. See you in a few!"

I pushed my cart out into the blazing afternoon heat and noticed my posture was straighter and stronger. I had no idea where the town of Tarboro was, no idea what the office was like, and no idea what type of people I would work with, but I was certain about one thing: my inner strength and willpower was coming back.

The twenty-five mile drive out of Greenville weaved like a lazy ribbon, passing long stretches of green pastures, huge ancient trees, and charming historical houses. I pulled up to the four-story brick building and walked up to the second floor to find Betty in Human Resources. The orientation from last week involved filling out paperwork and meeting my new co-workers in the Department of Emergency Services: Mike, the Director; Phil, the services and facilities manager; and twin brothers, Tim and Sam, who were the county's Fire Chief and Police Chief. The brothers were usually not in the office, so I shook hands with Mike and Phil and got settled. Everyone was very welcoming and kind - or maybe just eager for someone to finally answer the phone, take care of the mail, and keep things organized. I was the only female, the only person under forty, and the only one not born and raised in North Carolina. I was also the rare species who wasn't fluent in NASCAR-speak. I finally pronounced "Earnhardt" correctly after Phil spent two minutes repeating the name back to me as part of my professional training.

The daily rhythm invigorated me. Mike was the first one in the office every morning and the last one to leave at night, in addition to his National Guard responsibilities on the weekends. He was the strong silent type, so I poked my head into the other offices for updates and conversation. Phil shared slow stories about county politics. Tim described the latest county fires and how many volunteers showed up. And Sam's office quietly broadcast the ongoing chatter of the police radio since he was never in the office.

As I peeled an orange at my desk one afternoon, I realized I'd been in North Carolina for over three months and these were the first people I'd connected with. My motivation and discipline were back, my sleep routine was normal, and my eating habits were regular again. In some ways, the depression felt like it never happened, and yet it also felt like a new part of me that I didn't know existed before. Like a stranger showed up unannounced that I couldn't ignore because I needed to learn from it.

I finished the orange slices and started tossing pieces of rind into the trash can five feet away. Each toss moved across Tim's office doorway. The keyboard went quiet after my second throw. Every time I made a shot, he clapped; when I missed, he booed. Yep, these were my kind of people.

"Hey, Molly. Have a minute?" Tim beckoned from his corner of the world.

"Yep." I stood up and appeared in his doorway in three motions.

"What are your plans for Thanksgiving next week?" He reclined back in his chair, his right hand tapping on the wood desktop.

"Oh, um, I'm not sure yet." I forgot the holiday was already here.

"Well, my wife and I are hosting our family's dinner and we'd love it if you could come over and join us. Would you be interested in stopping by? It won't be fancy, just casual."

"Yes, thank you! I would be happy to be there."

"Great, we'll look for ya around four o'clock or so. And here's the address." He slid a piece of paper across the desk.

"What can I bring? I can't arrive empty-handed."

"A dessert of your choice would be great. Our family loves having too much dessert around." He laughed and patted his belly.

"Great, no problem. I'll bring a pie. And thank you for the invitation, that's kind of you."

"It's only because you made most of those orange peel shots. I have to be very careful about the kind of person I bring home to my family." He smiled and the phone rang; I swooshed back to my desk to grab it.

Thanksgiving Day showed up as a beautiful cornucopia of late fall: Marigold branches, red berries, orange leaves, and golden sunlight all guided me to Tim's house. Wearing shorts and a t-shirt in November was unseasonable to my Northwest traditions, and it felt delicious to have the sun on my skin as I walked up to the front step, pumpkin pie in hand. Tim's wife, Jennifer, ushered me into their festively decorated rambler with a scarecrow on the porch, rows of pumpkins in the entryway, white candles blazing in the living room, and hints of turkey, cornbread, and apple pie wafting just above my shoulders. Jennifer put a bottle of Cheerwine in my hand with a smile and said it was a Thanksgiving tradition to drink the cherry-infused soda pop before the main meal. Tim's mom said with a wink that it was only available in Carolina, so best to enjoy it extra slowly.

Ten of us gathered tightly around the holiday table with only a few inches between each place setting. I squeezed into my seat and found myself holding my stomach, arms, and breathe as close to my body as possible. The Thanksgiving prayer was spoken and we went from extreme silence to non-stop chatter in seconds. Jennifer asked about life back in Seattle and what the West Coast was like compared to North Carolina.

"Well, there are many obvious differences like the weather and food. I just ate grits for the first time a few weeks ago."

"What did you think? Were they good grits?"

"They were good to me, but I'm not sure if they were high-quality. I told my neighbor Lee where I ate them, and his face started to contort in a way that told me I did not choose the best restaurant for grits."

"We love our grits here in Carolina." Tim replied, as numerous heads around the table nodded. "So what else is different about being here? It's interesting to think about what we take for granted. I'd love to hear a fresh perspective."

"NASCAR is not a sport I'm familiar with, so it's been a new thing to understand while I've been here. Car racing is not something we see or hear much about in Seattle."

The table went quiet as blank stares of confusion spread around the table. Uh-oh.

I quickly added, "But I'm sure that will change later this year when Earnhardt, Jr. wins the next Daytona. Who wouldn't hear about that, right?" Everyone broke into smiles and head nods.

The evening ended a few hours later with friendship hugs and sincere thank you's. Jennifer and Tim told me I could visit any time, especially if I needed a place to visit over Christmas. I was leaving North Carolina in a few weeks to drive back home, but I told them this gathering had been one of the highlights of my time here. I walked backwards out the driveway, waving as I went, and balancing a few plates of leftovers. It was an interesting feeling to say goodbye to people knowing that it really was a true goodbye. It was highly unlikely our forks would be at the same table again.

A note from Lee was on my apartment door, offering turkey and mashed potato leftovers if I was interested. I knocked on his door to accept the invitation. I must be making up for those days of not eating. He clicked off the television and we pulled out our trusty balcony chairs to share a late dinner together.

"What are your plans for the upcoming holidays?" Lee asked after a sip of iced tea.

"Well, it looks like I will be leaving Greenville in a few weeks to go back home. I'm ready to be with my family again, especially for the holidays."

He nodded mildly. "A lot of people leave here. But somehow I've stayed. Glad you were my neighbor for a while."

I nodded in return. "Me too, Lee. Thanks for sharing your meals with me. You're a great cook."

"Happy to share with a nice young lady like yourself."

We finished eating in silence. Lee lit up a cigarette. The empty plates sat on our laps as the courtyard slowly faded into darkness. I felt a weariness coming over my body.

"Think I'm gonna call it a night, Lee."

"Sure you don't want some pumpkin pie? It's too much for just myself. We like to fatten up our neighbors here in Greenville, ya know. "

I smiled. "Sure, I can take a few pieces, why not."

He went into his apartment and emerged a moment later with a foiled-cover plate. "Here ya go, lady."

As I took the plate, he moved back and forth from one leg to another as if he was trying to go somewhere but couldn't settle on a direction. I stalled my exit.

"Say Molly, just wanted to let you know... I phoned up my daughter last week... and..."

I stood holding the pie plate as he moved uncomfortably, looking out over the grass.

"And, uh... it was really nice. Really... really nice..." His voice died out as he looked down towards his slip-on shoes.

I tried to catch his eye, but he was avoiding eye contact. "That's really great, Lee. I'm happy for you."

"Yeah, well, there are some things I needed to say and some things she needed to hear, so I think it was good for both of us." He nodded his head repeatedly, affirming his words, lost in another place. He continued, "Like you said, we each have a story. And I hope you know that every page in your story is okay. Okay, lady? It's 100% okay." He was looking at me with the same concentrated stare he used when he was talking about grits.

It was my turn to nod, affirming his words. "Yeah. Thanks."

"Now get on with yourself and have a nice night." Lee turned to grab his pack of cigarettes as I went inside. I heard him shuffling his chair around and then it was silent.

Inside my apartment, I stood against the front door realizing all of the people I was supposed to connect with here showed up in other areas of my life. Maybe this experience wasn't such a failure after all. Maybe this part of the story held more value than I could understand right now. Maybe I did everything okay, after all.

Over the next few weeks, I packed up my belongings after work and made travel arrangements for the drive home with my mom. We'd be heading south down to Florida to reach interstate 10 and take it all the way from Tallahassee to Los Angeles, then north up Interstate 5 to Seattle, avoiding the harsh December weather that most of the country was starting to experience. Planning the return drive reminded me that I hadn't talked to Jill much since I'd been here. I couldn't bring myself to tell her, or any of my other friends, the personal hardships I had experienced. A part of me wanted to keep it to myself.

For my final weekend in Greenville, I drove east to Cape Hatteras National Park on the Outer Banks to take in the fresh Atlantic Ocean air for the last time. Everything felt different by the ocean: The sky was clearer, the air was freshly exfoliated, the sounds of waves, gulls, and wind removed any debris you were willing to release. My foot hitting the sinking sand was the sensation of entering my favorite chapel.

The black and white stripes of the dominating lighthouse spiraled above the beach like a swirling chocolate and vanilla ice cream cone. A doorway at the lighthouse's base began the 248-step climb north, a full twelve stories above the wind-pushed sand, wispy tufts of sea grass, plastic pails of sand. I stepped out onto the top circular balcony, slightly breathless from the climb, and the spectacular view took all of my thoughts away.

Turquoise blue skies hung over endless navy ripples. The southern coastline reached out its right arm to elongate tired, stiff winter beach muscles. The northern coastline stretched out like a left arm extending its hand and fingers as far as it could go, just beyond eyesight, just enough to feel the full expanse of the coastline. I was the only person on top of the world on this December day, so I stretched my arms out to mimic the coastline's intentions, to feel wind gusts swirl through my hair and whisk away heavy thoughts. Sunbeams kissed every exposed patch of my face, neck, hands. I invited the salty air to cleanse away any internal dark corners as the rhythmic water beat up and down on the horizon. Gentle and fierce, the waves created a tempo that synchronized with my heartbeat and breath. All of the earth's elements were in harmony to create this space of serenity. The weather may change from smooth to turbulent at a moment's notice, but anything that was not destroyed was only made stronger, tougher, better. Sand that was rearranged by the crashing waves and galloping winds was not simply blown away; it was carried to a new landing place. Waves pounding on the shore took away what was complete and brought in new tidal treasures. The sun silently calmed, soothed, nourished, and reliably showed up for the next day's needs. In these last few months, I had felt the experiences of the sand, the winds, the waves, and the sun. And from this perch atop a beacon of light, a higher and broader perspective gave me a sense of detachment from the ground and an opportunity to observe the Divine perspective of harmony and peace that isn't always seen at eye level.

Inhale. Exhale. Release.

Inhale. Exhale. Release.

Inhale. Exhale. Release.

I glided around the balcony one more time, clutching to the black railing and the feeling of peace, and took in this grand perspective with gratitude. All was well.

Then I began walking back down the stairs, my breathing deeper, fuller, stronger. It was all going to be okay. I will drive back home in two short weeks. I will spend the holidays with my family and friends. I did the best I could during this unexpected time in my life. All was well. All was perfect today in my chapel.

I arrived back on the earth with a renewal of hope. *Something bigger was happening here.*

THE PLATFORM

As an official *FAUX* PARISIAN, one of my favorite daily adventures was discovering more metro platforms all over the city. I'd descend into the city's numerous cement rabbit holes and the air would become stuffier, dense with busy bodies. The dimly lit hallways felt safe, but I still moved at a quickened pace through the turnstiles and out onto the platforms. Rumbling echoes from the tunnels' activities could be heard in both directions, making it hard to decipher if a train was coming close or moving away. Automated signs hung over each platform announcing the minutes until the next train arrived, followed by a second train. Giant advertising images stretched from my knees to well over my head, looking down with authority. All of these details were consistent in every metro station, but the style and atmosphere was different at each platform.

The tin dome ceiling of the Arts and Metiers metro station felt like every whisper could be carried down the tunnels and shared with the city. The Bastille station had open-air platforms where the clouds and sun and rain and stars could make a passing appearance. The hyper pace and winding tunnels of Charles de Gaulle-Étoile felt like a never-ending whitewater rafting ride: sharp curves, up-and-down stairs, and side-to-side shoulders pushed me along as I tried not to get left behind in the backwash. A soft sophisticated vibe welcomed me at the Louvre-Rivoli metro station as enclosed display cases and dramatic lighting set the tone for the museum's treasures. Arriving at a new station was yet another introduction to one of Paris's multiple personalities.

And then there was the adventure of actually riding the metro and never knowing what I would find as the doors swung swiftly open. One morning, I boarded a metro car that was almost completely empty on one side. Everyone was standing in the middle or far end of the car, so I interpreted the space as an obvious place to find a seat. As the doors opened, I pounced to an empty seat and I sat down just as a foul smell hit me in the throat. I instinctively covered my nose and mouth with my soft purple scarf and looked around as the buzzer blared and the doors slammed shut, locking me into this decision. A homeless man was sitting on the train floor, humming loudly to himself, and chewing on raw sardines from a collection of opened cans. Each can was lined up in a straight row. I counted eight before turning my head towards the window and staring into the dark tunnel. The stench was overbearing even with all of the windows pulled down. We rolled into the next metro station a few minutes later and I jumped out to move down the train to another, less fragrant car.

But surprisingly, most of the metro cars were typically clean and almost always silent, like mobile libraries. There was rarely any loud talking; no lengthy conversations, no cellphones ringing, and very few distractions. Passengers read silently, looked out the window, whispered quietly in hushed voices, or stared straight ahead. Even packed cars at rush hour were gravely quiet as soon as the door buzzer went off and business suits stood shoulder-to-shoulder without making a sound except for a faint cough or a muffled sneeze. If a phone rang, it was answered briskly or immediately silenced and put in a pocket.

Then the library car would change to a circus car when the occasional street performer boarded with a song, a boom box, or a puppet show. They would quickly set up on one side of a car to entertain passengers and walked the full length of the car asking for spare coins. Beggars would swiftly make their way in one end of a car to pass around written requests for help and then exit out the other side and move on to the next car. All was silent again after the buzzer sounded and the doors forcefully whooshed shut.

I exited the cavernous metro stations with the anticipation that anything could be happening above ground: blazing sunshine, pouring rain, a protest parade, a crowded farmer's market, or complete silence. The unpredictable summer weather would change quickly from sun to clouds to hard rain and back to sun again in only a few hours. I learned to travel around the city with a purse that carried sunglasses, an umbrella, and my current favorite reading material so I could duck inside a cafe when the summer rain started to dampen my floral skirt and brown slip-on sandals. I would sit down and order a warm cup of *Mariage Frères* tea and hold it inside both of my palms as street puddles accumulated, buses hurled by, and people ducked under store overhangs to wait out the weather. Within twenty minutes, the hard rain turned into light droplets and the mighty sun emerged forward again. I grabbed my purse off the blue-and-yellow rattan cafe chair and headed towards the Seine for my walk home.

Most major cities in the world were built around a river or near a waterway. I always interpreted this as how the flow of the water sets the pulse of the land. I am regularly drawn to the pull of waves in any city, an unspoken magnetic connection that re-centers my own pulse and opens up more of my inner-world flow. As the city's aquatic boulevard appeared ahead, the sound of drumbeats and festival music also grew louder, as if the music notes were being carried on soft waves and slowly raised up to street level. I descended the nearest staircase to the Seine, and as the music became louder, I found I had magically arrived at an outdoor beach party.

Long winding strips of temporary sandboxes, about two feet deep, covered most of the cement walkways and created an instant beach. Blue-cushioned lounge chairs, giant beach umbrellas, and lazy sunbathers stretched for any rays they could find. A pair of women grabbed two lounge chairs that were abandoned during the rain and flung bright beach towels out from their canvas totes as a pile of magazines fell into the sand. I zigzagged slowly between palm trees in white planter boxes providing tropical shade. Their expansive shadows hit the uneven pavement below my feet and blew on the ground like leafy street sweepers. They looked completely out of place in this urban jungle, yet I readily welcomed their tropical vibe. The music I heard at street level had faded away as a parade of Brazilian dancers moved along the walkways, their bright feathers bobbing up and down in the crowds. The sun was now back to blasting at full July intensity.

I grabbed my shades out of my carry-everything-purse and stopped in front of a decorative sign: *Bienvenue à Paris Plage*. Welcome to the Paris Beach. From late July to late August, long stretches along the Seine turned the cement highway into an instant oasis. Walls of fountains cooled off sunbathers with mist sprayers. Children stared at flowing play fountains and tried to figure out the perfect timing for getting wet and outsmarting the water spurts. I watched them run through the random blasts, squealing with delight, and then turned around to do it again I weaved through a line of people waiting in front of an ice cream stand. The scenery changed from sandy beaches and loungers to long teak decks and patches of fresh grass. Café tables with umbrellas and deck chairs were sprinkled everywhere, almost all occupied, and people carried trays of sandwiches and drinks from a temporary café. A tempting whiff of fries sailed through the air but was quickly followed by a fishy smell from a passing river barge.

Amidst the laughing children, rows of tilted sunglasses, and bright tropical displays, a surreal feeling came over me. If I zoomed out of this location at this moment in time, I would see myself as a pin on a map standing in the middle of a Brazilian beach party next to the Seine river in Paris, France. I was not sitting at a desk, staring at a screen and willing the clock to tick faster to 5 p.m. I was not stuck in traffic or looking forward to only Friday and the weekend. I was experiencing one of my life's dreams because I gave myself permission to follow a heart-based choice and Trust. In an instant, I could flash back to feeling chained to the responsibilities of a mediocre job, waiting for *something* to happen, waiting for all of the pieces to line up perfectly in some fashion. Waiting, waiting, waiting. Like someone else had more control over my choices, or that I needed something outside of myself to decide for me, or I needed to have *all of this* ready to go before I could experience All of This.

And when I zoomed back in, it felt incredible to be in the middle of a Brazilian beach party along the Seine on a gorgeous summer day. I smiled big to no one and everyone at this realization, and turned around to walk back up to the commotion of the street.

I crossed the glistening gold Pont Alexandre III bridge and walked towards the golden dome of *Les Invalides* where Napoleon Bonaparte was entombed. Just think how different world history would have been if Napoleon had waited for permission to live his life and make his choices. Well, some figures in history might have appreciated that.

I turned right onto charming Rue de Grenelle and headed towards the Eiffel Tower off in the distance. A white utility van careened around the corner, nearly knocking over a line-up of tightly packed motorcycles. Drops of water came down as I passed under a balcony of flowers. Then I halted in front of an unexpected sight: a store window full of peanut butter, mustard, maple syrup, bags of little chocolates, and all kinds of American confections. *Hello, friends!*

How lovely to see all of you!

I pushed through the store's front door with too much force, a bell jingling erratically, and entered a delicious land of soups, bagels, chips, and cookies. *Glory day, we are united again!* I held myself back from doing jazz hands.

"*Bonjour, Monsieur!*"

"*Bonjour, Madame!*" The French man behind the counter barely turned away from the blaring television set.

Yes, I was living in a world capital known for its gastronomical masterpieces, but I felt like I had just found a treasure chest of forgotten foods from Misfit Island. I impulsively grabbed an insanely-priced-but-totally-justifiable bag of Cheetos and continued down the rows grabbing sacks of food. *I love YOU, and I love YOU, and I adore YOU, too.* The French man behind the counter turned away from the television and raised his eyebrows and moustache simultaneously.

"*Tous mes amis, Monsieur.*" All of my friends, Monsieur.

"*Oui, Madame. Les amis sont important.*" Yes, Madame. Friends are important.

I threw my head back with loud American laughter in front of the loud American packaging. He winked.

After completing my first lap around the store, the weight of the hand basket now hurting my elbow, I gathered myself together like an adult woman and walked around the store one more time, but during this round, I casually and discreetly returned most sacks back to the shelves. I could always come back. Tomorrow.

I paid for my American staples in euros and only computed the exchange rate for one item. Too much financial information ruins the fun.

"*Bon après-midi, Monsieur!*" Happy afternoon, Monsieur!

"*A vous aussi, Madame!*" You too, Madame!

The doorbell jingled wildly again as I exited back out onto the street, and as my hair turned to catch up with my head, a hidden box of grits caught my eye. Greenville. Depression. Cross-country road trip. Falling. In a heartbeat that life from seven years ago became present as if I had dinner with Lee on the balcony last night.

I walked toward the Eiffel Tower as the past rushed up behind me. When I returned home to Seattle after my time in North Carolina, and felt the safety of distance from the experience, I eventually dove into figuring out the spiritual purpose of my depression. It would have been easy to medicate, but that was not the right choice for me. It would have been even easier to attempt to sweep it all under the rug, say some happy affirmations, and "think positive thoughts" to move ahead. But that wasn't me either. That brief episode of depression revealed a new part of my self-identity that I hadn't seen before, and I didn't want to see again, and I didn't even want to claim it as a part of me. *Deny, hide, cover up, ignore.* But when I attempted to do all of that—and oh, how I did!—little triggers (a book, a movie, overhearing a conversation at lunch, or a lame public service announcement) brought me right back to the experience. And then it felt like there was a giant, intimidating monster shadow on the wall following me around, complete with fangs and spikes and claws and the ability to keep growing because I was keeping it in the dark where it could thrive and expand without boundaries. Until one day I felt really strong and had had enough. I turned around to face the monster with moxie and said, *"Alright, Bucko! I'm not afraid of you anymore! Let's DO THIS."* Because I was really only living in fear of a part of myself.

So I ventured into the deep questions, ugly self-examination, and messy emotions that lurked in the shadows. Ugh. NOT FUN. It was intense and initially not very gratifying. I wanted the answers to be a microwave dinner: quick, convenient, minimal effort, done!

Instead it was a process of planting the seeds (hurry up and grow!), harvesting the crops (discomfort and long hours), and then making my own homemade lasagna recipe with fresh vegetables (carbs always motivate me so they needed to be an incentive in there somewhere). At first I thought the depression was only situational—far from home, all alone, no social support, feeling like a failure—but I realized if I didn't look at the deeper messages from that experience, those same messages would come right back around in another form in order to get my attention. I learned where I felt separated from something bigger than me; the ultimate in being alone on this giant planet. I had collapsed into myself and couldn't see any way out.

One of the biggest revelations was how I have been a lifetime Empath and never even knew it, or even what that term meant. You mean feeling other people's emotions and assuming they were my own was a *thing*? I thought everyone could pick-up on others' reactions, emotions, and thoughts. In conversations, I could tell when someone was withholding information, off in another place, or being completely authentic and present. I picked up on messages from animals everywhere and felt a mixture of joy and sadness every time I paced through a zoo. Many friends and acquaintances, even coffee shop strangers, opened up to me about their life secrets and troubles as if I had a 24-hour light bulb over my head that said *Excellent Listener, No Charge.*

Through the years, I had unconsciously absorbed a lot of stuff that wasn't mine and had unknowingly created this ocean of loneliness and weight inside. I realized it became necessary to put up more energetic boundaries around that pattern for my own health and sanity. I still pick-up a lot of the thoughts, feelings, and energies swirling around me, I just developed a more detached way of observing them. *Not mine. Not mine. Not mine. And I love you anyways.*

Discernment also became my new go-to ally because I felt a hesitation around opening up. Many people can be unknowingly judgmental when they can't relate to something personally, but then I observed how I could also be just as judgmental about *them* in return, like a loop of energy that keeps circling and whirling between us. Judgment stops conversations from moving ahead, closes down options, and halts possibilities, not to mention the discomfort of being misunderstood and awkward silences. Besides, it was never about other people's thoughts and interpretations; it was how I was unconsciously judging myself. And it became clear to me which relationships and friendships were finished because of the necessity to value myself more than that connection. As I moved up, up, up and away from the limits of self-judgment and into higher atmospheres of self-love, some beautiful people I adored felt like rocks in my socks: uncomfortable, heavy, cold, hard. There was less of an energetic match between us as I changed and our relationship dynamic did, too. And like always, I sensed the confusion and hurt they felt as friendships changed, but I had to honor myself fully and completely. I could not hold back, or hide, or be untruthful in any manner. (*Open up more*, three stars.)

As I found my answers, I viewed the temporary depression in a new light: I did not fall down; I fell into myself more. The hollow, unconscious areas inside of me collapsed so a stronger foundation could be built, like a new platform for higher self-understanding. No one else could do the work for me, but no one else could take it away from me, either.

Then, just to prove to myself what I had learned, and that, oh yes, I could most certainly try again after Greenville, I moved to Portland, Oregon on a sticky-hot morning in July. *Fall down seven times, stand up eight*, as the saying goes.

The sidewalk was quieter as I approached the Champ de Mars, the lush long park in front of the Eiffel Tower. Buildings disappeared as the sky opened up higher and wider preparing for the grand view of the city's famous steel giraffe. The trees became denser, the air was softer with birds' wings and cotton candy clouds. I walked along one of the winding dirt paths that weaved through the park. Two joggers passed by going in opposite directions, both wearing bright yellow jerseys. The street noise came back as I approached a long parking lot crammed with high buses and tiny cars lined up in every parking space. I walked in the afternoon shadows of the trees, keeping the monument to my right, and found a vacant bench facing the silver spire. It really was an Eye-full of a Tower.

I sat down and wrestled the bag of chips open, knowing a tourist destination was a safe place to satisfy this impulse, and soaked up the sun's warmth even as throngs of sun visors and backpacks and herds of heads clouded the view. A man walked by wearing a Pebble Beach golf hat and light blue polo shirt. His wife drawled at him, "Keep up, Harold, stay with the group or you'll miss the bus." Harold then stopped, looked up for an Eye-full, and said, "Betty, I did not come here to rush back to the bus. I came here to see everything outside of the bus." I wanted to offer Harold a handful of Cheetos in support. And I could; there were no "Please Don't Feed the Tourists" signs in sight. But these little puffs cost way too much to just give away. So I squinted at the top of the Eye-full and all of the little figurines toddling around at its highest point. The elevators inside the steel legs ascended and descended rhythmically, as if in slow motion with the passing cloud puffs and the meandering flow of the Seine. Just stopping to take in how peaceful an environment is can do wonders for the—

"What? WHAT? No, no, we need more than that for this month. Are you kidding me? We have sales goals for a reason, they need to understand that!"

And then this guy showed up and sat down on the bench next to me. Dark blue slacks, white polo shirt, red in the face from yelling into his cell phone. Like a vertical version of the French flag.

"Well, get them to try harder than! We're behind right now and we can't risk another loss this quarter. This is NOT okay!" He huffed and puffed air into the receiver like a bull about to charge. I stood up to take my picnic elsewhere. Definitely no Cheetos for him.

"The numbers are the only thing that matter at this point, Charlie. The *only* thing."

The unwelcomed intrusion got me thinking about my time in Portland when sales goals governed my life every day and how all-consuming the pressure and numbers could be. Thankfully, I was able to get clear about my More Before and recognize it as another platform to jump from.

EVERY BAR STOOL AT KELL'S Irish Pub was occupied as I nudged my way up to the bar, squeezing through shoulders and sleeves, looking to grab a bartender's eye during the crazy Friday happy hour activity. I spied Mike's haircut through the crowd and moved in that direction to grab his arm. He signaled to the back corner where our group had claimed territory over a tiny table. He appeared five minutes later with pints in hand to pass around.

"Cheers to our branch! Cheers to our sales team, the youngest in the region!" Five pints of Guinness met over the middle of the table and five heads bobbed in unison as we clinked glasses.

Sophia, our assistant manager, chimed in. "Well, I'm proud of everyone, great job! And it's very cool since we're the youngest branch and we're on the new Regional Leadership Team. Congrats, you all worked very hard."

"So Molly, what did you spend your prize money on? It's pretty awesome to be one of the top performing bankers in the state in only seven months. That will be my award next quarter, by the way." Joann laughed and shook her blonde hair out as if getting rid of everything in her head from the week. She worked at a different branch and we became instant friends after sitting together during our Personal Banker Training Program. It was smooth sailing after we created a theme song for our new positions. Tina Turner's "Private Dancer" was the clear winner since we could easily incorporate Private Banker into the title. Dance moves behind a desk were still in the works and choreography gave us an incentive to continue with banker training.

"Well, I got four CDs with the cash, and then a new sleeping bag and stereo with the regional contest. Pretty cool stuff."

"Yeah, and don't forget the part where I had to spot you two bucks for going over the cash total." Mike laughed.

"That's what makes you such a top manager, Mike."

Sophia said, "Let's cheers again to the next quarter's sales goals and being the best!"

We touched glasses again just as live music started up in the background. Jerry, the silent fifth person, pushed back his chair and grabbed his phone. "Gotta take this call from my wife, guys. Talk to you all next week."

Four hands waved goodbye and then we quickly redistributed the chairs to take advantage of the additional space.

"What are you doing this weekend, Jo?" The music was almost too loud to talk. Mike and Sophia were huddled in close to hear each other.

"Oh, we're building a new shed in the backyard and I told my husband I would be around to help him. But that means I'll be sitting in the sun with a magazine watching him. You?"

"Oh, not much. I need to clean up my apartment tomorrow—"

"—exciting—"

"—absolutely thrilling. And then I'll see my mom on Sunday for lunch up in Washington. It's only a two hour drive to meet her halfway between Portland and Seattle."

"Nice. That's great your family and friends are within driving distance. All of my family is too close. I wish they were further away most weekends." She sipped her beer.

"Yeah, it's nice to have them within driving distance since I'm new to the city."

The band became louder as our pints declined. We each started playing with our phones and purses as an unspoken desire to call it a week circled the table. I finally declared I was "Friday night tired." All four chairs pushed back from the table and we weaved our wave towards the door.

"New quarter starts Monday! See you then!" Mike yelled down the street as we all went our separate ways. I silently held up the peace sign and climbed into my forest green Toyota Tacoma, tucking in my gray skirt so it wouldn't get stuck in the door.

Another week of hitting sales goals; another month of tracking numbers; another quarter of achievement and high rankings and making our regional manager proud. Now it would start all over again with higher sales goals to hit and even more numbers to prove. And I didn't care about any of it, at all. I had been going through the motions for the past seven months, and sure, the rewards and recognition felt good. But they were fleeting and only offered false security because it meant more was expected next time. It was eye opening to have reached a certain level of achievement and not to feel connected to it, like the cash moving in and out of my hands every day. Is this what I wanted my life to be about: quarterly sales, bank profit, and long commutes? I could feel a stronger underlining energy pulling me to search for *more* than this. More daily enjoyment. More creativity. More delight. More heart satisfaction.

I pulled out of the street parking spot and crossed over the Willamette River to get on the southbound highway. The truck's windows were cracked open to welcome the Friday night breeze inside, clearing out the thoughts and stresses from the previous week. The spring sun sank to pink and reflected in the river, like a flow of grapefruit water was meandering through Portland. The Friday night traffic was surprisingly light and my mind could wander effortlessly, easily without having to shift between gears or lanes. From this job and place right here, based on what I have and what I know about myself, what is next? *What would I do if I could do anything? What do I want my life to include? And can I summon the motivation to continue with the reality of right now even though I don't like it?*

Fair to say, my life could be separated into two main sections. The first twenty years were about being a daughter, teenager, student, and an emerging adult in the world. I was tethered to my parents and school, and luckily my choices expanded as I grew up. Then the next long-term phase of my life would presumably include the roles of professional *something,* wife, mother, and full-fledged adult status. The responsibilities would be greater, but hopefully, so would the joys and rewards. Which left me at this place now: in between these two main phases and questioning what I want to do when there were no tethers holding me to one place or anyone else.

There seemed to be an unspoken-but-known checklist that determined how far along we were in life based on professional status, marriage, house, and babies. I had none of these things and, truthfully, I did not want any of them now. Or soon. Even when the world seemed to be Built For Two most of the time, marriage and houses and babies all felt confining to me. And at the same time, I couldn't help but wonder if this perspective would put me "behind". *Was I missing out on my one chance to pair up with Mr. Right? Was I going to miss securing a great deal on a 30-year mortgage loan and forgo a stellar 401K plan? Was I terribly and irrevocably doomed by choosing to step away from the traditional path and instead head into unknown territory where no SUV-with-two-car-seats had roamed before?*

I wanted more in my life before I entered into something married or mortgaged. More *before* all of that. *More before* that revolved around being free, living unscripted, expanding my goals, discovering new sources of joy, thinking of a new idea and then trying it on for size. And more. Before. *So what would be on my More Before list?* The ideas came whirling in as I slowed down off the highway exit: travel, graduate school, live abroad, follow inspirations that move my heart, play with money I earn, explore new professional terrain, make time for creativity, and keep moving forward knowing that the right "everything" will turn up along the way. And more.

My apartment complex appeared on the left, the entrance flanked by blooming trees, and I pulled into my reserved parking spot. I turned off the engine and sat with my revelations. I could live by my own unspoken-but-known checklist, my More Before. And I could get through a full year of this job easier if I was able to view it as a starting point—a platform—for the next adventure, and more. *Perfect.*

I walked up to the second floor, unlocked the door, and threw my purse onto the dining room table. Two circling tails glided past my knees. I patted them one at a time; one warm from lounging in the sun, the other cool from sleeping in the dark on the duvet.

"Hi little muffins. Did you meet your sales goals today?"

They scurried into the kitchen. Dinner was being served a highly unacceptable hour late. I kicked off my heels and paused to see my art supplies and blank canvases sitting in the corner; another week untouched and ignored. My heart pounded with both desire and frustration. Always too tired, too busy, too much time spent commuting, and trying to stay on top of each day's priorities. Would there ever be time to create?

As of four minutes ago, I declared it a vital part of my More Before and I could not let my creativity collect dust forever. The art meant way more to me in the long run than the sales goals. I needed fresh momentum that served my highest good, and as I spooned cat food onto ceramic plates, I set the intention for the perfect solution to arrive from this platform. It had to.

THE BARS

SIZZLING SMOKE WAFTED UP TO touch the high ceiling of my kitchen as I placed two marinated duck breasts inside the tiny pan. Trisha stood up to open the giant window a bit more, then returned to the kitchen counter and nestled back into her bar chair.

"Okay, next question. Who is known as the first architect of the Louvre?" She sipped her wine.

"Oh gosh. Was it… Pierre Lescot?" I glanced over at Trish as she nodded yes, her nose five inches from the book. I haven't had an academic test in years, and yet the nerves came back quickly as if they had lived in a dormant volcano. Our final exams of the summer term started tomorrow. We spent yesterday afternoon staring at books and notes and pages at a cafe in Saint Michel. I flipped the duck breasts in the pan. "Anything else you want to add?"

"Yeah, Leonardo da Vinci came to France to share his expertise with the king when Italian styles were highly influential. Moving on. What do the fountains and statues in *Place de la Concorde* symbolize?"

"The two fountains represent the rivers in France and the surrounding seas: The Atlantic and the Mediterranean. And the eight statues represent the main cities of the country. Do we need to name the eight cities?" I moved the duck to our plates to let them rest and threw bright, firm green beans from today's market into the same pan. Trisha poured more wine into both glasses.

"Probably, yes. You know how thorough and detailed Dr. Brown is, especially after the quizzes we've had this term. We probably need to know the important architects, too. And the story of how the obelisk arrived in the square. And all of the history of *Place de la Concorde*."

"Right." I shuffled the green beans around in the pan. "I'm afraid to ask, but how many more sections do we have to cover tonight?"

She flipped through her notepad. This class was a six-week walking tour of the architectural and political history of Paris: from the city's original settlement as *Lutetia* by the Gauls all the way through every Republic and Empire; every monarch, president, and ruler; most monuments, museums, and *hôtel particuliers*; all of the architectural movements, influential architects, and significant symbolism of different structures; plus the city's parks, growth, and urbanization into the twentieth century. The details were overwhelming and mind-blogging, but also completely fascinating and enriching at the same time. I walked all over the city with new eyes and increasing appreciation.

"Quick change of topic. When do you have to move out of your apartment?" I stepped away from the two-burner stove and bit into a slice of baguette, my daily addiction.

"In a month, after the owner returns from summer holiday. I've already asked for help at the school, but everyone is getting ready for vacation, so…"

I moved the green beans around one final time, then pushed them next to the warm duck. "You can always stay here if you need a place to crash for a bit."

After unpacking my books, filling up the closet, and rolling my biggest suitcase next to the mini-fridge to keep it out of the way, my apartment felt slightly bigger than a pinky thimble. But there was always additional room for family.

"Okay, thanks. We'll see how my apartment hunting goes."

I slid two plates across the counter and handed out forks. "*Voila! Manger, manger.*" Eat, eat.

We each removed our tortoise-framed glasses to signal our brains were turning off, mouths turning on. A family with three young kids moved through the courtyard and doors slammed shut in their wake. A siren was heard in the distant. I opened the window even more to let summer inside.

Thirty minutes later, my hair up in a fresh new bun, we returned to studying without wanting to lose any momentum. The upcoming week of exams somehow felt connected to all of the other developments that could transpire in the next two years: New friends, travel, professional opportunities, and maybe even a Parisian romance for each of us? The energy was there and growing, like if we nailed this test, we would have more momentum in other areas of life. Trisha and I had bonded easily because our intuition was connected and weaved together in strong ways. We could both feel new dreams taking off.

Underneath my stack of notes, I felt an uplifting excitement that the energy would take each of us where we needed to go, and connect us with whomever matched that same energy. The jump to Paris was a fresh surge of joy, and the momentum would continue to move forward based on greater levels of trust and faith. Things were coming together perfectly even if we couldn't see any "proof" yet. But I felt the possibilities on some level because I had followed the momentum that had started for me two years ago in Annecy. And by trusting the inspiration, I had safely landed here.

"Couper les carottes, s'il vous plaît."

Couper is cut. Cut the carrots. Got it!

The instructor paced slowly behind us, our aprons crammed around the woodblock island. Her nose leaned in over each shoulder, surveying the work, and her pursed red lips gave away no information about the culinary craftsmanship she was witnessing. Her apron swayed gently with each pause-and-survey, pause-and-survey.

"Bien. Prochain, couper les navets, s'il vous plaît."

Navets?

Everyone grabbed from the pile of turnips and started chopping, so I did the same. From the corner of my eye, her well-coiffed hair floated around the kitchen again as all six of us worked in silence.

"Excusez-moi, Mademoiselle?" Her stern voice was suddenly loud in my right ear. Uh-oh. Being singled out in a French cooking class could not be a good thing. I stopped moving my knife.

"Oui, Madame?"

"J'ai dit coupé, pas piller et détruire." I said cut, not pillage and destroy.

She shook her head, then grabbed my knife to take over. I looked around at the other turnips; they had been cut with tender, loving perfection into slim slivers. Mine were a pile of slashed bits like I was chanting *die, turnips, die* with each stroke. I alone was about to ruin her *terrine de petits légumes en gelée*.

I stepped back from my overthrown cutting board. Another student smiled at me. I shrugged and smiled in return as Madame tried to salvage my mess. Alongside the terrine, we were preparing a main course called *suprême de loup aux deux artichauts*. My stomach had flipped and my face curled up upon reading the recipe. Supreme wolf with two artichokes? I had anticipated the French Alps being rustic and I knew French cooking could be, uh, adventurous, but I didn't realize we would be eating wild animals off the land. My hand sat on my stomach unconsciously as I held the recipe in the other hand.

Then Madame brought out a tray of sliced fish filets from the refrigerator and I noticeably exhaled, saved from the fate of biting into wolf meat. My relieved chuckling made her visibly annoyed, wringing her hands in her apron and twisting her face, as if we would be cooking something as uncivilized and disgusting as a rabid forest beast in her kitchen. In a superior tone, she explained that *suprême* was a filet of fish and sea bass was known as the" wolf of the sea." To be fair, there was no *de la mer* in the recipe title. Just one more instance where I was constantly learning how things worked in this country and trying to decipher the cultural codes.

Being a foreigner meant always trying to figure something— everything—out. The puzzle never stopped. I couldn't just put the Rubix cube down and walk away. I was fully submerged in the experience, sometimes swimming desperately for a lifeline, and most times just trying to stay above water and roll with the waves as they came in.

I had arrived in Geneva exhausted from twelve hours of travel and with high anticipation about this new land. A young French man at the airport had my name on a piece of cardboard, so of course I went with him to his shuttle parked out back. As with everything in life, absolutely judge a book by its cover, especially if the cover has clear blue eyes, a fresh haircut, and a dangerous grin. He grabbed my giant suitcase with a grimace and explained it would be over an hour drive to Annecy. I passed out almost immediately in the van, head against the window, probably drooling in my all-black outfit with jet lag abandon. The shuttle pulled up in front of a tan six-story apartment building with orange awning shades on Avenue de la Maveria just as I was coming back to life. He unloaded my luggage from the back of the shuttle and waved goodbye with little care. I fumbled for the code into the building and pushed everything into the tiny closet that was called the elevator. *Bonjour, chez moi.*

For the next five weeks, I shared the three-bedroom apartment with two other women studying French at the same school: Jessica, a stylish American from New York City, and Masami, a friendly Japanese woman who had been travelling around Europe for a few months. We quickly became companions and enjoyed wandering around town together, grabbing an evening beer, cooking meals with foreign ingredients, and cheering each other on with every little victory. Masami figured out how to use the washing machine that had no words, only odd symbols and weird compartments. Jessica discovered that we were supposed to bag our own groceries at the store after observing how annoyed the woman behind the counter was with us each time we visited. And I learned that there was an unspoken formal etiquette at the weekly farmer's market, especially at the fruit stands. Reach out and blatantly touch the fruit? You will be ignored. Pick up and bag the fruit? You were obviously trying to steal and would be publicly scolded. Wait patiently for Monsieur Fruit Stand's attention and kindly ask, *Combien pour trois apricots, s'il vous plaît? How much for three apricots, please?* Ah, now the code had been broken. Monsieur will triumphantly select the best apricots just for you, you, you as if no one else was on the street and he will invite you back to his splendid fruit collection next week. Once you are a regular, you can touch the fruit and bag it on your own, but first you have to earn the right. Demonstrating respect was key. And the French love authority; specifically, their own.

The three of us posted a schedule in the kitchen to show our weekly class schedule and to help plan meals together. But, of course, Fridays were the highlight of the week. When class ended on Friday afternoons, I dashed back to the apartment to pack a day bag or grab my weekend suitcase, then I caught a train to somewhere, anywhere, to see more of France. Life had new momentum on a train. I took day trips to new places on the Intercité trains that connected smaller towns and bigger cities. The train rocked rhythmically and pulled into yet another vacant village stop. No pedestrians, no children, no action on the streets, no movement of life at all. As if everyone was inside savoring a leisurely meal and did not dare reveal the secrets of their lives to window strangers. The greens, browns, oranges, and golds of September shimmered in every direction as the train carried on to the next *ville*.

The Friday night TGV train hurled south to Nice passing fields of lavender and open stretches of fading sun, every seat occupied with wide-brimmed hats, effortlessly chic sunglasses, or white polo shirts blazing against bronze skin. A book rested in my hands with the best of intentions, but the action outside the train was far more fascinating. Grand chateaus and tangled vineyards whirled by. Small towns would creep up to the windows, then quietly slip away. Signs on the side of the tracks faded in and out of focus. The rolling hillside would be close and imposing, and then distant and without consequence. The passing filmstrip constantly amazed and intrigued. Book pages were never turned.

In Nice, I slowly moved in and out of charming boutiques and expensive stores, walked along the *Promenade des Anglais* surveying the water and fashion, and rented a beach lounge chair and umbrella even though the hip afternoon crowds had already disappeared with the outgoing tide. I dined solo outside in the warm Mediterranean air, yet the restaurant tables were so close together that anyone sitting next to me felt like a dining companion. When the waiter sat another solo American woman at the table to my right, the meal turned into an amiable conversation over *salad niçoise*, our individual shrinking baskets of baguette slices, and a few pours of rosé. We chatted about feeling safe as female travelers and how strangers surprised us with extra doses of assistance. I shared with her that I was confused at the train station on Friday night, and two separate times someone asked if I needed anything. My dinner companion nodded in return, sipping her wine, then said, "I've only found open, generous people, and that's saying a lot considering the political environment at this time and how our President is not popular here."

It had been two years since the attacks in New York City and now we were at war. I was worried about how current politics would affect my travels, but most people I encountered only wanted to talk and learn more about the American perspective; why was war the first option and not the last one? And when I shared that I was in agreement with their perspective, that I had my questions and doubts as well, something lifted in their eyes; they thought all Americans wanted to be at war. Every conversation—with fellow train travelers, school colleagues, strangers—turned out to be eye opening for both sides and smashed inaccurate preconceived cultural stereotypes. "Dinner diplomacy" seemed more beneficial and accurate than turning on the evening news.

In Chamonix, two gondolas carried me up, up, up to over 8,200 feet atop Brevent, a mountain with a spectacular view of the town below. From way up here, Chamonix appeared to be sinking down into the earth between all of the mountains. Glaciers raced each other down the mountainside and the winner melted into the gushing river that ran wildly through town. I gazed up, up, up at the glistening majesty of Mont Blanc and felt like a dainty snowflake in its authoritative presence.

In Lyon, I tottered along the uneven cobblestones, ate a baguette sandwich in a grand square bustling with Saturday activity, and visited a local vineyard for an afternoon grape tasting. We toured the tangled lines of grapes (these are free to sample, right?) as the *propriétaire* reached down to show the strength of the roots and the complexities of the *terroir*. He led us down into the *cave à vin* where we drank the proof of his roots and *terroir*. The underground room was cool and dank as a wine storage venue should be, and sturdy thick brick walls with arches led to more rooms. Robust wine barrels displayed fresh wine glasses, brochures, and meager bits of cheeses and meats, but despite the rustic underground appeal, I found myself always looking for the entrance and the light on the floor.

In Grenoble, I strolled along the river, bought a beautiful heavy-to-hold grayish-blue sweater just in time for the approaching fall weather, and leisurely ate a banana-and-nutella crepe as a wedding commenced at a cathedral in the neighborhood square. Men stepped out of cars wearing tails and their best postures; women chattered away in colorful flouncy hats and luxurious silks. The congregation of suits and hats disappeared inside the church, and then a collective hush fell over all the outside spectators as a white angel appeared with a bouquet and long veil bouncing in the wind. The grand double doors of the cathedral opened slowly with strong, pushing arms. A distant organ began playing as the angel's train was straightened and smoothed down the cathedral steps. An elbow appeared next to her, and she started floating, floating, floating into the dark hallway until the last inch of her dress was devoured by the entrance. The heavy doors were slowly shut at the same moment every spectator in the square took a collective breath and went back to their Saturday life.

But it wasn't until the school's organized bus trip to Geneva to visit the United Nations' Palais des Nations that something bigger sparked alive within me. After taking a guided tour of the art-filled halls and listening to the history of the buildings, I stood in the back of the Assembly Hall where row upon row of long tables, chairs, and microphones were lined up in front of a grand central podium. The room easily accommodated thousands of global delegates. I stared up at the United Nations emblem on the back wall and felt the energy of the room shift to become both ancient and modern. like if I squinted straight ahead I could vaguely see an Ancient Greek Boule, complete with floor-length togas, dense white beards, and loud voices jostling to be heard, communing in the same place to advise, manage, and question the collective efforts.

When I looked up above all of the now-silenced noise, empty chairs, and invisible shoulders of delegates, I heard whispered languages, inquisitive sharing, and an intermingling of souls that were present for a shared peace mission. The room danced with possibilities, options, and solutions because the well-lit air wasn't vacant at all; rather, it was alive with a constellation of stellar possibilities and intentions for humanity. As if it was possible to reach up and grab a handful of stars that could possibly, potentially, maybe, serve and benefits millions. For all of the conflicts, disagreements, and wars in the world, this space with four walls and a high tray ceiling was dedicated to peace and cooperation. Few places on the globe could hold this type of energy and turn it into reality. It may sound naive, simplistic, or idealistic considering how imperfect human motivations and conflicting needs were always involved. But as ideals pull us up and reality pulls us down, it is the places in the middle where consensus develops and greater peace grows. And this is one such place. I looked around at the balcony seats and felt triumph as well as victory for the resilience of collaboration and the commitment to continually show up at the table.

Then the tour guide started to wrangle up the group, so I quickly took a few more pictures before throwing my red leather bag over my shoulder. A new question grew in my consciousness as we left the building and returned to the parking lot: *What energy did I want to create and contribute to in my professional life that could benefit the world? What would that be?*

On the bus ride back to Annecy from Geneva, I stared out the window as parts of life as I knew it flew by and disappeared. I had left Portland and banking behind, and now a bigger dream was appearing on the horizon. A new momentum was carrying me forward to this emerging dream, but I couldn't see the details or the timeline or how it would all fit together. A surge of fresh intention was creating movement, and despite all of the current uncertainties, I knew everything would come together in the best possible ways as long as I followed the uplifting flows of inspiration. And in the meantime, I could choose one thing:

Let the higher levels of Trust begin.

ENDURANCE

"**A**RE THEY COMING? DO YOU see anything?"

I raised my heels and chin up simultaneously, but still only saw the same haircuts and shoulders as when I was two inches shorter. International public events should have a mandatory policy like we all learned in elementary school class photos: Tall in the back, short in the front.

"Nope, nothing yet." My friend Aaron was visiting from California and since he had the advantage of being a foot taller, he was also responsible for passing information down to me with a foot-taller quickness.

"Wait!" I tilted my right ear up into the wind and brushed my hair back just in case those five strands were obstructing any potential clues. "Did you hear that? People are cheering louder, I swear."

He turned to look behind us. "Or else it's more response to the parade that already went by."

Brightly decorated floats with singers and dancing cartoon characters had streamed down the race route, creating greater anticipation and flurries of cheers. I spun around to check out the noise only to see an endless sea of hair and hats moving, standing, and bobbing behind us. The terrace of the Jardins des Tuileries had shrunk considerably as the population of Paris filled up the gardens and then overflowed down to the streets in all directions. We had walked along Rue de Rivoli, weaving between standing spectators and others reclined in folding chairs, to arrive at this elevated perch. Even a few ladders were propped on the pavement, right up against the street barricades, as vertical space above the sidewalk to fly flags and wait for the grand entrance. Up and down the sidewalks, people were packed tight, leaning over the barricades to get a better angle. I glanced up at the Haussman buildings lining the grand boulevards, and hands and flags waved mildly, saving their energy for the real event. An incredible surge of electricity was pulsing through every vein of Paris. Cheering in the distance steadily started to increase.

"Yes, they're coming! They are!" I grabbed his arm and jumped up again on my toes, lifting slightly off the ground with anticipation. All of the body shapes around us started to move with the same wave of excitement. The late July sky had recently brought us drippy gifts from above and the wet cobblestones made this final stretch down the Avenue des Champs-Élysées more dangerous. But no weather could detour the thousands who wanted to see this last leg of the event.

Suddenly, escort vehicles whizzed through the streets with wild speed to clear the route for the approaching cyclists, flying by like a pack of stampeding black horses. Then a crescendo wave of yelling picked up to our right until the loudest noises were all around us and a tight group plowed by at top speed, a blur of spinning wheels, bright colors, and one yellow thunderbolt. All heads rotated to the left in unison as the cyclists stormed passed and the wave of intensity moved down the street. Chaser cars came blaring through next, a few with cameras hanging precariously out of the windows. Then motorcycles weaved back and forth down the street with a camera operator facing backwards to capture the cheering scenery. The pulse of the street then returned to a normal heartbeat.

"Was that it? The Tour de France is now over?" I turned to Aaron, not hiding my disappointment that we stood here for over an hour to watch two seconds of blurs.

"No, I think they come around a few more times."

I lifted back up onto my toes, this time elevated by the excitement infused into the ground and the intensity covering the crowds.

A few minutes later, the peddling pack thundered by us again but this time they were less of a group blur and more of a straight line: two, three, one, one, one, two. We heard through an all-knowing voice in the crowd that they went halfway up the Champs-Élysées and circled around the Rond-Pont, came back down towards the Tuileries, cycled under the roadway between the Tuileries and Louvre, and back up Rue de Rivoli towards the Champs-Élysées again. The full loop repeated eight times. With each successive lap, leaders became more definite, riders appeared to slow down, and a couple wiped out, either from the wet roads or the competitive jostling. Every time the yellow jersey approached and then flew by, a higher roar moved down the street to escort him to victory at the Arc de Triomphe.

We counted eight laps, but it was no longer a race at that point as supposedly, due to the rain, the race supervisors had made the first lap the finale instead of the eighth lap. The crowds started to move towards the Arc de Triomphe for the trophy presentations and speeches. We could see a lot of movement that way, so Aaron and I opted to move the opposite direction, shuffling slowly and often sideways to move beyond the crowds and down to the street. Yellow T-shirts with new creases and countless souvenirs now appeared everywhere in the aftermath of the final sprint. Chairs and ladders were folded up; the barricaded roadway was completely empty while the sidewalks were crazy chaos. Crowded café tables discussed the high points, heartbreaks, and suspicions of the race, often followed by how next year would be different with a new route. There was always another July to look forward to.

We crossed the Pont Neuf bridge back to the sixth *arrondissement* and sat down at an open table for a well-deserved *café crème*. It felt amazing to lean back after standing for longer than anticipated.

Aaron and I met eight months ago on a plane. We were both departing from Tucson and I saw him in the gate lobby while waiting for boarding to begin. *He's cute.* End of thought. Then he sat next to me on the plane. Then we talked from take-off until landing, an easy, interesting conversation about his work, my plans, everything in between. Then we had lunch together at a restaurant in LAX before going to our separate connecting flights. Then we kept in touch with email and phone calls and long distance visits just to see where things went. My move to Paris was already underway by then, and just like the time when I met Trevor and was moving to Monterey, I knew one thing: *Don't give up your dreams for a boy.* Aaron was visiting Paris for three weeks and it became clearer during our time together that we were better off as friends. One of my favorite parts about traveling and going out into the world is you never knew whom you would meet and connect with.

Swarms of people, many wearing crisp yellow jerseys, began to pass down the street after the awards ceremony ended. Athletics reminded me about the importance of making a commitment to the endurance of your abilities and showing up—despite injuries, weather, attitude, unexpected changes—and having the experience because it keeps you in the moment. Enduring because you want it regardless of anything external. The journey was the reward.

Or you could stand on the sidelines and buy the jersey. Sometimes being on the sidewalk makes sense, but I'd hate to spend all of my life as a spectator of other people's choices.

Which was why meeting new friends from all over the world in Paris was such a joy. We were each going to school for different reasons, yet there seemed to be a common thread between us of living life on the front lines. Everyone had a story about how they arrived in Paris and what they planned to do next: Mohammed came from an affluent African family and would be responsible for developing his family's international business; Luigi, a loud Italian, had many professional talents, but none that spoke to his heart so he came back to school for fresh inspiration; Asma was living in Paris because her father was a diplomat here; Inga was a German woman avoiding her family's ideas about her life; Anna had a job back in Croatia when she was ready, but she yearned to be free; a few women from Morocco lived in luxurious apartments and showed up in the most fashionable outfits every day; numerous people from India were looking to expand their travel and language skills, and were always sharing notes together; and most of my American and Canadian friends started graduate school after years of working in the Real World and wanted a new dream to follow. All of us were transients on a layover between our former lives and the new life that was coming up on the horizon. We formed instant connections to help endure the discomforts of living with grand unknowns and to feel supported during a time of transition.

Many of us had left groups of friends and families behind that we yearned to see. Others from some African countries revealed they could not return to their countries due to political unrest or poor economic stability with no jobs. Hearing these perspectives put my own country in a new light, especially with gratitude that I could return home with my passport if or when I needed to.

When I met Elham, a beautiful Libyan woman with long dark hair and sharp almond eyes, the first thing she said to me while walking in Montmartre was, "I'm from Libya, and since you're American, you probably don't like me, right?" I was stunned by the statement and taken aback, but on some level, I also understood her defensiveness since interactions between our countries weren't always *chipper*.

"Well, no, because I don't know you. We can't always form our opinions based on the news media, right?"

She nodded. "Right! Well, maybe we'll get along better than our countries do." Her eyes crinkled when she smiled. A group of us was walking up the street from the metro stop Pigalle to go to a restaurant with amazing salads.

"Yeah, let's hope so. When did you arrive in Paris?" I asked, as we climbed the streets of Montmartre.

Our friendship grew slowly as we tried to figure out how we fit together and what we had in common. And as women, the one thing we certainly had in common was the need to be beautiful with minimal effort. A couple of weeks after meeting, when the August heat was regular and bothersome, Elham invited a few of us over to her air-conditioned apartment for mint drinks and threading services. Threading is the technique of using two pieces of string to pull hair, quickly and swiftly, out of unwelcome places, similar to tweezing. She confidently sold the concept based on her years of experience and how quickly she could do it. I volunteered to go first to get it over with, and because I didn't want to see another person in pain and change my mind.

"Elham, owwww!" Streams of tears moved down each cheek as she threaded my eyebrows. "This hurts more than I realized."

She giggled. "Shhhh, let me finish and you'll be happy with the end results." I focused on breathing. Two minutes later, I sat up and tried to wipe away the pain. She handed me a mirror so I could appreciate her work.

"See? Now wasn't that worth it? It hurts a bit, but you'll be happy for a while. I grew up doing this with my aunts and cousins and they all say it hurts less each time." Not only was beauty universal, but the pain associated with it was well.

"Wait, don't you have this threading done, too?"

"No way! It would hurt too much!" Then she threw her head back laughing. My jaw dropped and I picked up a pillow off the couch to hit her with it.

"I'm going to remember that, Libya!"

"I'll give you the best hookah flavor as a peace offering, I swear, I swear." She held up her left palm, still laughing.

"Trisha, you're next up." Trisha lay down for her turn as I sat on the floor and reclined against the couch, knees to chin, sipping the delicious mint tea. Elham's family's apartment in the sixth *arrondissement* was ornately decorated with beautiful oriental rugs, bronze bowls, silver vases, and giant pieces of furniture. Hardwood flooring stretched out in every direction and big windows were covered with luxurious curtains. It had that home-away-from-home feeling since every item had a family story. I looked outside the living room window and peered into other people's apartments and lives. A woman and two kids bustled about in their kitchens on the third level; a man on the fourth floor typed away on a computer.

I was crossing paths with many new friends from all over the world and we formed insta-families to make the temporary stopover more enjoyable. We were living for the long-distance rewards, like the promise of finishing a marathon, and yet had found batons of support along the way in other kindred souls who showed up out-of-the-blue and provided the necessary camaraderie and conversation for this leg of the tour.

AND THEN THERE WERE THE days when Paris sucked. Like any intimate relationship where you start to see the fullness and flaws in another, my relationship with Paris now revealed its ongoing faults, difficulties, and moods. Metro strikes were one of the city's worst personality traits. These all-day affairs brought the city to a paralyzing stop in movement, but not in daily needs; everyone still needed to get everywhere. Every strike was slightly different, but each one was incredibly inconvenient. Some metro lines shut down completely, while other lines had an arriving train once every ten minutes, or a train only went to a certain stop on the route and not to the end destination. The platforms would be stacked six people deep as every head vied for space on the next train, and when that train pulled into the station, no one would get on or off, and shoulders would still push harder for movement. Some metro strikes were scheduled, while others were impromptu. All of them made me wish for my own car like I had back home.

Unexpectedly, the city's air quality was terrible and I somehow developed a respiratory infection that knocked me out for three weeks; thankfully, school was not in session. Paris sits low in a bowl, which keeps air and germs stagnant in between the buildings, on public transportation systems, and covering every door handle. Luckily, the pharmacies were like street-corner doctor offices and I could hobble two blocks to find a remedy, then hobble back to my apartment and collapse on the futon for five more hours of sleep.

I was learning the language more each day and diligently focused on improving my accent, but I was also realizing my own shortcomings with listening to the words. I could read French pretty well, but when the language flew by my ears, I didn't always catch the correct tense or understand each word. My mind was always on, always alert, always aware, but all of the trying was also exhausting at times. I probably looked like a fool more times than I knew, but I had to allow that to be, realistically, part of the process. I was the outsider always learning and attempting and some days were just rougher than others. Living in a foreign country took effort and diligence because, as I learned during my time in Annecy, I was always, always, always trying to figure something out or how things worked. Once I had a victory, three more unknowns would show up creating a continual rocking between local confidence and visitor questions. I leered at tourists with their maps and cameras and guidebooks all wrapped up in their Paris rose-colored glasses, staying oblivious and idyllic in the safety of tourist status. If only they knew how the city turned on you when you had to call the electrical company, or sign-up for a bank account, or misunderstood instructions even after your best listening effort, or when you opened your mouth and revealed you weren't *really* French but an impostor.

But this was what it meant to be in a relationship with someone you loved. You gave your all each day to the best of your abilities, and then started fresh again the next morning with a new *café crème* in hand. Thankfully, Trisha knew the feeling and we could share our frustrations as they came up. And there was one common gripe we had against Paris: there was no good Mexican food anywhere in the city.

One afternoon in September, we sat down for lunch at a little restaurant on *Rue Saint-André des Arts* near metro Odeon. The menu declared fajitas, burritos, salsa, beans, and quesadillas, and we were both desperately craving the one food we couldn't find authentically made in the city. I wanted one of everything on the menu to make up for lost time, but ordered a single burrito instead, still skeptical about the final result. We waited patiently for the plates to appear in front of us, and when they did, it wasn't Mexican food of any kind I've seen before: spurts of cheez-whiz-like-cheese, smashed tomatoes for salsa, flavorless beans, crème fraîche instead of sour cream, and no rice. Trisha had a plate of wannabe-fajitas with equally dubious ingredients. We exchanged apprehensive looks as our waiter disappeared.

"Maybe it tastes better than it looks?"

"As long as it tastes like something."

We did our best to finish whatever was in front of us, but left unsatisfied and fifty euros poorer.

Paris wasn't perfect. And after five months together, I had learned to shift my expectations to a different place where I could roll with the uncertainties and keep persevering no matter how maddening, confusing, exhausting, and unsatisfying some days could be. The ability to endure the difficulties was all part of the package, and no one ever, ever, ever said it would be easy or simple. Every day required energy and concentration, and I knew I had it in me to keep this dream alive for at least another year and a half.

JUST AS NEW FRIENDS SHOWED up like batons in a relay race, new opportunities arrived out of the blue that brought in fresh motivation. One of my professors had arranged a meeting at the Organization for Economic Cooperation and Development (OECD) to learn more about the international organization from an American diplomat. In my true over-eager, dork fashion, I was the first name on the sign-up list. The first person at the designated meeting place. The first body to pass through OECD security into the meeting hall. And the first one with pen and paper in hand, ready for notes and insights, as we sat in an auditorium with about one hundred other attendees from all over the world.

Five minutes later, a young male walked out on the stage and introduced himself as a diplomat, originally from Houston, who had been stationed in three different countries thus far. He explained how he lucked out in a big way with this current post in Paris so early in his career since this was a highly sought-after location, and began to describe his role as part of the American Embassy's political department. He went on to speak about the OECD's purpose and its unique role in diplomacy with 34 member countries actively participating in economic stability and financial growth measures. I jotted down notes and was really impressed by his presentation and sharing. With time running short, he took a few questions from the audience, and just as I was about to pack up my notepad, he shared one more piece of information:

"For those of you in the audience who are Americans, the U.S. Foreign Service offers internships every term, all over the world, for full-time U.S. students. Almost every Embassy in the world uses interns, and each location has a different number of students they accept each term. The intention is for Americans to become familiar with the Foreign Service as a possible career choice, and to learn what happens in the real world of a U.S. diplomat. It is a great step to consider if you want to take the Foreign Service Exam. I was an intern, and that is where I learned everything I needed to know to pass the exam because Foreign Service Officers trained me and helped me prepare sufficiently. The positions are full-time, Monday to Friday, and not normally paid. I do not know all of the current requirements, but just go to the U.S. State Department's website to find the link for students. That will send you in the right direction. We're now out of time and I have to go to a meeting. Thank you all so much for being here! Hope it was useful information."

I was frozen with giddiness. I had no idea there were internship possibilities at the U.S. Embassy. Being a foreign diplomat had always sounded amazing and was a profession I had temporarily considered back in college. But the test was only offered once a year at that point and the timing didn't match up with my graduation plans. It would be worth exploring it more now since I had nothing to lose and it fit in perfectly with my graduate studies.

Later that evening, a loud, laughing group of us went to dinner at a charming little bistro that served the most delicious *confit de canard* and roasted potatoes. We shared a disappearing bottle of *Côte du Rhône* followed by divinely whipped chocolate mousse. After finishing the meal with departing *bisous*, I remembered on the metro ride home that I needed to do some research on this internship possibility just to find out if it was even an option.

I returned to my sweet little apartment around ten o'clock, yawning from the wine, and fired up the computer just to take a quick peek at the information. I turned on the soothing music of Ray LaMontagne and relaxed into my futon. As I clicked around on the website, my main concern was determining if there was an age limit for internships. I was not a 20-year-old college kid trying to pass a summer; I was a 29-year-old graduate student with years of work experience under my belt who wanted a quality opportunity. After surfing every tab and section a few times, it became clear that any age was eligible as long as I was a registered student pursuing an undergraduate or graduate level degree. If I was pre-selected, then I would have to pass an extensive United States government background investigation.

I felt excitement rising within my gut at the opportunity, but there was one big unknown, assuming I was accepted: I did not get to select the city or country I was assigned to. And due to the thousands of applications they received every term, I could only select the region I wanted to work in which was as vague as Western Europe, Eastern Europe, South America, North Africa, etc. Summer was apparently the biggest time for internships, but the due date had already passed for that term. To qualify for an internship for the next term, applications were due -

Wait a minute. I glanced at the calendar.

Today? Blink, blink.

Crap. *Yep, today.* My computer's clock now said it was almost midnight, but that meant is was only 6 p.m. in Washington, D.C. The applications were due by midnight Eastern Standard Time. I had a few hours left to go for it. I took three deep breaths and started tapping away at the computer keys to write-up my Statement of Interest, fill out an extensive questionnaire, and submit my geographical preferences. My head spun with all one hundred different bureaus and offices within the State Department that offered openings, but luckily I could narrow down my top choices based on location.

Two hours later, I double-checked my essay, re-typed parts of it, and then sent away the final draft. I threw my head back on the futon and stared up at the ceiling. How incredible to attend this presentation today, find out about this opportunity today, and discover the deadline was also today. Everything lined up perfectly, and when this type of synchronicity occurred, I knew something bigger was underway. Maybe even something amazing was happening. Maybe?

I shut down the computer and fell exhausted back onto the futon. I wrapped myself up in my duvet as if angel wings were holding me tight and lovingly flying me to everything my heart could wish for.

STYLE

WINTER ARRIVED CALMLY AND WRAPPED itself around Paris like a cashmere shawl. More steam appeared in the bakery windows, more tightly knotted scarves adorned the streets, and the air's edginess caught in the back of my throat a little more each morning. On my way to class one December afternoon, I realized I did not have a suitable, long winter coat because I normally drove everywhere in the winter months. This was the first time I had to walk outside in the frost before boarding a warm bus or a protected metro station. I strolled by beautiful boutiques every day with tantalizing outfits, but because I had to adhere to my student loan budget, I had to demonstrate great restraint by not buying every charming shirt and chic skirt I loved. However, I could definitely justify a winter coat investment because if I froze to death, I wouldn't be able to pay back my student loans. So I took it upon myself to study French style and decipher some of the fashion codes in order to find the perfect coat.

Window after fabulous French window, there was always something eye-catching on display. An unexpected hem length, a diagonal stitch, a rare accessory, or a pair of colors that wouldn't logically seem to work together, and yet, with French flair, the odd color combinations managed to look desirable, such as a marmalade orange and lemon yellow skirt with a tan top. I absorbed the color schemes and trends, trying to understand how the effect looked chic without being coarse. Over and over again, the oddest blends created the most amazing appeal, like a mustard yellow paired expertly with aubergine and red to create a warm winter ensemble. After staring at numerous windows on my street, I finally spotted the fashion secret:

most palettes were a combination of two dominant colors held together by a neutral, such as charcoal grey, beige, light grey, or chocolate brown, which enhanced and complimented both colors. White and black were not always used, so the neutral shade made for unexpected sophistication: Emerald green, navy blue, and charcoal grey; butter yellow, baby blue, and a cool beige; soft pink, solid magenta, and light grey. The more unexpected the combination, the higher the chic factor.

Another observation I noticed with French clothing was that every woman, no matter her age, size, or shape, wore clothing that fit her figure and showed off the female form instead of hiding underneath excessive layers or billowing shapes. Belts showed off the hips, well-cut tops accentuated the bust properly, skirts and dresses had feminine flare, and structured tailoring brought out the best of the body, allowing confidence to shine through. Size didn't matter as much as wearing the clothing well and with pride in one's body.

And then there was the all-important scarf that accompanied almost every female, and many men, regardless of season or time of day. In summer months, scarves were tied around shoulders to protect from the sun, or carelessly put in a beach bag as an extra piece of fabric to sit on. In winter months, they were everywhere and the bright colors enlivened any dark, drab day. But I also realized scarves had another less-obvious function. It required the eye to travel up to the face. If chosen well, scarves highlighted one's natural beauty and special features softly while also being stylish. It was both functional and fashionable; yet another way to demonstrate individuality and personal features.

With these unspoken rules on display everywhere—a chic color palette, clothes that accentuated the female figure, and an accessory that brings the eye up to the face—I noticed another theme on the streets of Paris. The subtle message was "This Is Me." There was a quiet confidence that exuded pride, ownership, and care for one's body and self without blaring a "LOOK at ME" message out into the world. Although some women took that approach, too, and wow, they did not leave you much room on the sidewalk since they owned the full street.

I was inspired to use all of this carefully researched data to find myself a smashing winter coat. But after two weeks of looking in department stores, perusing smaller shops, and picking through boutiques, I came up with nothing that fit my style and minimal budget. Every coat was either wildly expensive or wildly bland. I bundled up with more layers as the temperature dropped and my anticipation grew. I continued to hold the intention for a gorgeous, stylish winter coat that I could afford and would instantly love. I decided to choose to enjoy the discovery process and maintain confidence that the best possible coat would find me even though I was becoming borderline desperate.

After exiting the metro one morning, I decided to turn right instead of left on Rue Saint Charles. I wandered up toward the Eiffel Tower, passing a newsstand, real estate office, and *brasserie*, and found a few clothing and home stores I hadn't seen before. I quickly browsed through each one, uninspired, and as I was about to exit back out onto the street, a rack in the far corner caught my eye. Dark shoulders with collars were lined up in the shadows. I turned around and walked to the discreet corner rack where five black-and-white plaid bouclé wool coats were hiding; the only clothing items in the whole store. My heart jumped as I slipped one off the hanger, slid my arms into each sleeve, and instantly felt ten degrees warmer. I spun in front of the nearby mirror used to make the store appear bigger. The coat hit the top of my knees, had a flattering slim waistline, two big pockets in front and a nice collar. I searched for the price, but there wasn't a tag on this one. I grabbed another coat, and instinctively my hand came to my heart. *Only fifty euros.* That's the price of a crappy over-priced *faux* Mexican meal. I looked up at the storeowner, who had been watching my whole performance, afraid he would tell me this price was a mistake. But I didn't want to give him the chance to do that. I walked up to the counter and pulled out my money right away.

"*C'est parfait, Monsieur. Je l'adore.*" It's perfect, Monsieur. I adore it.

"*Oui, Mademoiselle. Ils sont arrivés ce matin et j'ai presque les ont renvoyés puisque nous ne vendons pas de vêtements.*" Yes, Mademoiselle. They arrived this morning and I almost sent them back because we do not sell clothing.

He shrugged in that nonchalant French manner and handed over the receipt. I glided out the door wearing my new coat home, feeling warm and cozy and fabulously French for the first time in weeks. I didn't want to take it off once I got home, so I grabbed my rolling laundry cart full of dirty clothes and sashayed to the *laverie*.

After loading up the washing machine, I decided to take my coat home the long way through side streets, empty laundry cart in tow. I halted, cart bumping into the back of my knees, in front of a charming little shop with a pink cursive sign: *Visagiste*. Beautician. The shop's menu promised facials, waxing, skincare services, and massages. Yes, please; one of everything. Considering I saved money on my winter coat, logically I now had a little extra to spend on a facial for my birthday. Well, an early birthday present since my birthday was not this month. Or even next month. But the occasion was coming up soon-ish, so if I had a facial now, I wouldn't spend the money later. Completely logical.

A chime rang as I gently pushed the white door open and pulled my cart in behind my legs. The smell of sweet beauty stuff instantly lathered my body. No one was at the front counter as I turned to face the shelves. My pulse started to drop, drop, drop as all of my senses were overtaken by the power of beautiful oils and soft warm air filled with lavender and vanilla. Eyes closed, body warm in my new coat, slowly rocking side-to-side in all of the yumminess, knees relaxing. I could stand here making sniffing noises all day if only —

"*Bonjour, Mademoiselle.*" Back to earth. I turned around to greet Madame.

"*Bonjour, Madame. Je voudrais prendre un rendezvous pour un soin du visage pour cette semaine, si possible?*" Hello, Madame. I would like to make an appointment for a facial for this week, if possible?

"*Oui, bien sur. Voulez-vous un rendez vous pour cette vendredi? Ou samedi?* Yes, of course. Would you like an appointment for this Friday? Or Saturday?

She glanced down at her book again. "*Ou cet après-midi?*" Or this afternoon?

She probably took one look at my winter skin and realized I was an emergency situation. Her other hand was probably pushing a red button under the counter to signal an on-call beautician to the shop.

"*Cet après-midi est bien, Madame. Merci.*" This afternoon is fine. Thank you.

Madame wrote down my name and kindly said to come back at two o'clock to meet with Sylvie. I returned home to drop off my laundry cart and look up important phrases I may need during my first-ever French facial appointment:

Please don't make me cry anymore: *S'il vous plaît ne me rend pas plus pleurer.*

Stop waxing or I will call the police: *Arrêtez de cire ou je vais appeler la police!*

May I live here and be your beauty prisoner: *Puis je vis ici et d'être votre prisonnier de beauté?*

A gentile woman in her twenties was waiting behind the counter when I entered the tiny, succulent shop for the second time. Sylvie led me down a narrow spiral staircase to the basement where the light dimmed to a soft glow and vanilla aromatherapy filled every corner. She handed me a lavender chenille robe, and after changing, I poured myself onto the facial table. Soft music played in the dimly lit space and my eyes closed themselves too easily. Sylvie started to knead my shoulders and whispered a few questions about my skincare and beauty routines. I managed to whisper back that my skin was sensitive, I drink lots of water, and I have no special requests or needs. Just keep rubbing.

Before beginning the facial, she offered to wax my eyebrows, which really translated to, "I'm sorry no one told you sooner." I had no energy to explain Elhram's threading skills and I didn't even care what Sylvie did at that point. I already was the liquid wax, soft and melting in her hands. I managed to say "to cry" and "sensitive" in a full and complete sentence before she began. Sylvie gently and lovingly waxed my brows with so much care that my small tears were probably more from the affection than the pain.

Then she began the facial process, and I was gone. Over. Out. I vaguely recalled my face being steamed... and then my hands being massaged... my shoulders being rubbed again while a cool compress covered my face... and then my décolletage was smothered in a thick cream that smelled like the most decadent honey vanilla on the planet. Cocooned in a lavender chenille robe, lathered in rich creams, smelling like yummy-goodness in a dimly lit Parisian basement; this was absolute paradise. I should have removed the clock battery before she started so she couldn't see when the hour was over. I had never experienced a facial like this before; it relaxed and soothed every one of my senses into a state of utopia.

Then way too soon, Sylvie leaned into my ear and whispered softly that my service was over.

And I responded with a definitive, "*Non.*"

She laughed lightly. "*Désolé, Mademoiselle.*" Sorry, Mademoiselle.

I murmured in my trance, "*Je vais vivre dans cette chambre... ma nouvelle maison...*" I will live in this room... my new home...

She giggled and turned the dim lights up a bit before quietly closing the door. I opened one eye. If I locked the door from the inside, what could they do? I could stay in here as long as I wanted and just enjoy the love in the room. I opened my other eye. Unfortunately, there didn't appear to be enough honey-vanilla for a long period of survival. And who would do the rubbing, anyways?

I slowly managed to gather my clothes, but lost my balance while trying to step back into my jeans. I put my shirt on backwards, eyes half closed, then had to try again. I patted down my hair and then remembered to put on my shoes. I stumbled up the stairs to find the light of day and Sylvie was smiling softly, her head tilted to the side. I tried to move my face into a smile. I handed her money and she handed me her card. I made an appointment for next month. Birthdays are so great.

I staggered home, unintentionally doing my best impersonation of a mid-day alcoholic, and thinking about how my laundry cart would have been a welcomed stabilizer. I fumbled with the door keys and managed to stand up long enough to see my soft-yummy-goodness of a face in the mirror. Then another idea popped into my head: I should get a sophisticated French haircut for my birthday, too.

THIS APPEARED TO BE THE correct address, but there was nothing in sight that resembled a hair salon. I stepped backwards into the street to look further down the road in both directions, then peered back up at the Haussmann building in front of me, double-checking the address on *Rue des Notre Dame des Victoires*. The number straight ahead matched the address on my sheet. This must be it.

I pushed the buzzer that unlocked the giant door, stepped into the quiet interior courtyard, and adjusted my eyes to the dim lighting. A plaque on the wall listed all of the building occupants with the *D. M. Salon* to be found on the second floor. I ascended the majestic spiral staircase, the smooth carved banister in my hand, and reached the second floor with a single door as the only entrance option. A small gold plaque next to the door stated simply and eloquently *D. M. Salon*.

I pulled the door forward. No movement. Then I pushed it. No movement. I tried the whole routine again, and still nothing. I had used doors before and thought I had them pretty well figured out -

"*Bonjour, Mademoiselle. Bienvenue!*" Hello, Mademoiselle. Welcome! A model-esque African woman opened the door widely, her hair going in all directions and bright red lipstick framing incredibly white teeth. She was gorgeous, and perhaps it was only her beauty that could open the door. She generously welcomed me inside *D. M. Salon*, hairdresser and stylist to international models, exotic fashion shoots, global magazine covers, rich Parisian women, and now someone who fitted into none of those categories: me. But based on a friend's recommendation, knowing the right phone number and owning a credit card secured me an appointment at this exclusive salon. *Of course* the place was not at street level. That would be so pedestrian.

I took a seat in the foyer while the model disappeared. I discreetly glanced around, and then realized the salon was a minimally decorated, spacious Parisian apartment converted into a place for beauty. Every vantage point showed off chic and trendy taste: beige paint, big potted trees in the corners, original hardwood floors, chaise lounges, and over-sized paintings hung on numerous walls. The entry way was adorned with covers from ELLE, Vogue, Marie Claire, and various photo shoots. Sounds of chatter floated through the space, but it was hard to decipher where people were. Then an unexpected giant caught my eye to the left. I leaned forward to see the most unexpected visual delight: A full-size stuffed ostrich stood proudly in the main room. A real ostrich, in all its feathered-glory, stationed fully erect in perfect posture, staring out onto the streets of Paris.

A cool, calm, and collected person would have glanced at it once and looked away, as if having a giant ostrich was the new version of the family dog, but I was not that cool, calm, and collected person. I was incredibly intrigued. I tried to get a new angle from my seated position, tipping over slightly off the chair, my hair nearly touching the ground as I twisted and turned to see it more. Are those the bird's original feathers? The real feet? Are there other stuffed animals in the back rooms? If I tilted my head a little more, I should be able to see if this was a Mr. or Mrs. Ostrich—

Then the lovely model's feet echoed into the entryway as she returned holding a tray of sparkling water. I sat up promptly and regained composure. You don't want to be caught messin' around in a place that stuffs former living creatures.

Then the lovely model escorted me through connecting rooms to the hair washing stations, which appeared to be the dining room. A swinging door to the side led to the kitchen where the faint sounds of cappuccinos being frothed could be heard while my own head was frothed and massaged and whipped around by an assistant. After ten minutes of thoroughly cleaning every hair on my head, Barbara, the stylist, retrieved my hair. I followed her to a back bedroom as we passed through two rooms that looked down into an interior courtyard. Several hair stations with giant mirrors covered the floors. I sat down and realized I forgot to study up on French hair phrases.

Luckily, Barbara spoke some English, so with our combined Franglish we arrived at a mutual understanding of the desired mane outcome. After the session was underway, I couldn't resist asking her about the giant bird. She said the salon owner was Australian so the ostrich was a reminder of his homeland. *Ah, logically.* Cans of Foster's beer and a photo of the Sydney Opera House would be so pedestrian.

After an hour of chop-chop-chopping, I was coiffed and curled with layers of various lengths in all the right places. This was worth every birthday justification I could conjure up.

"Je l'adore! C'est parfait, Barbara. Merci beaucoup." I love it. It's perfect, Barbara. Thank you very much.

"Je vous en prie." You are welcome.

She smiled and removed the black robe, then walked me to the front living room. If Barbara and Sylvie went into business together, I would come financially undone. And love every bit of it.

My reflection bounced in the store fronts all the way back to the metro. Birthdays are so great. And only a month to go before it arrived! I wondered what I'd get from myself next. Being in the high of a moment did wonders for the spirit. It felt like a bigger energy was pulling me forward as my heartbeat pulsed to a higher vibration and new swirls of possibilities were arriving at my feet.

I crossed over to the metro entrance as a well-dressed man, tall and dark and dapper in a navy suit caught my eye, or all of my bouncing hair caught his. He nodded his head slightly and smiled in a way that only French men can do; a subtle communication of respect, appreciation, and desire. He turned around to reveal a cellphone up to his ear, and after another glance my way, moved down the street towards the Bourse. *Don't chase him just because you have bouncy hair confidence.*

Months before moving to Paris, I had dreamed about my potential new life and how the romantic possibilities could unfold. A French man who spoke just enough English in his sexy, alluring fashion would obviously play the role of The Guy. He would make dull words desirable and desirable words dangerous. I, of course, would have some type of magical American-woman effect on him with my butchering of the language, questioning his worldviews, laughing too loudly in public, and showing no restraint around desserts. All of my mistakes and *faux pas* would make him swoon. Our relationship would evolve to meeting his family for long weekend lunches at Les Deux Magots; socializing with his European friends after work; lazy strolls through weekly markets; traveling to picturesque regions of France; and exploring the *arrondissements* of Paris together. We would be inseparable, eager to create a life together, and move towards the expected next steps of house, marriage, kids. Easy and obvious, that's the road we would follow. *Paris parfait.*

That thought returned as I bounced down into the metro tunnel. If only I'd had a clue about how things would really unfold. Oh, silly me. *Silly, silly me.*

DOUBLES

Spring STARTED POPPING UP ALL over the city. Stores set out bright ceramic pots and fresh-to-the-touch gardening supplies, outdoor café tables came out of hibernation, and the sun extended its curfew a few minutes each day. Windows in my apartment building were propped open longer during the day to welcome in vernal blue air from the passing clouds. Even the children's voices in the courtyard were rejuvenated as they bounced balls and ran through every open doorway with glee. I kissed my winter coat *au revoir* and put it in the back of the closet as I transitioned into a soft green jacket paired with light, flowing scarves.

I had been in Paris for almost a year, and as much as I loved the city, I also realized how much I regularly craved peace, quiet, and more living space. The option of being *away* from the city and near more green grass, fresh air, and less noise became very appealing after the cramped, closeted days of winter. Considering the trials and realities of finding my first place in Paris, I had no expectations that I could find a bigger, brighter apartment. But it never hurts to try.

After a few inquiries and following my gut instincts, I serendipitously found a bigger apartment for less money in a charming village twenty minutes outside of Paris. The new residence was surrounded by lakes, rivers, walking trails, ducks, chateaus, and fresh air that provided a grand escape from the loud, crowded city. Plus, the real selling point about this apartment was that it had one of the rarest things to be found in a metropolis: a garden. My own green space with a private place to sit outside in the sun. The apartment was better than I could have imagined, but there was one drawback.

It was currently being renovated and wouldn't be ready until the middle of April. Luckily, Trisha was well settled in her apartment and she offered me a pillow to sleep on.

A week after I gave notice to my current proprietor that I would be moving out, she hosted a Tuesday afternoon open house for potential renters to view the apartment. I sat on the couch to watch the process and answer any questions, if needed. The first six visitors were a mélange of foreigners from Japan, Canada, Sweden, and Germany who all communicated their interest in the apartment eagerly and directly. Each one left their contact information with my proprietor and said they were available to sign the lease now. Then, a young French woman came in towards the end of the hour with all of her documents in hand. She stayed less than five minutes, did not ask many questions, and said she would like the apartment if it was still available. After everyone filed out, trying to hide the desperation in their eyes, I asked my landlady how she felt about the prospects. She said it went very well and she was happy to offer the apartment to the French woman. She had a good job and all of her documents were in order, so they signed a lease on the spot. *I knew it.* At least I wasn't imagining how things worked here. It was like no one else even stood a chance once there was a French prospect in the bunch.

I had to move out by the end of March, so I packed up my four suitcases, plus an array of acquired household possessions, and slowly moved everything over to Trisha's apartment for storage while my new home was nearing completion.

My 29th birthday in late March arrived on a Tuesday, and my oh-so-thoughtful gift from the city of Paris was an all-day transportation strike on the subway system, train lines, and all city buses. There were also a limited numbers of taxis on the streets since most of the taxi drivers were participating in the strike, too. Every loose taxi was being hunted down quickly by desperate travelers. I put on my most sensible shoes for the thirty-minute walk to school, and quickly discovered how getting around the city was a complete headache no matter which route I took. Congestion was above ground, below ground, and on the sidewalks. This did not bode well for my birthday festivities, which had been planned for weeks. Over twenty people RSVP'd *oui* to a celebration at Culture Bierre on the Champs-Élysées, but now I doubted its success since transportation was nearly at a standstill around the city. I made a frowning face at Trisha during class. She tossed her hand and said not to worry about it, everything would be fine.

The sidewalks were bulging with people in every direction on my walk home, and I realized I would have to leave extra, extra early to make it to dinner on time. With my right palm up in front of my closet, I vowed not to sacrifice a cute outfit or the perfect shoes for the transportation madness. *The (birthday fashion) show must go on.*

Trisha and I arrived on the Champs-Élysées thirty minutes late, after miraculously finding an available taxi. We entered Culture Bierre, a grand restaurant with three separate levels of experiences, including a formal dining restaurant, a beer counter, a gift shop, and a packed downstairs club with pumping lights, music, and dancing. We weaved our way downstairs and found our friends in a private section of the bar marked off with a velvet rope and soft white curtains. Two long tables overflowed with tall drinks, multiple conversations, and a few bouquets of flowers. I took off my coat to settle in and exchanged *bisous* with my friends.

After an hour of chatting, laughing too loudly, and picture taking, a guy I'd seen around school a few times entered our special space with a friend, and he said hello to some people at the other table. He was a Turkish version of Gerard Butler: strong build, dark features, alluring confidence. His intense brown eyes connected with my green eyes a few times and I quickly averted his gaze with slight discomfort. *Was I being hunted?*

A few minutes later, the Turkish stranger abruptly squeezed himself into a spot on my left, physically separating Trisha and I from our conversation.

"How are you?" he asked, staring intently at me as I picked up my wine glass and my face contorted into slight annoyance. "Fine. Trisha and I were talking, and you just sat down between us where there is obviously no room. That's a bit rude." I said lightly.

"I wanted to sit next to you, so I made room for myself," he stated matter-of-factly.

"Obviously," I replied, equally matter-of-factly. Another sip of wine as silence descended between us. Then Trisha and I continued our conversation as the Turkish stranger leaned forward to talk to other people at the table. He leaned back and started saying a bunch of numbers to the side of my face. Interrupting. Again.

I turned to him with more annoyance. "What are those numbers? And why do you keep repeating them?"

"It's my phone number."

Pause. "Why are you telling me your phone number?"

"So you will have it to put in your phone."

Who was this guy?

"You can keep repeating the numbers all you want, but I'm not going to add them to my phone."

"Why not?"

"Because I don't call boys."

"Well, I am not a boy. I am a man." He sipped his beer.

"Then if you're a man, I don't have to explain the concept to you."

He furrowed his brow and looked away. The arrogance of his approach was such a turn-off. After a few minutes, he moved to another table where his friend was sitting. *Easy come, easy go.*

"How was your conversation with Turhan?" Trisha leaned in to ask quietly, smiling.

"I wouldn't call it a conversation. He was trying to give me his phone number, but I've never even talked to him before and he didn't make the best impression."

"I've heard he's cool and really smart. An engineer or something," Trisha said.

"Huh, cool." Pause. "But if he's so smart, why was he giving me his number instead of asking for mine?"

Trisha shrugged. "Don't know."

I shrugged.

The evening continued until midnight, and then the reality of hunting down transportation encouraged us to get home. I left holding bouquets of beautiful flowers, a camera full of great photos, and a huge feeling of gratitude in my heart. *Awesome birthday.*

As I pushed through the front door of Culture Bierre and onto the sidewalk of the Champs-Élysées, the Arc de Triomphe loomed a few hundred feet away, an incredible, illuminated sight after midnight. The eternal flame danced in the center, never distracted by the endlessly circling, chaotic traffic. I breathed in the stars shining brightly above as Trisha managed to hail down a taxi for our ride back to the fourteenth *arrondissement.* The cab maneuvered through the open streets, passed over the sleeping Seine, and off to the west, the Eiffel Tower sparkled and twinkled wildly in the twilight, then suddenly faded to silence. The night was ending, but it also felt like so much was dawning.

A WEEK AFTER MY BIRTHDAY, I did something very odd and completely out of character: I stayed late at school to do research. Sitting down at an empty table in the vacant library, I opened my laptop and bent over to rummage through my bag as legs passed by my chair. I sat back up and Turhan was suddenly standing next to me. He put his bag down on my desk, not saying a word.

"Hi," I said, glancing up.

"Hello there." He said in a deep voice while staring down at me. I shifted my weight uncomfortably. *Maybe I am being hunted.* He casually looked away and took a sip out of his water bottle while surveying the library. I typed in my computer password.

"So... do you have class now?" I asked, trying to break the awkward silence.

"Yes, I do." He put the water bottle on the table to stake his territory. "I came early tonight for class, which I never do. I am normally late because I have to work until six o'clock."

"I stayed late after my class tonight, which I never do, either. I need to get some things done."

He nodded and pulled up a chair to sit down next to me. I signed into my email account as we sat in shared silence. No new email in the last thirty minutes, hate that.

After glancing at my screen, Turhan moved my laptop over to his side of the table and began composing a new email. To himself.

"So you're sending me an email from myself?"

"Yes. I'm including my email address and now I have yours."

I've never met someone from Turkey before. Is *force* a standard Turkish communication style?

As he typed with intense focus, I discreetly watched his movements. His brow furrowed slightly as his hands typed quickly; he was decisive, clear, in charge. He smelled masculine, clean, sexy-musky in his striped long-sleeve shirt and jeans. Small butterflies flipped around in my stomach. *He was cute.* My shoulders relaxed a bit. There was something unexpectedly comforting about his confidence; like I could rest my head on his shoulder and he would take care of everything.

Yet I had learned through my previous dating experiences that it was important to be observant of his character at the beginning. And to not rush the process. *And do not initiate.*

I was "that girl" who previously called guys up and suggested hanging out, going out, why not? I was empowered, confident, fun! I could do anything I wanted, including taking charge of my romantic life, and if I wanted to ask a guy out, I could. So I did.

Until.

At a certain point, I didn't like the dynamic and found myself scrunching up my nose at him because on some level I didn't respect him. As if I didn't view him as... *a real man*. He didn't earn me, he didn't do anything to get my time, and since I was the prize, he needed to put some effort into winning me over. The kind of man I am attracted to goes after what he wants in life, in a career, in a woman, and he isn't afraid to take the reins.

Hence, I didn't call boys.

Hence, I was sitting next to a man from Turkey who was now *telling* me, not asking, that we were going out to dinner next week.

I watched him intently for a moment. "Is that a question or a demand?"

He shrugged. "Maybe it's both. I want to take you to dinner. I will email you back with more information."

Then he grabbed his computer bag and water bottle, and disappeared to class. I stared at my computer. I had completely forgotten what I was doing in the library. I packed up my stuff and grabbed a bus to Trisha's apartment. He *was* cute.

Turhan sent a brief email the next morning, not that I expected anything else:

"Are you available for dinner next Tuesday or Wednesday? And is there any kind of food you do not like?"

We exchanged emails a few more times, and after giving him my phone number, he called promptly to finalize plans for Tuesday night at a traditional French restaurant in Saint Germain that one of his co-workers had recommended. He asked a co-worker where to take me to dinner? That's cute. Duly noted.

Tuesday night arrived quickly because it was the only date I kept staring at on my calendar. Trisha and I were at her apartment determining what I should wear as she moved pans around the stove for her dinner.

"So, what's the plan for tonight?" she asked excitedly from the kitchen.

"We're meeting at seven o'clock at the Saint Germain des Pres metro stop, and then going to dinner at a French place his co-worker recommended nearby."

"Ohhh, sounds romantic. Saint German is so cute." She giggled.

"Yeah... I just... I don't know. I feel sorta *laissez-faire* about this date because I don't have any expectations. I don't know *anything* about him. What if we don't have anything to talk about and the conversation is awkward? What if it's awful and I want to leave early!"

"No, it will be fine. You'll have fun! It's a first date! In Paris!" Trisha couldn't stop smiling. I changed my shirt for the second time. Nothing looked right.

"But if I have any problems, I am going to text you. Then call me back with a reason why I need to leave, ok? I need a rescue plan, just in case."

"Alright, just in case." She rolled her eyes. "But it will be fine…"

"Okay, you're right. It will be fine. And!" I walked into the kitchen and reached into my computer bag. "Look at what I got today at the library." I handed her the book I pulled out.

"What is that? You got a book about dating?"

"No! I found a book about Turkish culture."

"Oh, nice. Are you gonna bring that along on your Parisian date?" She laughed.

"No! I was just kinda curious if there was anything I should know, or not do, or… I don't know. I don't know anything about Turkey, so it doesn't hurt to read a bit."

"You're a dating scholar—researching, studying. Are you bringing your notes along?"

"Yes, I am definitely bringing notes tonight. I will be prepared for either an essay or multiple choice tests on Turkish culture, thank you very much."

I looked in the mirror and then changed my outfit two more times before finally deciding on one of Trisha's shirts.

"Hurry up! You have to go! What if he doesn't show up at all?"

My eyes grew big. "I can't believe you just said that! Shoot, I'm late!"

She laughed again before sampling her dinner from the pan. I grabbed my purse and bolted down the stairs, heels clipping-clipping-clipping on each step. She peered over the stairwell. "Have a fun time! Be a good girl! Don't leave my top at the restaurant!" She thinks she's so funny.

I arrived at the metro stop coiffed, polished, and primped five minutes after seven o'clock, but no Turhan. I circled around to make sure there was no other entrance; still no Turhan. He said this Tuesday, right? Or was I at the wrong metro stop altogether. I stared casually down the street in both directions; no Turhan. I waited, waited, breathed. My phone now said 7:15 p.m. and my stomach churned more. Am I being stood up? I turned around to start texting Trisha, and then heard a deep "*Bonsoir*" in my ear. I spun around, hiding my relief.

"You said seven o'clock right? Or are you always late?" A little attitude just to show I was aware of how he was making an impression.

"*Désolé,* I am on French time." Big smile, both arms thrown open wide. He *was* really cute. "I went home after work to shower and change because I wanted to look nice. Do you like my shirt?"

I softened. Duly noted.

"Ahh, okay. But don't keep me waiting for too long next time. Maybe text or something." Even if his reason was valid, I didn't want it to become a standard practice.

We walked through the buoyant atmosphere of Saint Germain in search of the restaurant, and almost passed the entrance because it was discreetly nestled in between two other dominant doorways. We stepped inside quietly, not wanting to disturb the intimate atmosphere. The lighting was warm with cozy booths and numerous quiet conversations underway. It was the perfect place for a first date. We nestled into a table for two as delicious plates of food were served all around us. I leaned over and whispered that his co-worker made a good recommendation. He nodded in agreement. The waiter brought menus and placed clinking glasses of water on the table. Turhan made a few wine recommendations and asked me what I liked. After agreeing on a bottle of red, I dove in with my burning questions.

"So, I'm going to cut right to the chase, which I know is very American of me. Why didn't you ask for my phone number the other night instead of only yelling yours at me?"

"Because I didn't have my phone with me, so there was nowhere I could record your number. And I figured I would see you again at school and I would run into you there."

"Ahh, okay." Nodded my head, moved the fork around on the table. "And how did you know about my birthday party since we've never met or talked before?"

"I heard from a few people at school that the hot girl was having a birthday party so I decided to come. My friend and I went to dinner first then came over to the party."

My face scrunched up. "Wait. What other girl was having a birthday party that night?"

He smiled and winked at me. Or maybe it was an eye twitch. People do have eye twitches, so I didn't want to assume anything on a first date—

"*Bonsoir, Madame, Monsieur. Ce soir, je vous propose...*" Good evening, Madame, Monsieur. Tonight, we offer you…"

The server launched into the specials in beautiful detail, and after careful deliberation, we chose our entrees. Wine glasses were placed in front of us and filled as if they were liquid gold. I glanced around the small, cozy space with dark wood walls and flickering candles. Then the server left us to our first date. Turhan raised his glass in a toast, and I followed with mine, feeling butterflies again. *I'm sitting in a romantic restaurant in Paris with a sexy foreign Gerard Butler-lookalike. Be cool, mind your manners, don't burp.*

He leaned in and put his elbows on the table. "So how did you find this school in Paris?"

I leaned in to answer, and our conversation took off. It went everywhere. We talked about everything and anything that came to mind. I told him about my past ten months in Paris and how hard it was to find an apartment; he understood completely. On his own, he got nowhere. He found his place because a French friend helped him and assisted in the rent negotiation. He had been in Paris for over a year and wanted to get his Ph.D. after completing his M.B.A.

Plates of beautiful food arrived and still our conversation eased on. He poured more wine into our glasses. I glanced around the room, and we looked just like every other couple: leaning in, talking quietly, listening intently, wine disappearing. We talked about school, friends back home, our parents, and what we've discovered so far about Paris. No dull moments, no awkward silences. It felt like we had shared numerous meals together before and this was just another dinner conversation between us.

Eventually the server stopped by to remove our empty plates and the weightless *carafe du vin*. I glanced at my phone to check the time.

"Oh wow. It's been nearly three hours."

"Nooo, really? Wow."

"It feels like we've been talking for an hour."

"Yeah, it's a good sign." He smiled. A hand dropped the check on the table.

"I know you have to work tomorrow, so let me know if we need to go soon..."

"No, it's fine. We can check out another place if you want?"

I nodded yes as Turhan reached for the check. I grabbed my purse in case we were splitting it and he looked at me in alarm, shaking his head no as if insulted I would even offer. *Just kidding.* I put my purse down.

We exited the restaurant and entered the cobblestone street to find that Saint Germain was alive with music from different bars. People strolled hand in hand and glowing street lanterns warmed up the late evening chill. Turhan suggested we have a drink at a bar and led us to a place with dark lighting, jazzy music, and television screens playing soccer games. We found a corner seat, placed our drink orders, and continued talking in the dim light. I eventually excused myself to use the bathroom and text Trisha an update: "Everything is going great; I have not been tested on my understanding of Turkish culture yet; and sorry, I lost your shirt somewhere between dinner and drinks, but at least my bra is super cute."

We left around midnight when the streets were a little quieter and the café chairs a little emptier. In the middle of the street, Turhan suddenly stopped walking and turned his back to me, signaling at his shoulders. I froze looking at his back. I knew I should have studied that book on Turkish culture more.

"Come on!" He pointed again at his back.

Then I intuitively figured out what he meant and our first date ended perfectly: he carried me piggy-back style through the cobblestone streets of Paris to the metro station, my small arms wrapped around his strong neck, his big arms holding my legs, me giggling in his ears as people moved out of the way for us.

He stopped at the metro entrance where we met five hours earlier. He kissed me goodnight, sweetly, and then winked again — or his eye twitch reappeared — as we turned to go in different directions to our separate train platforms. His metro arrived first, and he waved to me from across the station as the train disappeared into the tunnel.

I floated back to Trisha's apartment on heart-filled adrenaline and turned the key softly in the door. She sat up almost instantly, ready for the full report. I told her all of the highlights as I washed my face and changed my clothes.

"I don't know anything about Turkish men or their dating practices. I feel the need to proceed slowly and be cautious about this, just in case."

"Yeah, I get it. Just wait and see. It could be really fun, you never know."

My head hit the pillow suddenly exhausted.

I glanced at my phone occasionally the next day, trying to be casual, but there were no rings coming through and no missed calls. His name had not appeared in my email inbox yet, either. My day was busy with classes, research and errands, but I kept thinking about different parts of our conversation. Then I turned back to studying for my upcoming test. *If he's smart, he'll call.*

The following day, I went to class in the morning and then visited my new apartment in the afternoon. The apartment's renovation work had been delayed a few more weeks, and I wanted to check on the progress and take some measurements. I unlocked the front door of the apartment with high hopes of progress and cleanliness, but was only met with disaster: the place was still a complete mess. In every direction, the floor was torn up with nails and boards lying everywhere. The bathroom was crammed with tools, supplies, and tiles that needed to be placed on the walls. No appliances were installed in the kitchen or bathroom. Every surface was covered in dust and grime. There was still no room to store my luggage or boxes because the hardwood floor was not finished. And the French workers hadn't even shown up today. For no reason at all. *Groan.* This project was supposed to be completed next week, but at this rate it would certainly take much longer. I didn't want to overstay my welcome at Trisha's place and I was more than ready to have my own space again. But surveying this scene, all of my confidence vanished. I could barely walk through the front entrance. The mess was everywhere. I closed the door and felt disheartened by the delays. My skin was covered in dust as I walked back to the metro.

Somewhere in my purse, my phone rang.

"Bonjour?" I answered absentmindedly.

"*Bonjour*, Molly. *C'est* Turhan." My posture straightened.

"*Salut, Turhan! Ca va?*" Hello, Turhan. How are you?

"*Bien, merci, et toi?*" Well, thank you. And you?

"*Bien…*" Good.

Pause.

"So…" he said. "I had a good time the other night."

"Yes, I did too, that was fun. Thank you for dinner." I entered the above-ground metro station and stood on the platform.

"You're welcome. I had a friend in town visiting yesterday, so I took him to dinner last night and we were out late. That's why I didn't call yesterday."

"Oh, good. That's nice of you. Sounds like you have a lot of friends coming to visit you." The metro pulled up to the platform, and I stepped back to wait for the next one.

"Yeah, everyone wants to come to Paris." He paused, then continued. "So, I wasn't sure if maybe you wanted to go out again…"

He said hesitantly.

"Yes, I would like to go out again, that would be nice." Happy smile on my face.

"Okay, good. How about this Saturday?"

"I already have plans Saturday night, but I could meet earlier in the day, if that works for you." Silence on the other end. I really did have plans Saturday night but I didn't want him to think it was with another man. "I'm going to a friend's birthday dinner at a restaurant in the twelfth. We could meet in the afternoon to do something or make plans for another day if that's better for you."

"Let's meet at one o'clock on Saturday."

"Okay, great. I know what we can do. I'll email you the information." The next metro car was pulling in to the station.

"Good. Talk to you soon. *Ciao.*"

"*Ciao.*" I stepped onto the metro with an extra bounce.

Saturday turned out to be a beautiful April afternoon. Turhan and I met at Parc Bercy in the twelfth *arrondissement*, a lesser-known area of Paris along the Seine with a park, restaurants, and shops. We strolled through the park and ate a late lunch at a local brasserie. Our conversation was easy and enjoyable as we learned more about each other's families, friends, and life in Paris.

A few nights later, Turhan and I met on the Champs-Élysées to go to a movie after work. Then on Sunday, we ate a late brunch at a café in Bastille and wandered the corridors of the endless Bastille farmer's market. We bought fresh vegetables imported from the outskirts of the city, sampled varieties of cheese from hearty *fromagers*, watched the street musicians perform, and enjoyed a second cup of coffee at a corner bistro. A perfect Paris day.

The more time I spent with him, the more I enjoyed being in his presence. There was a comfortable ease between us that felt both calm and intriguing. Our lives and backgrounds were so different, but our chemistry was effortless. No awkwardness or strangeness, just ease and simplicity. We continually talked about school, Paris, friends, school friends in Paris, past relationships, travel, religion, work, the French, and any other subject that came up over dinner or as we wandered. We held hands on the streets and exchanged hello and goodbye kisses regularly. I started to understand more of his facial expressions and picked up on when he raised his eyebrows in surprise (about a crazy French tradition), or in shock (typically about an overpriced item), or in disbelief (about a ridiculous piece of information in the news).

Over the following weeks, we met for a movie one night; went out to dinner another night; and cooked dinner at his place. I heard him use the word "girlfriend" about me, so I used the word "boyfriend" about him. I rested my head on his shoulder as often as I could.

And the completion of my apartment was delayed yet another week. I showed up to check on the progress and inspect the work.

"*Bonjour!*" I called, unlocking the front door.

"*Bonjour, Mademoiselle!*" a male voice responded from the main room. I walked inside to see one man on the phone in the kitchen, another smoking in the garden, and the third adjusting a screwdriver like it was a complicated piece of machinery. The new floor was installed and the painting was done, but the bathroom was still a disaster, the kitchen needed to be finished, the main room required finishing touches, and the baseboard still had to be nailed back on every wall. All of my possessions were crammed in the unfinished bathroom waiting for me. The landlady had stopped by occasionally to check on their progress, but she was busy with other things and couldn't be there every day. The project was now almost a month late because there were no consequences or incentives for the work to be done; the workers made more money with each delay.

The man in the kitchen stopped talking and the air was silent. Time to apply pressure.

"*Monsieurs, s'ils vous plait. Je dois emménager dans l'appartement ce samedi. Je suis sans abri.*" Gentlemen, if I may. I must move into the apartment this Saturday. I am homeless.

They nodded as if I just offered them a glass of water and then slowly wandered outside to take a cigarette break. I glanced around exhausted at the mess of a place that was supposed to be my new home. Frustration ran through my veins. No one was holding them accountable. If left unattended, they could easily make this project last another three weeks unless something changed. I grabbed my purse and went to the garden.

"*À demain, Monsieurs!*" See you tomorrow, Gentlemen! Each face looked at me with a puzzled expression.

The next morning, I arrived with my class notes and books in tow, and set up a place to study in the garden. Then I started unpacking my belongings, stacking glasses in the cupboards and brewing fresh coffee. I sat outside on the patio and declared it my space so the workers couldn't escape there with extended breaks. I walked through each room regularly, nodding and smiling, offering fresh coffee. All of us were cramped into a small space, but the windows and doors were open to keep air and fumes circulating. I asked them questions about things I didn't understand and quickly became an on-site pest. They hammered and nailed and painted, but still disappeared by two o'clock each afternoon. After two days of this routine, I finally realized there was one thing that would get them moving even faster.

When they returned from their two-hour lunch break the next day, I picked up a paintbrush and offered to finish painting along the trim. Three faces stared at me in shock.

"*Ce n'est pas un travail pour une femme!*" This is not work for a woman! The foreman declared, visibly insulted. I shrugged like I was clueless and didn't mean to offend.

"*Je peux vous aider à travailler plus vite si vous avez besoin de plus d'aide?*" I can help you work faster if you need more assistance?

Disgust was dripping from their faces. As if I could perform their work.

The foreman puffed up his chest and stepped forward. "*S'il vous plaît, amusez-vous dans le jardin. Nous finirons le travail bientôt.*" Please, enjoy yourself in the garden. We will finish all the work soon.

I sat in the garden and read a magazine as the hammering and movements grew faster and louder inside my new home. By the middle of the afternoon, another worker had appeared. I smiled and wondered why I didn't think of playing that card earlier.

By Friday afternoon, enough of the renovation was completed for me to move in. The new furniture from Ikea had been delivered, the hot water usually worked, and the electricity was properly turned on for the new outlets. There were a few incomplete items, but the workers said they would return one day next week to finish everything. I didn't want these final projects to be continually delayed, so I told them my boyfriend could also help if they needed any assistance.

The foreman puffed up his chest again. "*Nous allons terminer tout ce mardi après-midi.*" We will complete everything by Tuesday afternoon.

I smiled with appreciation. "See you Tuesday, then!" They grunted and walked out the door.

The space was finally livable. I rented a car for the weekend, and Turhan helped me move all of my remaining possessions from Trisha's place to my new apartment. I scooted my whole luggage collection, all of the same bags I hauled up to Francine's place a year ago, into the closet and put a few essentials on the bathroom ledge. Turhan and I arranged the furniture and stacked some books on the shelves. I couldn't wait to get fresh flowers from the local market on Sunday.

We finished up a few more tasks, then headed back to Turhan's apartment for a late Saturday dinner since I didn't have any food in the fridge yet and the paint fumes were still lingering. I closed and locked the front door. The workers will never know if I slept here or not.

In only a month, I had a brand-new apartment and a sexy boyfriend. Could more good news be on the horizon?

IT HAD BEEN MONTHS SINCE I applied for the internship at the U.S. Embassy, and I hadn't heard anything about it yet. Over grilled salmon and broccoli one night at Turhan's apartment, I told him about the internship and how much I would love the opportunity to work in a diplomatic office, even if it meant moving to another European city and then coming back to Paris to finish school.

He stopped chewing and raised his eyebrows. "Hmmm. Well, we'll have to wait and see what you hear about this opportunity."

I looked up from my plate. I hadn't put the pieces together until right now that a job could take me away from him. My heart sunk a few feet. I didn't want to contemplate a long-distance separation. My time in Paris had improved greatly since he had been in my life: more friends, more social activities, a fuller weekly schedule, a hand to hold. I changed the dinner topic.

At school the following day, there was an announcement posted about an upcoming trip to the U.S. Embassy in Paris. The visit had been arranged by a professor to meet with Foreign Service Officers and discuss current international diplomatic issues. Being allowed access to the U.S. Embassy was a *big deal* because it was not a place any visitor could just stride into and tour around, much less meet with diplomats.

Being a determined nerd, I was again the first name on the sign-up list; the first person to arrive at the meeting place at Place de la Concorde; and the first one in line, along with Trisha, to go through security, passport in hand. Everyone handed over all of their electronic items: no phones, no cameras, no iPods allowed.

Our embassy host guided us through the imposing front doors and ushered us up a grand central staircase. Artifacts of French and American relations were in the hallways and rooms; plants sat in the corners; the floors echoed with discreet whispers and impatient high heels. We entered a massive boardroom with wood panels and grand portraits on the walls and took our seats around a central wood table. The décor was simplistic, masculine, and austere. Trisha and I exchanged looks and sat up straight in our chairs, trying not to giggle. Things are always funnier when you're supposed to be quiet.

Three Foreign Service Officers entered the room and sat down at the far end of the imposing table. They introduced themselves as being from the political, economic, and financial departments, and then we each introduced ourselves and where we were from as if we were important, too. We discussed diplomatic duties, how diplomacy had changed in recent years, and how Foreign Service Officers had to adapt to living in a different country every four years. I was the big nerd asking every other question to get as most information as possible. Trisha silently smirked at me.

After the session, we were escorted back through the security checkpoint to collect our electronic possessions. Our group returned to the chaos of Place de la Concorde and Trisha finally had a chance to tease me about my non-stop questions. I turned on my cell phone while simultaneously firing off five questions at her about her experience today as she laughed up into the sky. When I glanced down at my phone, I had a new voicemail waiting.

"Please hold. I'll have more questions for you in a moment." I put the phone to my ear.

She turned and started speaking German to our classmate, Miron. He was from Serbia and very cute; they obviously had a little flirtation going on, but both of them played it cool. She regularly denied their mutual attraction like I was blind and couldn't see it oozing out of their body language. They needed to be dating. She routinely shrugged it off but hid a smile at the same time.

As I listened to the voicemail, my face contorted into confusion. The message was from a woman at the U.S. Embassy asking me to call her back. I turned around and stared at the building we just left. Someone from the Embassy called me while I was inside? How did they get my phone number? Maybe they were calling with one more answer to one of many questions. The traffic of Place de la Concorde was incredibly loud, so I hit replay to listen to the message again. Then my eyes grew bigger than my ears as I finally deciphered the information correctly.

"Oh my god! Trish!"

"What!"

"It's the U.S. Embassy... in GENEVA! They are offering me a position!" We stood in simultaneous stunned silence before breaking into a hug.

"No way! That is incredible!" Then we stared at each other again in wonderment at how this *one* call came during the *one* hour on the *one* day we were inside the U.S. Embassy in Paris.

"I bet I'm gonna work for the U.S. Ambassador," I said, winking at her. Since when did I start winking?

"I bet you'll BE the Ambassador." She laughed.

"And I'll make relations with Turkey a priority."

"Well, you already have a book on Turkish culture to put on your desk."

I called Turhan right away to tell him the exciting news. His enthusiasm was forced.

"Wow, that is really great. Good for you. How long is the position for?"

"I think a few months. Maybe three or four? I'm not sure yet. I need to call the woman back tomorrow to find out more information. She is gone for the rest of today."

"Okay, well, we'll figure out what to do after you speak to her."

A mixture of gratitude and disappointment ran through me as we hung up. I wished I had received a phone call from the U.S. Embassy in Paris about working there because it would be so much easier and simpler. But I couldn't pass up this opportunity. *Don't give up your dreams for a boy.*

My pulse started racing when I realized Geneva was where this dream began, and my intention was coming full circle. I had stood in the United Nations Office, connecting to this energy, and now I would be a part of the energy. Whenever I let go of the expectations of how something could happen, I was dazzled by the synchronicity and energetic alignment of how it arrived in my life. My heart ballooned up to the sky.

Miron, Trisha, and I started walking towards the metro as I listened to the message for a third time. Thousands of people applied for these positions every term and only around twenty people were accepted, at the most, for each post. And I couldn't get over the fact it happened while visiting *this* American Embassy.

After playing phone tag for a few days, I finally spoke to Judy in Geneva about the responsibilities and priorities of the position. The main area of responsibility was event planning for a major international refugee convention and she said I was her first choice out of hundreds of applicants because of my education and experience in event planning. I was humbled and blushed, shaking my head in shock. She arranged for me to talk to other people in the office to find out more information and ask questions. I spoke with three different people and everything sounded interesting and stimulating, except for one thing: temporary housing was typically in the Marine barracks. I would have my own room, and there were other possibilities if I wanted to rent a place elsewhere in Geneva, but this was the living situation most people chose for the short-term and to save money. Living with a bunch of twenty-something military boys? Early wake-up calls, late night bar hopping, stinky laundry, and who knows what else? I didn't like the idea at all, especially when I had a boyfriend. One big negative to this otherwise positive opportunity.

And that was when I realized another concern. If I left Paris, I would have to move out of my apartment and find another place to live when I returned. Or pay rent in both Geneva and Paris simultaneously. But I didn't have a budget that covered two rents in two expensive European cities. And the thought of looking for *another* place to live when I returned to Paris to finish school sounded dreadful.

School was another factor. While in Geneva, I would have to take a term off from school and that could potentially put me a full year behind in my degree program because some classes were only offered once a year. Being behind would be costly since I would have to stay a year longer and take out one more student loan to cover living expenses in euros. And did I want to delay completing my degree? My stomach knotted up more.

I thought getting this internship would be a great opportunity that would coincide with my studies and life in Paris, not create more burdens. It was turning into a hard decision with significant pros and cons. I wished I had some more options to consider, but I didn't. *Ugh.* I sent out silent intentions for the best possible solution to present itself, whatever that may be. I needed to make a decision soon, and of course I had to follow the opportunity. But what if this choice created negative ripple effects in every other area of my life?

Gratitude for clarity. Gratitude for the opportunity. Trust in the process.

HEART

AFTER LIVING IN PARIS FOR over a year, I came to terms with the fact that I was somewhere between a permanent tourist and a temporary local. I was not French, but I didn't feel completely American. I was more than a visitor, but not a citizen. I knew more information about Paris than the average tourist, but I certainly didn't understand everything about how this city worked. Every day I tried to be open to learning something new while also being thrown a little off balance; the seesaw of living in-between cultures and not fully belonging to either one. And to be experiencing this blurry status with another person who was also a foreigner created an incredible bond between us. It changed and expanded everything because now I had someone else in my daily life who *gets it*.

Turhan and I celebrated when one of us figured something out or noticed a new way that things worked ("Ohhh, the kiosk is the faster way to buy the monthly metro pass!"). We supported each other in moments of confusion about how certain things were done ("It's okay to cut in line at the grocery store, but it's not okay to be *rude* while doing it. It's about being *discreet* while cutting in line. Being rude is unacceptable."). We were learning how to navigate the language barrier in unfamiliar situations and how not to appear stupid ("Say *comment* and lean in when you want someone to repeat a sentence. Then it looks like you couldn't hear them and they will repeat themselves, instead of the fact that you didn't understand what they said in the first place.") We shook our heads in frustration when information didn't make sense ("Strikes against the government happened regularly around the city and the strike had to be registered first to be legally allowed. But usually the strike was against the bureaucracy that was requiring them to register their strike in the first place."). Other times, we just shrugged our shoulders and said, "This is France" instead of searching for definite answers. Through the rough bumps of feeling like an outsider, it was comforting at least to know we were in it together.

AT SCHOOL THE FOLLOWING WEEK, I ran into the Director in the hallway and shared with her both the excitement and the unknowns of my internship opportunity. She listened intently and made some good points about how special this opportunity was and I wouldn't want to waste the chance and regret it later. She said not to worry about finding a place to live in Paris when I returned; things would work out like they always did. And as for school, I might be able to do a long-distance learning situation while I was in Geneva. She was willing to work with me and find some solutions. I nodded along. Her encouragement helped me relax a bit, but I still didn't feel completely clear about what to do.

I sat down at an open computer in the computer room to check my email and found an interesting message in my junk folder from the U.S. Embassy in Paris. They were asking for my response. *To what? Did I sign up for something during our recent trip? Did I unknowingly agree to something while firing off my long list of questions?*

I re-read the message and noticed another email address referenced in the "to" field. My heart jumped. On my initial application for this position, completed after a long day and many glasses of wine, I must have used another email address that I only sometimes used (and mostly forgot about) for professional purposes. I feverishly logged into that account, and -

"Oh my gosh!" I jumped up, knocking my chair out behind me and throwing my hands over my mouth. Everyone stopped tapping on their keys and stared. Two emails were waiting in my other account: an acceptance email from two weeks ago and another one that said I needed to respond by tomorrow.

"Sorry!" I whispered apologetically. "I can't believe it! I was accepted to the U.S. Embassy in Paris, too!"

I slinked into the library to look for Trisha and didn't find see her, but I did run into a few people in my degree program who were sitting around chatting. I shared the news, bubbling over with excitement and relief, until one girl interrupted me with a hardened voice and steel blue eyes.

"Wait a minute," She began. "You were accepted into not one, but two Embassies?"

"Yeah, I can't believe it…" Shaking my head in disbelief.

She stared at me. "I have applied six times for those jobs and have never been accepted."

Oh no. I tried to inhale my last words.

"Thousands of people apply every term for those special opportunities and *you* got two slots from two highly desirable locations?" Her face conveyed controlled anger. "My dad is a Foreign Service Officer and helps me fill out applications every term for a position. I needed this type of internship for my career. I needed this experience and these references on my resume. I can't believe *you*" — fierce annoyance on her face — "got a spot that someone like *me* should have." Cold eyes.

I stared back at her for second. "I guess God loves me more than He loves you, sunshine." Shoulder shrug. Smile.

Just kidding. I didn't say that.

Instead I replied, "Wow, I didn't realize people applied for this opportunity so many times." I really didn't. I had no clue. And if she hadn't been so rude and hostile, I would have *maybe* offered to pass her name along to Judy in Geneva. But my mouth never offered that. She slammed her book shut and packed up her bag. A few of us exchanged silent looks, then I returned to the computer lab for my bag.

Turhan was in meetings all afternoon so I couldn't call him until later in the evening. As classes finished for the afternoon, I left school with a few friends to indulge in a *kir royale* at a café down the street. We situated ourselves at a corner table in full view of the passing sidewalk show and city activity. The waiter was unusually attentive and brought continual bowls of peanuts. The sun sank lower as we chatted away and tables filled up with more after-work drinkers. Parisian life moved around constantly as the sky turned to darkening shades of blue.

After two glasses of bubbly, (Or was it three? Or four glasses? What number comes after four?) I called Turhan in a bubbly voice with my bubbly news about staying in Paris. He had already left work and was about to get on the metro so he couldn't talk for long, but he was very happy to hear this development. No forced enthusiasm in his voice this time.

"Come over to my place. We'll go to dinner to celebrate. I gotta go, the metro is coming."

I hung up and stood up with slightly wobbling feet. I bounced my bubbly self over to his apartment, bounced through the front door he held open for me, and bounced to the couch as he changed his clothes in the other room. I put my feet up on one end of the incredibly soft couch and rested my head on a pillow.

"Are you hungry?" He yelled from the other room. I was pondering this question very deeply with my eyes closed.

He appeared in the doorway. "Why are you sleeping?"

"I'm not sleeping, I'm awake." I opened my eyes widely to prove my point.

"So are you hungry for dinner? What do you feel like?" He asked again.

"Well, I'm kinda hungry... but I have been celebrating my new job... for a few hours now..." I closed my eyes for a second. A quick second.

He walked further into the room. "Let's walk to Bastille and eat at a restaurant there."

I stared at his physical outline from my pillow. Did he know he was standing sideways? Quite impressive.

I raised my right hand with a pointed finger. "Turhan," I began in my mature, intelligent voice. "It is very important that we are respectful of each other's cultural differences. And one of the main cultural differences between Seattle and Turkey is that we eat and sleep at different times."

He stared down at my random thoughts. "Those are called time zones."

"Yes, EXACTLY. *Time zones.* So we must respect each other's different time zone needs." I nodded sideways on the pillow in agreement with myself.

He sat down next to me on the couch to assess this situation better. "You have been living in Paris for a year now and so have I. We have the same time zone needs."

I continued. "But, it is okay for those needs to be different at times. It's peerrrfectly okay." I was nodding my head on the pillow still. Or was the pillow nodding under me? "And considering the time it is right now, we shouldn't talk too loud or we'll wake up Moscow... shhhh..." Finger to my lips. Eyes closed for just a fast second. A really fast second.

He stared with a slight smile on his face. "How much champagne did you drink?" I raised one hand and twinkled my fingers. With sound effects.

"And you haven't had any food?"

"Yum. Food is good."

He grabbed my twinkling hand and held onto it. "Do you want to stay in and we can celebrate tomorrow night?"

"Okay... yeah... sure." I smiled with my eyes open. I think they were open.

He winked at me. I winked back. Except my wink turned into a loonnng sloowww blink. And my eyes slammed shut until morning.

MONTHS BEFORE WE MET, TURHAN had been going to salsa dancing lessons every Friday night at a Latin bar in his neighborhood. It was his weekly fun and a needed release from his desk job and stuffy colleagues. I loved dancing, and felt so lucky that this sexy man was now teaching me the basics of salsa dancing. I had never salsa danced before, although I have taken many dance classes, and this style was completely different than anything I'd done before because the movement was in the hips, in the rhythm, and in the flow. It was not the counting choreographed steps I was used to following. So I just trusted his lead and followed wherever he took me as he demonstrated basic maneuvers and patterns. In his living room and in the kitchen, we practiced steps, movements, and counts. He had many moves memorized and knew which way to spin me around the hardwood floors. He was patient, instructive, and in charge as he pushed me out, then pulled me close. With each routine, I had more opportunities to kiss his cheek while he concentrated on the moves.

Salsa classes were offered on Friday nights at two different times for two different skill levels: 8 p.m. for beginners (me) and 9 p.m. for intermediate dancers (him). After the classes ended at 10 p.m., the dance floor opened up for everyone to shake, twist, and turn to the pulsing spicy beats. Note to self: do not get in the way of the regular Cuban movers and shakers. They were hot stuff and not afraid to twist and turn on toes anywhere they pleased.

After going salsa dancing a few Fridays in a row, Turhan introduced me to some regulars he knew as we stood on the dark sidelines watching the bright dance floor action. I had a beer in my right hand and Turhan was talking to three people on my left side; I nodded *bonsoirs* and exchanged polite smiles with his friends. The music was loudly pumping and thumping, so talking was difficult because every chat turned into a shouting match. A few amazing dancers had captured my attention and I was watching them intently while Turhan took my left hand and said something that sounded like "must have taken it off." Then he put his hand on my stomach and appeared to nod eagerly at the group while I watched the dance floor, trying to remember the dance moves we just learned.

I turned to look at him, and his three friends all leaned over with big smiles and said something that sounded like "*Felicitations*" Congratulations. I nodded absentmindedly in agreement with whatever they were saying, doubting my ability to hear anything correctly with this loud music. As I put my beer up to my mouth, their smiles quickly turned to looks of horror.

One woman leaned forward abruptly to shout something that sounded like "*...pas bien pour le bebe...*" ...not good for the baby...

I whipped my head with shocked eyes to look at Turhan, who threw his head back in laughter and winked at me. What a troublemaker.

I then leaned forward to yell something that hopefully sounded like, "*Desolee, n'est pas vrai. Il n'y a pas un bebe...*" Sorry, it's not true. There is no baby.

Their faces showed immediate confusion as they turned to look at a laughing Turhan. He grabbed my left hand again and asked what happened to the ring, pretending to search for it on the ground. I just stared at him, shaking my head, as he performed his entertaining antics. Then throwing his head back in laughter again, he pulled me onto the dance floor, leaving a group of people confused in his salsa-shaking dancing wake.

Turhan and I regularly went to a Turkish restaurant in his neighborhood when he was craving food from his homeland. A Turkish couple owned the place and greeted us warmly each time we entered. Turhan liked going there for the food, but also so he could speak Turkish. He missed his language and enjoyed any opportunity to use it. I hadn't realized what that must be like, never using my native tongue. We spoke mostly English to each other on a daily basis, and occasionally conversed in French when we were both inspired.

I settled into a corner table while he chatted freely with the restaurant owners and any other Turkish patrons who happened to walk inside. He returned to the table with a tray of delicious, bright food.

"How long have you been studying and speaking English?" I asked while setting food in front of me.

"I started learning English in fifth grade." He took a bite.

"Wow, that is amazing, because the Turkish language was required learning for all fifth graders in America, too." I replied with certainty between forks of food.

He stared at me with his dark brown eyes and said something in Turkish.

I stared back blankly. With a slight shoulder shrug, I said, "Well, we didn't study it in sixth grade *too*. Just fifth grade and then most people switched to Spanish that they completely forgot before turning eighteen."

He smirked knowing I was kidding and took another bite. I was certainly happy to visit Turkish restaurants regularly so he could speak his language and I could eat the delicious food.

We routinely bought basic Turkish ingredients at the store so the necessary components were always in the fridge: feta cheese, yogurt, hummus, fresh vegetables, olive oil, and always, always, always, tomatoes. The unspoken rule was that tomatoes were served with every meal: at breakfast with eggs and a baguette; at lunch on a sandwich or as part of a salad; at dinner cut up into slices as a side with any entree; and as a snack to be eaten while standing at the kitchen counter, holding off hunger between meals. In fact, Turhan needed to see at least three red shapes in the refrigerator drawer to get through the next meal. If there were less than three, we needed to make a trip to the store and stock up. This meant we were always buying tomatoes.

If we stopped by the store for dinner ingredients, we bought tomatoes for the next morning. If we went to the store Saturday afternoon, we picked up enough tomatoes to last through Monday because the grocery stores were closed on Sundays and we might not make it to a Sunday farmer's market. If we went to the store for any other reason and bought cheese, toilet paper, or chocolate, it was always a good idea to pick up more tomatoes too, just in case. *Just in case.*

And sometimes, it was funny for one person to say "Potatoes? You want how many potatoes?" to entertain herself and get a wise-ass response from the other person. But that only worked the first few times because then he didn't respond at all to the stale joke, and getting a wise-ass response was the whole point of the exercise, anyway.

As my second summer in Paris arrived and the city gradually warmed up, we quickly went through vines and vines of tomatoes. Vegetables, fruits, and other seasonal delicacies changed at the farmer's markets to signal that summer was officially here. Baskets of strawberries, bundles of asparagus, bright peppers, and beautiful ripe melons filled up the street-side stands. The early morning sunrays could damage fruit, so many bundles were pulled back under the awnings of the stands. Vendors regularly handed out samples of sweet apricots or ripe grapes to herald the arrivals of their latest grand possessions.

Another signal that summer was nearly upon us was evident in how the walking pace at the weekly market changed as more tourists streamed into the city and waddled through the stalls, touching fruit, picking at displays, yelling in non-French words, and generally annoying vendors. These little behaviors were not always a big deal and could be politely ignored. But at this time of year, rudeness could be an especially sensitive issue because there was a secret about the city that many invading tourists did not know: Parisians started to turn crabby in June. The longer days, the bright sun, the open windows, and the desire to bask in warmth translated to a deeper issue that Parisians were ready *now* for their annual month-long holidays in late summer. No more city life, city pace, crowded streets, or public transportation woes. When summer weather arrived, the anticipation of escaping the city was turned up intensely. And Turhan was no exception.

He worked a standard business day and regularly heard about exotic holiday plans from all of his French colleagues. At this time of year, it was the daily conversation topic during coffee breaks and lunch. He was definitely ready for a break from work and school, and I was never one to disagree with a vacation idea. He brought the topic up almost nightly over dinner. Possible places to visit rotated with every evening entrée:

Monday: Over chicken, rice, and tomato slices, we should definitely go to the Canary Islands.

Tuesday: With spaghetti, a tomato salad, and baguette slices, we were off to Spain. Somewhere on the beach.

Thursday: Salmon, rosemary potatoes, tomato wedges, and slices of *pain au campaign* were almost gone from our plates when it was decided that Nice and the Cote d'Azur would be grand. Except, I vetoed this option because I had already been there and would prefer a beach with fine grain sand, not big rocks. And these potatoes weren't cooked enough.

Sunday: After finishing off the remaining slices of a mozzarella and tomato pizza, our bags were destined for Northern Italy. This was *definitely* the locale we decided on. At least until we saw another enticing vacation poster in the metro corridors and then maybe a new destination should be researched and considered.

The following Tuesday, Turhan rushed home from work, and with complete certainty, said we had to go to Corsica, an island in the Mediterranean, for our holiday. It was the best option of all. He had heard amazing things about the island from his colleagues who all said it was beautiful and special. We can go to the beach *and* go hiking in the mountains, plus there were many little towns to visit all over the island. And perhaps best of all, it was not as popular as other Mediterranean hot spots because ongoing conflicts between mainland France and Corsica kept many French people from going there.

"Great. Sounds good to me." I responded, shuffling around him to take dinner out of the oven. "And perfect timing because the baked penne is finished. Step to the side, please." While handling the hot entrée, I nodded in his direction that the tomatoes needed to be cut up. I may not be fluent in Turkish, but I am fluent in Kitchen Code.

We discussed the trip options in more detail while eating, then left the dirty dishes on the table to make our definite-for-sure-no-turning-back-now travel reservations for a week in the middle of July when he could take time off work. We found a beautiful rental cabin with an amazing view of Ajaccio, Corsica's capitol city, and secured a rental car so we could explore the island in every direction. The hiking trails were supposed to be the best in Europe and the beaches were noted for being some of the best in the world.

Once our destination was in place, I noticed a distinct change in my disposition. I was sick of the city as well and now joined the ranks of Parisian Crabbiness. I felt more impatient about clogged city life, loud traffic, and stuffy air with each passing day. I couldn't wait to be on the beach, in the sun, inhaling clean air, and in a world where laundry didn't exist until we came back home... only a month to go.

For the next few weeks, I busied myself with classes, schoolwork, and meeting Trisha for lunch. We hung out at a café in Saint Michel or a bistro in Saint Germain, then walked around the city and chatted endlessly, ducking into air-conditioned stores to cool off. After sharing our first year in Paris together, Trisha and I had a very easy and intuitive relationship. We regularly exchanged knowing looks about anything that may be happening around us—conversations, events, school, friends—and were constantly aware of our foreign surroundings. Many of our school friends had already graduated with their degrees and subsequently left Paris, so we were making the most of our quieter social lives. She had summer travel plans of her own coming up in a few weeks that would take her back to the United States, followed by a few weeks in the Philippines. Her family had connections in many locations, along with residences in Switzerland and Germany, so I could never keep up with her travel plans. One of my favorite things about Trisha was that she was a conscious explorer, ready and willing to go out into the world on her own and as necessary. She had a 24-hour stopover in Dubai one time, and fearlessly toured the city for a few hours as both a tourist and an observer attempting to understand the cultural practices. She quickly learned that riding a bus in Dubai meant women sat at the front and men sat at the back, unless you were married; then a man can sit in the front with his wife. At a fast food restaurant, there were different lines for men and women to order food. She covered herself up as necessary so her clothing would not be offensive. And even though these customs and practices were foreign to us, she felt safe because the men inherently protected the women and took care of them. She witnessed a comfortable dignity and an insightful perspective on the differences. Her travel inspired me.

The hot, slow days of July eventually passed, and soon enough Turhan and I were landing in Corsica. Located south of France and to the west of Italy, the island was surrounded by deep azure blue water that twinkled in quiet lagoons and safe inlets. Beaches lined every side of the island with carpets of perfect beige sand and mountainous terrain interspersed with rocks, trees, and curving roads. Together it created the appearance of a thousand puzzle pieces scattered over a land mass and held together by the clutch of Mediterranean water. It was highly possible we would want to lose our return tickets home.

Every mile away from the airport was a mile away from our former reality. We passed signs written in French and Corsican and gorgeous beaches sprinkled with only a handful of people. We passed the town center and turned up toward a small mountain off in the distance as a man fed his cows from a pail. We followed the road as it twisted and turned through pastures and clusters of homes, believing we might be going in the wrong direction, until the picture of the cabin on the website appeared in front of us. Our vacation cabin was perched on the side of a mountain facing the sea and the city. Three flights of steep stairs led up to our quiet getaway as we hauled our luggage up to a new altitude. A balcony overlooked the majestic views and a side patio had an outdoor eating area. Inside, there was a main living area connected to the open kitchen, a master bedroom, and a huge bathroom. The cabin was advertised as being recently renovated, and every surface was shiny, polished wood. We did the usual all-over-inspection of our temporary home, investigating every closet and cupboard to see what was at our disposal. It was so lovely and peaceful. Sleeping in this quiet would be a dream.

But as it turned out, it was only quiet for another moment until we met our new neighbors. Two little cats sauntered along the front patio welcoming us with Corsican meows.

"We have a welcoming committee," Turhan announced.

One *chat* was fluffy and observant, parading along the parameter of the patio rail. The other was tiny and scrawny, obviously younger and very inquisitive. I dropped everything to go outside and speak French to them. They individually came up to my legs for an introduction and personal meow sessions. Each one took their turn to meow, move away, and then come back like a soft boomerang. They made me miss my two cats even more. As I gave them tons of attention, Turhan inspected the barbecue on the side patio. His masculine armor didn't allow him to admit how much he liked our little visitors, but as soon as I went back inside to finish unpacking, his camera was readily taking pictures of them and I could hear him talking to them.

After settling into our new tropical mountain home, we ventured to the grocery store to pick up food, beach essentials, and a map of the island. Our store basket was full of items for all three daily meals, and as we reviewed what we needed for the next few days, I gleefully realized something important.

"Do we need to buy cat food, too?" My nurturing excitement could not be hidden.

"For what?" He said absentmindedly.

Incredulous stare. "For the true purpose of our trip: o make friends with the locals!"

He shrugged and continued inspecting the tomatoes. I went to grab a small bag of cat food. No animals will starve on my vacation! Not that they were starving, hungry, or even skinny; just friendly and welcoming. I was excited to lure them into my personal space. Apparently I really missed my cats.

When we returned to the cabin, Turhan started the barbecue outside as I chopped the vegetables inside. I discreetly watched as he abandoned the grill to look around the stairs, patio, and backyard to find the cats. I heard him talking to them again in a matter of moments. Big smile.

The following day was our first full day on the island, so we set off mid-morning to find the perfect beach. That task only took ten minutes, including stopping to ask locals for directions. The white sandy terrain spread out before us with only a few human dots occupying the precious land. We became two new dots on the sand, lying on our towels with the cooler and under the huge beach umbrella we found at the cabin. The umbrella turned out to be the most important piece of equipment we brought because the Mediterranean sun was pounding, intense, and persistent. Turhan's 100% Turkish skin tanned to a beautiful dark caramel with ease, but my Irish ivory skin had to sit in the shade with envy for most of the day. He sprayed on SPF 10 and relied on it lasting for a few hours, while I layered on SPF 45 every hour, on the hour, or paid the burning consequences.

Our holiday itinerary included driving, exploring, hiking, and relaxing on the beach. We toured the island by driving north, south and east, trying to cover as much terrain as possible without overdoing the hours of driving. The island distances were not far, but the long windy highways and two lane roads made for extra slow travels at inconsistent speeds.

We glided through charming mountain villages, slowed down for strolling cattle on the road, waved at ambitious hikers and bikers, and followed hairpin corners only to be met with incredible sea vistas around every bend and curve. The middle of the island had the most diverse topography, so we followed the main roads to the prominent hiking trails and spent a day playing along the mountain river and hiking. We ventured higher up into the hills, away from other people and their conversations, trying to find the next best picture to take and the path less followed. All was peaceful and serene as we hiked, until a huge, imposing bull with small horns was standing less than three feet away from us, munching on grass behind a boulder. The bovine stared at me, and then gave a slight huff through his nostrils. I reversed.

"Honey, we should go back down…"

"Why? It's just a cow. It doesn't care about us."

"It snorted at me! And I think it's dominating this piece of land. I don't trust wild animals in their own environment…"

Turhan stood with his chest puffed out and stared at the bull for a moment, positioning his dominance in the situation. Then in a deep, low voice said, "I will save you from the cow."

My laughter reverberated throughout the canyon, head thrown

back in the wind.

Then the bull huffed again and started to pick up a foot to move toward us. I grabbed Turhan's bicep and moved behind him.

"Honey, I'm not kidding! Let's go back the way we came up, just to give it some room."

He stood in solid dominant posture while I continued with my reasoning. "And I swear it's the same cow we saw walking along the road two hours ago. I can tell by the green tag on its ear."

Turhan huffed through his nostrils as I turned to reverse down the rocks and through the jungle of trees, ushering an unconvinced dominant male back down the mountain to the safe edges of the river. We stood in the shade along the water.

Glancing at him, I said, "We were lucky to escape. Because do you know what else wild Corsican cows like to eat besides grass?"

"Tell me," he said while taking a new picture of a village in the distance.

"Turkish skeptics." Then I turned on my heel to go find a place to pee in the woods as he laughed. Then Turhan went back up to take a picture of the bull.

As we returned home each evening, the two little felines came around to greet us while we were barbecuing dinner or sitting on the patio watching the city sparkle at twilight. Then one morning we woke up to find a little dog running around outside the front door. And then it was running around inside our cabin as we started to pack up towels and load an empty cooler. The furry little grey pup was the same size as the cats, but louder with toenails that scampered quickly across the wood floor. He walked triumphantly through each room, inspecting everything we were doing, and then scuttled back outside and disappeared. The owner of the cabin came around to apologize for the intrusion; the animals were accustomed to having visitors and playing host to the cabin. I told her it always made my day to see her animals running around.

We spent a long morning leisurely touring Ajaccio, walking along the waterfront and through the historic old town now populated with typical touristy shops. Along a side street, we passed the birth home of the island's most famous native, Napoleon Bonaparte, which was now a national museum. It was closed in the morning, so all I could do was guess about the life that occurred inside those four walls. Maybe Napoleon's furniture was lower to the ground but over-sized to make up for the lack of height.

We left the capital city to return to our favorite daily task of finding a new beach on a different part of the island. We discovered a new place every day, and each beach was wide open with lots of room to spread out our towels and hide under the requisite umbrella. We swam, napped, ate, read, and played ping-pong for as long as the sun allowed us. The water was always bath water warm and the sand was hot to touch, so the distance between towel and water was strategically short. We enjoyed the last rays of the sun until it sank behind the mountains, the last remaining witnesses to a Mediterranean sunset.

I never wanted to leave.

Unfortunately, the date on the calendar eventually matched the date on our return tickets and we had to leave the big beach umbrella behind. I tracked down all of our temporary animals to say a proper goodbye to each one individually. *"Au revoir, ma petit ami. Je t'adore and tu me manqué chaque jour."* Goodbye, my little friend. I adore you and I will miss you each day.

We reluctantly made our final descent from the mountain top oasis to the business of the airport. I couldn't bear to look at people who were disembarking from flights and just beginning their vacations. I couldn't bear to see their excitement over arriving. Instead, I scrolled through my pictures as a way to lengthen the holiday while we waited for our flight. I hoped it was permanently cancelled.

Upon stumbling back into Turhan's stuffy apartment, the warm Mediterranean air, carefree days, and regular trips to the beach were replaced with the bores of dirty laundry, an empty fridge, and hot city air with no breeze. No more beaches to run off to in the morning. No new hiking trails to discover. No fuzzy leg rubs from fuzzy friends. No reasons to keep the camera handy. The vacation was officially over.

And so was the honeymoon phase of our relationship.

A few nights after returning, we finished dinner at the pullout table in the kitchen. There were only a few bites left on my plate that I wasn't going to eat, so I silently slid those last pieces over to Turhan's plate knowing he would eat them without missing a beat. It was good for male muscles to consume more calories, except pastries and desserts, of course.

The stack of dishes at the sink had piled up quickly and I offered to clean them because Turhan needed to finish a project for work. I was not in any rush to jump up and get started though, so I lingered with wine glass in hand and watched how he leaned into the plate to meet all food with eagerness. His mouth was maybe ten inches from the plate; this was not his posture on our first date.

"So honey, what's the plan for this week," he asked in between last bites.

"Hmmm. I don't have much planned. I need to go to the Embassy for my security interview and I have thesis research to work on. But not much else. What about you?"

"I work, I sleep, I get up the next morning, and do it again. That is my plan every day." His voice was deep and serious, but his tone was mocking. I smiled. He makes me laugh.

I stood up to take our dishes to the sink. "Let's go to a movie after work one night. That would be fun."

"*Bonne idée.*" He stood up to clear the rest of the table. "But I have a visitor coming, so I don't know which evening will be best yet. Maybe Friday we can do that," he said as he stacked items next to the sink.

A visitor? I took my confusion out of my head and into the air. "A visitor? Who?"

"A family friend is coming to Paris for a few days and I offered my couch. It's what we do in Turkey. We always welcome people we know who are traveling to our city."

"Oh, that's nice. How long is he staying?" I picked up the first of the dirty plates. How did we use so many dishes in one day?

"She will be here for two or three nights. Not sure of her schedule yet."

She? I felt something in my stomach turn. I stopped scrubbing and let the water run. This was not the gender I was expecting to hear. He pushed the pullout table back under the counter and put the butter in the fridge. He squeezed my waist, kissed my neck, and then walked into the bedroom to sit at his desk. I stood silent and confused.

I continued doing the dishes, but at a much slower pace. I had questions, but I forced myself to finish the plates and cups first while I got my mind around this. I felt caught off guard. I felt uncomfortable. A woman is staying here. *Here.* On his couch. In this cramped space. In this small apartment with a single bathroom and very little privacy. My stomach turned some more.

I needed more information before jumping to any conclusions. She could be an older woman, or a friend of his father's, or a married mom, or… something like that. I needed more facts. There was no need to sprint ahead to a scenario that didn't exist. I focused on the dishes.

Before the last cup was cleaned, my mind had wandered from the fun we'd been having these past few months to the reality of a healthy relationship. That reality included talking about things that made us uncomfortable. If we can't communicate about the awkward situations and tougher topics, then how far could this relationship really go? Not far. Not far at all. I needed to talk about this.

I turned off the water and walked into the bedroom. "Hey, do you have a sec? Are you near a breaking point?" I sat down on the edge of the bed, cross-legged.

"Sure... of course." He closed his laptop and turned to face me.

"Well... it kinda threw me off that a woman would be staying here with you." Pause. "What kind of family friend is she? Is it someone you know well?"

He shrugged. "She is a friend's sister that I've met a few times. She is coming here for business. My friend asked if I would mind if she stayed here so she doesn't have to pay for an expensive hotel room in Paris."

"Oh."

From his expression he didn't think it was a big deal. My stomach thought otherwise. I continued. "It just..." Pause. "It just makes me uncomfortable that another woman would be staying here in your apartment with you. If it's a business trip, wouldn't the company normally pay for a hotel room?"

"Yeah, I guess, but the company is not paying for a room, I do not know why. Why are you uncomfortable?"

"Because a woman is staying at your place and there isn't a lot of privacy or extra room here. Is she, like, a friend of your parents? Is she older and married?" Maybe if I said those descriptions they would be true.

"Nope, she's our age, in her 30s. She is a friend's sister, which means she is like family to me." His tone was becoming more defensive. "I would never be attracted to her. Never."

"Well, you can't just control who you are attracted to, even if it is a friend's sister. And that's not my point. I'm just uncomfortable that another woman would be in this small space with you. Your apartment is..." I looked around to find the word "...intimate."

"I will get up in the morning, shower, go to work, and come home late so she can have her own space. It's not a big deal." His tone was more defensive.

"I know it's not a *big* deal, but it still feels weird to me. I know your morning routine and how you walk around with a towel after a shower, how you get dressed in the morning, all of that. There isn't a lot of privacy here; your place is small…"

"My apartment is not small." His tone bristled and his eyes became more intense. He grew up in his family's two-bedroom apartment with a balcony. I grew up in a five-bedroom house surrounded by green land in every direction. We had very different concepts of what constituted big and small living spaces. Our different cultural perspectives had officially collided. Proceed delicately.

"Your apartment is a good size for Paris. I'm not saying there's anything *wrong* with your place…" Pause. "The issue is that I want you to hear my feelings, and how uncomfortable it makes me that another woman will be staying in this apartment with you."

"I do hear your feelings. You are uncomfortable with another woman staying here." He said it like I was being totally insecure and completely ridiculous. I considered a different tactic. "Okay, so, what if the situation were reversed. What if some guy was coming to stay with me for a few nights in my place. How would that make you feel?"

He shrugged, then said "That wouldn't happen. No guy would stay with you in your place. That is not something a guy would do."

I stared with slight insult on my face. "Yes, it could happen. And if it did, what would you do? How would you feel about that?"

"If that happened, I would invite you to stay at my place and then he would have your apartment to himself. It would work out fine." Good point. But not my point at this moment.

"So then, what if for this situation you come stay with me at my apartment and give her your apartment for the visit?"

"She is a guest to the city and as her host I will need to take her to dinner one night and make sure she is taken care of while visiting. Plus, your apartment is far away from my work and it is easier for me to get to work from here."

I stared at the window curtains. I did not feel like I was being heard. My hand moved from my forehead to my chin to my heart. Was I overreacting?

"Turhan… I'm getting frustrated. I'm trying to tell you how I feel and why I don't like this situation, but I don't think you understand me. I'm trying to say that—"

He abruptly stood up. "I know what you're saying!" He started pacing, hard. "But this is the situation now and it is something we do in Turkey for our family and friends. It is our culture and it is polite. We take care of people who come to visit."

He was defiant. I was frustrated. We didn't look at each other. This wasn't good.

I broke the silence. "Okay, I understand that. I do, I really do. You want to be a good host and to take care of a friend's relative. But at the same time, I think my feelings about being uncomfortable are valid."

He didn't say anything. I continued. "Besides the fact that you just told me this news tonight—"

"—because I just found out myself and didn't think it was a big deal—" Loud voices.

"—I am a reasonable person. I understand you want to be a good host. But it is awkward for me to have another woman stay in your confined, personal space, and I'm frustrated you can't understand that. I trust you, but I trust my feelings about this, too. You're making the choice to have her stay here with no concern or regard for me."

I moved to the edge of the bed to stand up. "You're more concerned about her comfort than mine."

He leaned back against the desk, arms crossed over his chest, head looking down. "Well, there's nothing I can do. Arrangements have been made and it would be rude to cancel now."

I just wanted to get some fresh air and fresh space. It was frustrating to have this heated conversation after a great vacation together.

"There are other hotel rooms in this city, and there are other ways to be a good host." I walked into the hallway. "And I'm upset that we are obviously not understanding each other...I want you to be a good host, but I don't think you are thinking about my perspective in this situation. I mean, it would be one thing if there was a separate room for her, separate space, more privacy. But there's not."

Tired. I grabbed my coat and purse.

He followed me into the hallway. "It's after ten o'clock. Why are you leaving?"

"Because I need some space." I walked to the front door, putting on my coat. "I'll talk to you later." I opened the door without waiting for a response.

My face hit the fresh air and I couldn't stop reviewing the situation. One of the hardest things was that we were not at the same starting point definition about space and privacy. If he was American, he would most likely understand what I meant about his apartment being small and intimate. But, if I were Turkish, I would understand the cultural expectations and the need to be a welcoming host, regardless of apartment size. So the perspective that we were not each other's cultural equivalent was a wash. I arrived back at my apartment ready for instant sleep. I didn't want to spin in this anymore.

The next day, Turhan and I didn't talk at all. I focused on my thesis research, went to the Jardin du Tuileries with a book for an afternoon coffee, and finalized my plans for an upcoming trip home. I was returning to Seattle in a few weeks to sell some of my furniture that was taking up valuable space in my mom's garage, and to bring my two cats to Paris. I would be here for at least another year, if not longer, and I missed my little furry friends. I couldn't wait to have them in my daily life again. And it would be great to sell my furniture and have some more cash in my pocket. The euro was killing my dollar bank account.

I went to my security interview at the Embassy and returned to my apartment in the afternoon. The phone rang and it was Turhan asking how my interview went.

"It went great! I still don't know where I'm working in the Embassy. I'll find out later."

"Good. I'm glad it went well."

"Yep."

Silence.

"So..." he continued, "Do you want to go to a movie tonight or tomorrow night?"

"Sure, either is fine. But don't you have to show your visitor around."

"My visitor is no longer staying with me. I helped her make other plans."

My heart smiled. "Oh... thank you, honey. I really appreciate that you made that choice."

"You are welcome." His voice was strong and proud. "Let's meet tonight on the Champs-Elysees at 6 p.m. for a show."

"Okay, sounds good."

"*Ciao.*"

"*Ciao.*"

I hung up with a big sense of relief. I hadn't realized this issue was weighing on me so much. This wasn't just about our cultural differences, communication abilities, or hosting a visitor. It was about taking care of each others' heart. At the end of the day, would we choose each other?

I grabbed an umbrella and headed out the door to catch an early metro train into the city, wanting to walk before our rendezvous and give my thoughts some exercise. I'd had a big realization lately that filled me with incredible hope and prospective fear. *I'd always been searching for this life. Here. Now. Today. This was it.*

After my experiences in Monterey, Greenville, Portland, and Annecy, my roots and heels had sunk in here as they had never done anywhere else. I felt grounded and connected, yet excited about what was coming next. I was familiar with Paris and its personality, but knew there was still more to discover, and do, and experience. I liked moving easily around the city, the interesting new people I was continually meeting through my international friends, and the easy manner in which people gathered in restaurants without relying solely on technology as the form of communication. I liked that my friends lived all over town and were eager to experience all the city had to offer. I liked knowing my neighborhood well and yet still had new areas of town to explore.

I exited the metro at Place de la Concorde and turned up toward the Arc de Triomphe standing at the top of the Champs-Élysées. The sun faded in and out behind the clouds. Traffic whizzed by in controlled chaos. I weaved through tourists on the wide boulevard as different languages passed through my ears, my hair, my mind. I had grown accustomed to Paris's ebbs and flows: the traffic surges, the sidewalk choreography, the change of seasons, the dance of the metro, and the pace of daily life that one becomes connected to unconsciously. I felt comfortably positioned between stimulation and predictability. And my life here was also an easy gateway for venturing out on day trips to nearby palaces, castles, villages, and adventures, plus traveling to other parts of Europe easily, cheaply, and impulsively. The close proximity of different countries, cultures, languages, food, and history reminded me of where I was today, and where I could go tomorrow. And that could be as simple as a walk down the Champs-Élysées while feeling the Parisian summer air in all its complexities: Warm, smoggy, still, intense.

I crossed over Avenue Montaigne as the quiet stretches of grass became buildings, banks, stores, and restaurants where Paris expanded outward into the commerce of modern life and walked the streets with pedestrian authority. I was certain of one thing: *I really liked Me in Paris.* I was challenged to be broader and better than I'd ever been before. My senses were alive and loving it and my heart was connected to this life in a way I couldn't completely describe or fully understand. *I just felt it.* This was what I've been searching for my whole life, and I had found the right fit. Finally. I knew without a doubt I wanted to stay here and continue down this path. I had one year left before I finished my Master's degree, and I believed there must be a way to make this lifestyle permanent.

I glanced at my watch and then glanced up to see Turhan standing outside of the theater. We kissed hello and bought our tickets. He winked at me as we entered the dark movie theater. I leaned into his shoulder as we reclined in our seats. My heart had never felt fuller. I couldn't bear to think of it being any less. I couldn't bear to think of anything changing. How could a dream finally become reality and not stay that way?

FLEXIBILITY

ONLY ONE PART OF MY life remained in Seattle that now needed to be put on a plane. Make that two: my favorite felines. They had been staying with my mom since I moved, and it wasn't until I saw the little Corsican cats that I realized how much I missed them. They have been my little furry family for years that grounded me and provided a routine to daily life. After being apart for over a year, they were my responsibility and I couldn't pawn them off on family anymore. It was time to pack up their kitty knapsacks and have them join me in my new apartment, complete with a garden, fence, and place on the kitchen floor for their dinner bowls.

The elder cat was a six-year-old Maine Coon that I adopted when I lived in Portland. Rather, she picked me when I entered the shelter and she started purring up a storm the moment we locked eyes. I held her against my chest and she rubbed into my neck with her long whiskers and sweet disposition. Sold. I initially named her Jezebel, but that changed immediately when her personality became apparent: precious, innocent, sweet, teeny-tiny body. Her name was now officially Kit Ten. Not "kitten"; Kit Ten. Two words, two syllables, clap it out.

My other precious feline was a crazy little bundle of cuteness, only two years old, which came into my world when a previous cat had died. She was a Torby (combination of tabby and tortoise) with orange, yellow and brown coloring on her little body with a white chest and four darling white paws. She was small in size but loud in noise, meowing and talking often. Her given name was Peppurr, but that name didn't stick, either, and she preferred to be called Kitty.

Small, pliable and a complete baby most hours of the day (except when she was being crazy and aggressive).

With the names Kit Ten and Kitty, there would never be a doubt about what type of animals I had. Just wait until I start naming children. Whose names I already had figured out and squared away: Sale, Rent, and Lease. Because then every house, car, boat, and item for purchase would legally be for them. My daughter, Sale, would be accustomed to seeing her name everywhere, as in House For Sale—"A free home for my baby girl!" Car For Sale—"Get behind the wheels, sweetheart, it's all yours!" Treadmill For Sale—"Jump on the rubber mat and punch up those digits!" Of course, we would need to have a talk when she was older about things being "On Sale" because some things, such as teenage boys, should not be "On Sale."

In mid-August, I traveled back to Seattle with the intention of selling bedroom furniture, dishes, books, and a dining room set I no longer needed, and would then fly my little felines with me across the Atlantic. It was an efficient, practical plan that made sense. But now that it was time to put them on a plane, I became fraught with anxiety and could not sleep well for nights. Preparing the cats for international travel involved more steps than I originally anticipated: requisite visits to the vet for updated shots and health examinations; Obtaining approval from the United States Department of Agriculture for live animals to leave the country; Official documents had to be signed by all designated authorities and legible in both English and French; and then I had to prepare their crates in the best, most comfortable way for a long international flight. I padded their crates with foam to help temper the loud noises and hopefully protect them a bit from stressful flying conditions.

Then there were the things that were out of my control. I was not able to book them in the cabin with me, so they had to fly as cargo in air-pressurized compartments and then I would grab them at baggage claim. Luckily, quarantine was not required when traveling to France so I could pick them up upon arrival. Our travels took us from Seattle to Chicago with a slight layover, and then Chicago to Paris; no direct flights were in operation. It turned out every location where we took off and landed could not be warmer than 85 degrees, or animals could not fly safely. Not a reassuring fact considering it was the middle of August. And I discovered it was not a good idea to sedate animals during travel because the medication could have harmful effects on their hearts and little nervous systems, especially with the altitude changes.

Even as I did everything that was recommended, none of these preparations took away the emotional uncertainty I continuously felt about taking them on a long-distance flight. I considered not taking them at all, but that didn't sit well with me because I loved them, I missed them, and I knew the travel was a short-term event whereas being a family together would be a long-term reward. Plus, animals were flown all over the world every day and the airlines were equipped to handle their travel needs. The adventure would turn out okay once we returned safely to my home in Paris, snuggled up to take a nap together, and life would continue on as normal, only better. *Yes and no, but still go.*

Despite the rationale and pep talk, I was still not sleeping well. The morning of our flight I felt sick to my stomach and more nervous about flying than I had ever been in my life, which I'm sure their furry instincts picked up on. Clearly I was the one who needed to be sedated. Just knock me out now and allow me to wake up in my apartment, please.

My mom and I wheeled their crates up to the airport counter to check-in for the flights. My foot was tapping anxiously and unconsciously as I remembered to calm myself down; all would be fine. The flight attendant checked our flight path and said it was a miracle: this was the only day all week the temperature would be below 85 degrees in Chicago, so the cats could fly. I nodded in positive agreement; this must be a good omen. Then after checking baggage and final details, the two crates disappeared into the back luggage section and tears welled up a little in my eyes as if my heart was out now of my body and out of my control. It would all be okay. It would all be fine.

Upon boarding the first flight in Seattle, I stopped in the plane doorway to ask the senior flight attendant that both cats were on board and safe. She immediately went to verify and asked for my seat assignment. A few minutes later, she loomed overhead with a reassuring smile and a thumbs up signal. Then the captain stopped by my seat.

"Well I checked on your cats myself, just to make sure their cabin was all set, and both of them were alert and looking around, obviously curious." My shoulders dropped four inches.

"And, some good news about having this precious cargo on board is that we are given flight priority if the runway is busy, so we'll be sure to get to Chicago soon and safely." He nodded.

"Great, thank you. I really appreciate hearing all of this." He turned and went back up the aisle.

I exhaled and focused on relaxing as the remaining bags were loaded into the plane down below. All would be fine.

Four hours later, we landed safely in Chicago and I darted off the plane to search for a window in the airport to watch my two felines be unloaded from the plane. I spotted their little plastic beige boxes sitting vulnerably on the tarmac under the giant, expansive, metal wing of the plane. I couldn't leave the window until I saw what happened to them next. As the baggage carts and food vans whizzed by, I caught a glimpse of movement inside both crates and gave a silent cheer. After about ten minutes, a cart stopped right in front of them. A young man jumped out and picked up Kit Ten's crate. I watched as he peered inside and talked to her. He then picked up Kitty's crate and put her gingerly into his vehicle, talking to her as well. My heart smiled to see someone acknowledge them as live creatures and not another set of black suitcases. I finally left the window to find something to eat. It was going to be okay.

After two hours of waiting in Chicago, the longest part of our journey was about to begin. I boarded the international flight and again asked the greeting flight attendant if he could confirm that the two cats were safely on board. He said he would look into it while I took my seat.

Fifteen minutes passed while most passengers were loaded and seated, and still no word back yet on the felines. I went up to the front of the plane to confirm all was well with Monsieur Flight Attendant, and received the second thumbs up of the day: "Yes, they are on board! All ready to go!"

Exhale.

I returned to my seat and flipped through a magazine, relieved that all had progressed easily so far. The plane was about to take off, so I buckled my seat belt and started to relax for the long haul flight. It was going to be okay. Nothing to worry about. I flipped through pages of ads and articles.

Then a booming voice came over the seats. "Will the passenger with the two cats please identify themselves to a flight attendant?"

My stomach dropped to the tarmac. *Relaxing over.*

I pushed the red button above my seat and Monsieur Flight Attendant walked briskly toward me. He stopped at my row, put one hand on the back of my seat, and loudly stated, "I'm sorry, but the cats can't be on this flight."

I stared up at him stunned, speechless.

He repeated, "We can't put them on the flight today."

"Why? I was just told they were already on board and safe..." I stuttered, not understanding what had changed in only minutes.

The cabin grew quiet and more ears perked up to hear the developing details. He finally said, "They can't fly today because of a mechanical issue. There is no heat in their cargo compartment. They would freeze to death on this flight." The visual of that outcome froze *me*. Monsieur Flight Attendant was not winning any points for his bedside manner.

Holding it together, I asked, "So, what are the other options then?" Focus on a solution. He said he would check and dashed off.

I continued to breathe deeply while staring at the front of my magazine, remaining calm.

Monsieur Flight Attendant returned to my seat a few minutes later, and as if addressing the whole flight, said there were a few possibilities. The cats could stay in Chicago overnight, safe and secure in the cargo holding area, and then take the next flight to Paris tomorrow. He paused as if this was the best option. I stared up at him in disbelief. Leave them behind in a strange city for at least 24 hours while I flew to another country and had no way of checking on them? Completely ridiculous.

"Well, what is the other option?" Even tone of voice.

"Or you can get off the plane and get re-booked for tomorrow's flight with them. It would be the same flight as this one."

Numerous eyes were now watching our exchange. "There is room for me and both cats on tomorrow's flight? You're sure?"

"Come with me," he declared.

I jumped up to follow him to the front of the plane. He spoke to a man with a walkie-talkie who confirmed that he could put all of us on tomorrow's flight. They both stared at me expectantly for a decision. The plane was now fully loaded; every passenger was seated and seat-belted. With no time to weigh all of the pros and cons, the only thing I could do was follow my gut. I rushed back to my seat to grab my purse and magazine. Then I walked off the fully loaded international flight to Paris five minutes before scheduled departure.

The speed of this last-minute development propelled me into survival mode. For the few seconds I had to think about it, I knew I could not leave the cats behind in a random city overnight while I went on to another country. Who would be taking care of them? How would I be able to check on them and ensure they were on tomorrow's flight? How would I know they even made that flight and were not delayed again? What if the temperature was too high tomorrow and they weren't allowed to fly, and were stuck in Chicago for who knows how long? And how could I ensure they made it through French customs if I wasn't traveling with them? Plus, they would then be traveling for nearly 40 hours and would need more food and water. I wasn't going to leave them behind like excess baggage. We were a traveling family.

I marched back up the plank into the terminal escorted by Head Airport Guy and his walkie-talkie. Two airline employees at the desk started making hotel arrangements for this temporary situation. One asked Head Airport Guy if the cats could be put in the passenger cabin for this flight, but he said French customs does not allow animals to be transported into the country that way. She then asked if they could be put in the captains' quarters, and he didn't respond. He was reviewing papers with flight information and walked away urgently with his head down.

I was successfully booked on the following day's flight to Paris by one agent as another made calls to local hotels. She found a hotel that accepted animals, but then proceeded to tell me the airline doesn't pay the $50 additional fee for pets to stay in hotels; I would have to pay that charge. I stared at her in disbelief for a split second. Then I chose my words very carefully.

"The reason I am not on that flight is because my animals would die, per a flight attendant. I made every arrangement that was my responsibility for them to fly internationally—reservations, medical examinations, pre-flight requirements, USDA approval—and I paid for their tickets over a month ago. I understand that things change and emergencies happen. And if this were my fault, I would understand that the additional charge was my responsibility. But this situation is not my fault, nor anything I have control over, so no. I am not paying a $50 fee on top of my international plane ticket, two paid animal fares, and the inconvenience of being delayed for 24 hours after I was told everything was fine."

I held her eyes as she blinked back at me with no words. Little did she know I was well trained in staring contests due to my experiences with French government officials. Suddenly Head Airport Guy came back and interrupted our non-verbal exchange.

"Excuse me, ma'am. What does your baggage look like?"

I turned my head. "Both suitcases are blue. But how will you be able to find my bags?"

He responded with a blank look. "We have to unload the whole plane."

My eyes became saucers. The whole international flight had to be unloaded?

He continued. "The FAA requires that all checked baggage must accompany the owner. If you get off the flight, your baggage has to go with you. It could take two hours to do that."

Instant guilt flooded through my veins. I had no idea unloading the flight would be involved. The mechanical issue was obviously unexpected and last minute, and thank God the problem was found before take-off. But again, I was not going to desert my animals at this point and get back on the plane. My gut said to stick with my decision because I also felt like these people were trying to pressure me into what they wanted me to do without *getting it*. This wasn't about keeping an extra, over-sized suitcase behind; it was about two little beating hearts. Something did not feel right.

"So there is no other solution?" Pause. "Are you sure unloading the plane is the only option and there is nowhere else to fit two cat crates on that giant plane? I want to be on that flight."

Head Airport Guy quickly walked back toward the plane with his walkie-talkie to his mouth. I turned back to the counter agent, ready to finish our unsettled business, when Head Airport Guy returned by my side less than a minute later. "Hey, everything is fine. We found a solution. The cats are on board and you can get back on the plane."

Hold up. "You just found a new solution that didn't exist before? A safe area for them with no worries about any mechanical issues mid-flight or anything?"

"Yes, the cats will be fine in a safe area. You can get back on the flight now." A very content look sat on his face. Where did this sudden solution come from?

"So, I can get back on this flight—" And then it hit me. "—and you can avoid unloading the plane, having a two-hour international flight delay, and dealing with any backlash about not finding a place to put two small cats on a giant plane." He gave a silent huge smile.

"But where are my cats then? Are they with the pilots?" He didn't respond and only gave me a sideways look that could be interpreted as meaning "maybe." Then he quickly walked me back down the ramp to get on the plane.

Except when we arrived at the end of the plank, the 787 aircraft was already closed, sealed up, and ready to roll away from the ramp.

The flight was now about to leave with my cats and my baggage on board, but without me. *Awesome.*

Two airline employees began banging on the plane door and caught the pilot's attention. Then two flight attendants reopened the door with shock all over their faces, exclaiming loudly, "What is going on?!"

I brushed past them and walked to my seat while Head Airport Guy gave them a brisk explanation. I heard a few people whisper, "She's back..." as I returned to my vacant seat. Inquisitive looks came from every direction. If only they knew the two-hour delay they would have faced if I *wasn't* back on the flight. We all avoided a CATastrophe.

Cats on board, luggage on board, I'm on board, and the plane finally backed up two minutes later. I said a silent apology to my fellow passengers for the delay but at least we were only 15 minutes late for departure. And we didn't sit on the crowded runway for long. Perhaps the cats helped us get a priority take-off.

I tried to read, tried to watch a movie, and tried to sleep to get my mind off the unknowns of the nine-hour flight. I was curious where they were stored but quickly reassured myself that the crew wouldn't put them on board if there were doubts about their safety. Whenever I felt stress or worry creep in, I visualized giant angel wings wrapped around each crate, keeping them safe and cozy and protected from everything as we made this journey together. All would be fine. Wherever they were, they were safe with angelic protection. *Yes. Yes. Yes.*

Monsieur Flight Attendant and I exchanged interesting looks as he walked up and down the aisle handing over food, refilling glasses, and answering questions. He passed by my seat with eyes that said "We're talking about *you* in the back." But if he could translate my expression, he would know, "See, no animals had to die or be harmed in the duration of this flight."

Once I had a glass of wine, shoes off, and the cabin lights were dimmed, I realized the cats must be in the captains' quarters and perhaps the pilots ignored French customs requirements because they did not want to unload the full international flight. That would explain why they didn't tell me exactly what the last minute solution was.

The other thought that kept creeping up during the flight was about Turhan. I had asked him repeatedly if he could meet me at the airport to help move two cat crates and two pieces of luggage home, as well as be there for emotional support. But he pushed back each time and said he couldn't miss work, even for a few hours. His career was important to him and he didn't want to risk his job in any way. I steamed inside and denied my anger; a part of me couldn't accept that he didn't understand how stressful this was for me. I had called him from Seattle the day before flying and again asked for his help, if only for a few hours. He finally said he would try to be there. A part of me was relieved that he changed his mind, but another part of me was stunned that it was so much work to get his support. As the clouds passed by outside, I hoped he would keep his word and show up. After this ordeal, I would be beyond exhausted and would just want a shoulder to rest my head on.

Travel always required a certain amount of flexibility, of being open to unexpected possibilities and last minute changes as they came up. But I had never experienced it to this extent before. I couldn't allow myself to think of all the ways this could have gone wrong or been much worse, and it was because of how intently I followed my gut and intuitive hints even when there was no proof they were "right." Yet they always proved to be, as if those angels that were flying with the cat crates and guiding our plane to safety had a direction communication path to the best possible outcome for everyone.

Our flight arrived in Paris half an hour early. I gathered my personal items and made my way to the plane exit. As I approached the last doorway, Monsieur Flight Attendant was speaking to a very intrigued French Airport Guy. I heard him say a few phrases.

"...*la femme avec les chats... pas une problème maintenant, mais avant le vol...*" ...The woman with the cats... not a problem now, but before the flight...

"*Excusez-moi, Messieurs. Bonjour.*" They stopped talking immediately and stared at my French words.

"*Bonjour, Madame.*"

"*J'ai les deux chats. Elles sont avec les bagages, oui?*" I have the two cats. They are with the luggage, yes?

"*Oui, oui, avec les bagages.*" Yes, yes, with the luggage. French Airport Guy nodded enthusiastically as Monsieur Flight Attendant continued to stare in shock.

"*Merci, Messieurs. Bonne journee!*" I winked at Monsieur Flight Attendant since apparently winking was something I now did. Both turned away to find something else to look at.

After the nine-hour flight, the light at the end of the airport tunnel was seeing two familiar crates waiting for me in baggage claim at Charles de Gaulle International Airport. A young airport clerk was standing next to the luggage cart where the crates were stacked. My heart swelled as I saw one little nose sniffing the air in one crate, and in the other, small movements of life under the soft blanket. I ran up to them, gushing like a complete fool, and both cats perked up when they heard my voice. We made eye contact as Kit Ten rubbed against the front door of her crate, and Kitty gave a scared little meow from under her blanket. Poor babies. They had a long, scary day in a loud space. And maybe had to endure pilots swearing at them.

I added my two blue suitcases to the luggage cart and began to push through the crowds as nearly everyone who passed by leaned over to peer in at the animals and say hello. The enthusiasm and curiosity around the two animal crates was like I had a celebrity smuggled inside these little plastic boxes. People stopped and gawked, trying to say *bonjour* and peer inside as if Tom Cruise was being transported via pet crate. Make that TomKat.

I slowly pushed all of my possessions, both those with and without paws, through the arrival gates. The customs officers stood around making hand gestures, glancing left and right occasionally, and barely cared that I was pushing live animals passed them. Maybe French customs already checked their kitty papers upon arrival? Please tell me all of the pre-flight preparations were not a complete waste of time. It would have felt a bit more satisfying if someone stopped to request my papers, but no official seemed to care about my crates. I wore my now-normal French blasé expression and continued pushing on through the exit.

Turhan was standing anxiously in the arrival section, rocking from side to side, and I finally let out a big exhale, relieved to have support after sixteen hours of stressful travel. All was well.

We loaded into a taxi for the ride back to my apartment, one cat crate in the front passenger seat and one in the back between us. Turhan only rode with us halfway because he had to go back to work. The taxi driver took pity on me and helped move the crates and luggage into my apartment building's lobby.

I closed the front door to my apartment, and then bent over to open the front doors to the two crates. One cat dashed out eagerly; the other took a slow step and glanced around first. Then each feline tentatively ran along the wall, pause and sniff, stop and look. After inspecting the apartment for a few minutes, they curled up together on a blanket behind the futon. I followed their lead and crashed into my own catnap immediately.

Both felines slept in the quietest, darkest places they could find for two full days. I watched them slowly scope out their new tiny living quarters one evening as I prepared to start work at the American Embassy the next morning. I was over-the-moon excited with stomach butterflies to prove it, and yet had no idea what to expect or what I would be doing inside the walls of diplomacy. I had walked by the Chancery building at the base of the Champs-Elysées numerous times with curiosity and wonder since France was the United States' first diplomatic mission abroad with Benjamin Franklin as Ambassador. I couldn't believe I would be going to this place every day.

Like an eager student anticipating the first day of school, I laid out my clothes for the next morning and made sure my workbag was packed with First Day essentials: pens, notepad, laptop, unscented hand lotion, a granola bar, the right lipstick, emergency hair clips for a "good hair day gone bad" scenario. Unfortunately, I was still contending with jet lag and waking up before 10 a.m. the past two days had been difficult. I set the alarm clock extra early just in case my body fought back and didn't want to wake up and be an adult the next day.

Kit Ten and Kitty walked around and stared up at the walls regularly, disbelieving there weren't more rooms to explore. Kit Ten rubbed up against my calves, purring, trying to entice me to her food bowl for more. Kitty sat and meowed in the empty bathtub. I tried to offer her words of perspective about her new life:

"At least we are all together and a family again, Kitty."

"Meow."

"This new place will get better in time."

"Meeeow."

"The garden will be a lovely place for you to investigate when the weather improves."

"Meow."

"Transitions can be hard, but you're going to love France."

"Meooow."

"Now stop meowing."

"Meoowww."

It was early September and the air was still warm and stuffy in my small place at night. Unfortunately, there were no screen doors or screens on the windows, so I typically left the kitchen window open slightly to allow fresh air to circulate and the sliding door was cracked an inch.

With everything set for tomorrow, I fell into bed and tried to force sleep to arrive. Kit Ten was curled up at my feet, her little weight a welcomed presence for the past few nights. Kitty sat in the bathtub for a while longer, and then made her way to the bed. Relaxing and drifting, I reviewed what was needed for tomorrow... remembering all of the particulars of a daily work life... wondering where I will grab lunch... wearing high heels in the metro everyday might be painful... hope I hear my alarm —

BAM!

Something crashed. Or fell. Or closed. I sat up in darkness, squinting. Then jumped up to go to the kitchen. A tail was snapping back and forth on the outside window ledge.

"Kitty!"

She turned to look at me briefly and paused. Then she jumped down to the garden.

"Kitty!"

I ran to the sliding door and saw a little shadow dash into the bushes. Then it jumped through the front gates of the garden towards the street. Running to the front door of my apartment, I shoved my feet in shoes and grabbed keys. I dashed out the front of the building, doors banging behind me, whispering "Kitty!" loudly with each step. I ran around the front of my building. I glanced under bushes and looked in low, dark places.

"Kitty!"

I stopped to observe. Everything was quiet at this midnight hour. Nothing moved.

"Kitty... Come back..."

I walked with stealth silence along the sidewalk, ducking and glancing around corners and through neighbors' gates. She had never been outside before and had always been an indoor cat. She was skittish, fast, and anxious. Her fear of noises could make her run far and fast.

I didn't know which direction to go. She could have gone anywhere, any direction, any place. The possibilities were endless and there were no boundaries.

"Kitty... Kitty?... Where are you?" My voice increased in desperation.

Nothing answered. Nothing moved. Nothing meowed. The streetlights hummed as the only steady witnesses to this escape. I stood in the middle of the deserted street intersection right outside my apartment building, looking left then right in the moonlight. One hand was in my hair, the other was covering my mouth. My mind was foggy in disbelief. Kitty was gone?

I surveyed everything, trying to take in the best possible route to follow. I stared straight ahead for a few seconds, then turned around to look behind, trying to catch any type of movement. Nothing. Nothing at all.

I waited, and looked, and did nothing for a few more minutes. Then I hobbled slowly back to my apartment, stopping to glance around every few steps. She hated the trip over here. She didn't like the new small space. She didn't know where she was. She hated me for this decision to move her to France. She wanted to go back to her previous life.

And now Kitty was gone. The night took her.

STRENGTH

THE NEXT MORNING, I MIRACULOUSLY woke up on time for my first day at the Embassy, but my heart was heavy as I threw back the bed covers. I immediately rushed to look in the garden for a furry body hiding under a bush or waiting to come back inside, but saw nothing. I had left the kitchen window open all night in the hopes that Kitty would return on her own. She hadn't.

I crammed myself onto the standing-room-only 7:07 a.m. metro train that was filled with complete silence. My mind *wanted* to think about how to find my little cat, but I knew I *should* be focused on the first day of work, all of the people I would meet, and remembering where the restrooms were located in the giant building. I still had no idea what department I'd be working in and I hoped it was an area I had some actual interest in understanding. Ever since I found out I was accepted into the program, I had been focusing my intentions on working in the Ambassador's office. I knew I had the sophistication, work experience, and ability to do a great job, but the odds of that happening were so slim. The Embassy had many departments and offices, hundreds of people on staff, and a number of other professionals who could do the job. The Ambassador may not even have an intern in the office. But it was still fun to daydream about it.

After checking in with the security department and completing the typical initiation tasks, I met the other interns and exchanged pleasant conversations, but I also felt a quiet dread growing inside. They were all seven to nine years younger than me with little or no work experience. My prior responsibilities included managing people, hiring, training, coordinating events for hundreds of attendees, running meetings, and delegating tasks. But now I showed up here with intern status, and it hit me that I could very well be relegated to menial offices tasks, like filing papers, making labels, and possibly being regarded as naïve and inexperienced. My ego flared up. I hoped this wasn't a huge step backwards and a long-term mistake.

Assignments were handed out, and I received a name to report to in another building. For some odd reason, the name looked vaguely familiar... but how? I didn't know anybody at the U.S. Embassy. I grabbed my bag to go to a place that no other intern was assigned. I hoped this was a good thing.

Security escorted me to the other building and through more safety measures. Then I was led up a grand staircase to a quiet hallway and passed through glass doors to a row of offices. The name on the piece of paper in my hand was the name on the first wall plaque, so I knocked gently on the closed door. The door swung open and standing in front of me was the speaker who introduced me to the possibility of working at the Embassy in the first place: Kevin. Of all the hundreds of people who worked at the Embassy, in front of me stood the person who spoke to my classmates and I all those months ago about diplomacy. Now he would be my supervisor. And I swear we were nearly the same age.

We made introductions and exchanged pleasantries, and then I told Kevin he was the catalyst for this opportunity for me when I saw him speak months ago.

"So that means you've been in Paris for a while?" He leaned back in his cushy chair.

"Yes, over a year now. I have one year left to finish my Master's degree in international relations and diplomacy. This internship worked out great because I wanted to stay in Paris, but was originally offered a job in Geneva."

He raised his eyebrows. "Really? That's unusual to have two offers. So you're interested in being a Foreign Service Officer?"

"Maybe. That's what I want to find out. Internships are about test-driving a job, right? I've never had an internship before. This seems more like a full-time job, which I prefer, and I was intrigued by all of the experience I could gain."

"Yes, this is a full time job from nine to five every day. You are treated and regarded as any other office personnel and we expect you to fully participate in our daily duties. It sounds like this was a perfect opportunity that coincided with your education and living in

Paris. There is a lot to do in this office and I'm sure you can handle it."

"Yes, I'm sure I can too. But I have to be honest—I'm not really clear yet what I'll be doing here..."

"Oh, they didn't tell you?"

I shook my head. "No, I just walked in the door a few minutes ago and the whole morning has been a whirlwind of activity. I know you are a speaker, so I'm curious what my role is since I'll be reporting to you."

"Well, there are many things to do here in the Front Office."

"The Front Office?" Confusion crossed my face. Obviously I didn't know the lingo yet.

"Yes, the Ambassador's Office is also called the Front Office. You are the only intern assigned to the Ambassador's Office and to assist with all of her needs. We do the public relations work, meeting notes, write and review the correspondence with Washington, help with events. A lot goes on here. Can you handle it?" His tone was a challenging smirk.

My throat was dry and I was doing my best to keep my excitement professionally contained. "Can I handle it? I was MADE for this type of work! I'm going to be excellent at this job."

He nodded approvingly. "Good. Then I'll have you start by cleaning up my desk."

I stopped abruptly to stare at him, his messy stacks of paper, and the challenging smirk that hadn't left his face. He was testing me to determine how far his authority would go. I chose my words wisely.

"It might be a much better use of your resources to have me take care of more important priorities than filing papers. Besides, this desk doesn't look that messy to me. Everything is right where you want it, right? You're in control of what's in your space?"

He glanced around briskly. "Hmm. I do know where everything is on this desk..."

I nodded in agreement. "So then, there's probably very little to actually organize, and there are better uses of my work experience and education level than being your maid."

He stood up. "I think you are going to do well in diplomatic relations."

Kevin walked to the door and announced we were going to make introductions around the office, but first we would grab a cup of coffee.

After passing his initial test, we established an easy rapport.

Kevin was a very smart man with incredible knowledge of politics, world events, and the inner workings of diplomacy. Originally from the Midwest, he was only a year older than me and said he enjoyed pushing interns around because it was what he went through when he was an intern. He earned points for his honesty.

He had lived in Paris for nearly two years with his wife and young child. His previous posts in the Foreign Service were two African countries and an Indonesian capital, and each station lasted between two to four years depending on the needs of that job. Kevin explained that it was rare to find a post in a top European city this early in his career; being stationed in Paris, Rome, London, or Barcelona usually only happened after putting in years and years of service.

A thousand questions ran through my mind as he chatted away. I interjected, "So how did you get placed in Paris then if it's so competitive? How do you determine where you'll go next? Do you get to choose your next location?"

"Well, it was an interesting sequence of events that transpired. A last minute opening happened here when someone else moved to another post, and I knew the person who made the decision about hiring this job post. So it was timing and contacts and the fact that I was ready to make the last minute change that got me this job. My wife was excited to be back in Europe so I had her support, which helped."

"Does your wife work at all? She must not in order to move around based on your job?"

"She can be employed here in France because she has work papers, but no, she doesn't have a "regular job" if that's what you mean. She is a full-time mom and that is very important to us, obviously. It can be hard to have two working professionals in the Foreign Service. Some couples make it work though, and some locations are harder to be at, in general." We sat down in the break room, coffee in front of us.

"Those posts are called "hardship posts" and every diplomat serves in one at some point in their career. You can have a few hardship posts before receiving a preferred post, but the hardship posts are actually desired by some people because there is a high level of morale and the opportunity to wear many hats at once. Those locations are great opportunities to get a lot of experience in many areas."

As he talked, I realized this break room coffee was actually quite good. But I didn't want to admit that on my first day. What kind of reputation would I be creating for myself if I said I enjoyed forty-cent coffee?

He continued educating me about the life of a diplomat. "In terms of locations, there is no choice in the beginning. All Foreign Service Officers go through job campaigning every few years to determine their next posts. We submit a list of the top ten cities we want and then see how it plays out with the open jobs available, skills, seniority level, and networking. I start campaigning for my next post at least a year ahead of time. Sometimes two years."

"Wow, two years of campaigning for your next job? So you basically have to always be cultivating relationships and planning for the next place?"

"Yeah, exactly. So if a job post is for four years, let's say there is the first year of figuring out the job, two solid years of job competence, and then the last year is finishing up tasks and getting ready to move on to the next place. There's a rhythm to it that I like, but it's not for everyone."

I nodded quietly. Good information to know.

We walked back to his office and Kevin said that the Ambassador was out of the office and would return next week. I relaxed knowing I had a few more days to orient myself before meeting her. Her office door was open for cleaning, and I peeked inside to see a number of pictures with her and Colin Powell, the President, and other high-level politicians. I also noticed how plush and divine the carpet was. Wish I could take off my high heels for just two seconds.

Kevin escorted me to an office space that I would share with another diplomat who would arrive in a few weeks. I put my bag on the empty desk and took note of the cabinets, supply closet, phone, and whether any of the pens still had ink. I spent the rest of the day reviewing information and figuring out my schedule for the week. The office had giant windows with a lot of sunlight blaring through. I stared up at the sky and had another one of those unexpected moments of life reflection. Two years ago, I had been sitting at another desk, miserable and unhappy with my daily existence, and in a relatively short amount of time, I had created a new life that inspired, uplifted, and motivated me because I followed my heart. I had set the intentions, took action, trusted the process, released expectations, and now here I was: Drinking a second cup of forty-cent coffee in the Embassy and loving it. As I looked up at that sky with slow passing fluffs, I also knew it was the same blue canvas that Kitty was living under. I took a deep breath and resolved to look for her again tonight.

After work, I walked to the metro and called Turhan to chat about the events of my first day. He suggested we meet for dinner to talk about everything, but I declined; I had to go home and see if Kitty was back yet. *Just in case* she was home or trying to get home or sitting in the garden. We made plans for him to come over the following night after work to help me look for her, if needed.

I rushed through my apartment door yelling, "Kitty! Kitty!" and put down my bag, but there was no sign of her. Kit Ten was curled up on the bed and stretched to come meet me. I kicked off my shoes, picked her up, and strolled through the studio apartment three different times hoping that Kitty was hiding somewhere inside. Nothing. I checked the garden and under all of the bushes. Nothing. I changed into jeans and proceeded to walk around the neighborhood for over an hour looking for her. Nothing. I tried to put her out of my mind — *she's okay, she's an animal with survival skills, she'll be back soon* — and focused on my wardrobe choices for tomorrow.

My first week at the Embassy flew by with the usual beginning activities of a new job. More introductions, more tours, detailed explanations, continual questions, hunting down answers, trying to remember names, attempting to get up to speed on new topics, and low expectations for producing anything yet. Life was busy and full, and I loved having a daily work routine again, even as I dashed off to classes in the morning and then returned back to work in the afternoons. I bustled over to big meetings at the OECD and observed the inner workings of modern-day diplomatic conversations both formal (sitting behind big desks with loud microphones) and informal (quiet voices walking through the hallways, coffee mugs in hands). It was fascinating and intriguing; I wanted to soak up as much as I could every day.

But in the back of my head was always the fact that Kitty had still not returned home. For the past week I had been out looking for her every evening at dusk with dry cat food in each hand, yelling and whispering "Kitty... Kitty..." in as many places as possible. It became a habit that I couldn't go to sleep without knowing I at least *tried* to find her and *tried* to do something to bring her home. She had never been outside of the house before, much less gone for a whole week, and I knew she was scared and hungry. I doubted there were many sources of nutrients in this French village, unless she was eating croissant crumbs and *chausson aux pommes* scraps, which I would approve of since those should never be wasted.

Turhan and I spent the weekend putting flyers up all over the town. He made photocopies at work, so we decorated the town—legally and illegally—with an image of Kitty, the particulars of her personality, and the phone number to call if she was seen. By Sunday evening, a few phone calls had come in from eager people wanting to help, saying they saw her by Monoprix, or in the parking lot, or on a particular side street. But by the time I rushed over to the named location, it was not Kitty that I found but rather a similar looking cat sitting nearby or running off. My heart soared in anticipation only to be crushed by reality.

The following Monday, I had an appointment to officially meet one-on-one with the Ambassador. I had seen her picture, of course, and saw her return to the office Friday afternoon, but I had not spoken with her yet and I was nervous. I had no idea what to expect, although Kevin and others in her office expressed high regard for her abilities, demeanor, and professionalism. But no such luck at garnering any more insights. Turned out everyone I worked with was respectful and professional. Or just observing me first before divulging any more information.

I arrived early to work to move things around on my desk and make sure I had what I needed for our meeting (which was nothing, really). I entered the lobby of her office five minutes early to show I was punctual and responsible, and to chat with her assistant, Sue.

Sue had been working for the Ambassador since her appointment began three years ago and took her position of guarding the Ambassador's schedule and duties very seriously. She was the one person in the office who "knew all" and could grant, or deny, access as needed. I sat on the lobby couch exchanging small talk with Sue, all the while resisting the urge to push my toes into the plush, thick carpet. It was so tempting, though.

Right on time, the Ambassador's office door flung open and she made a strong entrance into the lobby. She had short, stylishly coiffed blond hair, eyes that sparkled with intelligence, and a well-tailored navy pantsuit that flattered her soft complexion. Gracious and smiling, she invited me into her polished den. I followed her into the office as she closed the door behind us. High ceilings and big windows with dramatic warm curtains allowed light to stream in effortlessly from the left. A seating area was in front of the windows as the Ambassador welcomed me to take a seat on the couch.

"Would you care for water or coffee, Molly?"

"Water would be great, thank you."

A striking wood desk commanded the back of the room with a wall of large bookcases behind it, all decorated with books, pictures frames, and trinkets. To my right was a small circular desk for meetings and work gatherings. Fresh flowers sat on most tabletops. The ubiquitous neutral colors enforced the feeling of diplomacy. Again, I resisted the urge to take off my high heels and give in to the beige carpet softness.

The Ambassador was a career politician who landed this prestigious post after being a Congresswoman for years. She was skilled in the art of human interactions and communication, and I had no doubt she was a keen observer of human behavior and relationships; I sensed her personable qualities right away. My immediate impression was that she was very astute and very little got past her because she was always taking in the surroundings, reactions, and conversations of those in her regard. She would definitely notice if I took off a shoe.

We chatted amicably about the workings of her office, what she expected and needed from my position, and the current priorities she was focused on. I took notes actively and asked questions along the way. A few times she nodded thoughtfully before answering, and always demonstrated that she was present in the conversation. The half hour flew by, and as our time ended, I left feeling she was well placed in this role as Ambassador. I sensed goodness about her I couldn't quite describe and I even wondered if I was idealizing her in some capacity. I felt proud to be in her office, and I hoped to do the best I could for her in the short time I was here.

The rest of the day was filled with meetings, note taking, and office mingling. I made the rounds to speak with every Foreign Service Officer who was available to ask them a few questions about their job and priorities with the hopes of understanding everything better. The conversations were endlessly fascinating. One senior officer was a noted expert on Chinese relations. One female official was married to another Foreign Service Officer and she talked about how tricky it was to find a joint post where both of them could be stationed. One man told me about his life before the Foreign Service when he was in the private sector and made more money, but this was really the job of his dreams. Another officer had been to more than twenty countries in his career and was thrilled to be in Paris, finally. I heard how all diplomats' children went to international schools, not to mention the amazing education they received outside of the classroom. Even though they felt lucky to be in Paris, they all knew this time wouldn't last long; it never does. Many mentioned how they were in the process of campaigning for their next posts. Every diplomat had stories they were proud to tell, and I sensed they also had stories they could never tell. Obviously those were the ones I wanted to hear the most.

On the metro ride home, I remembered a book I read when I first arrived in Paris called *A Lady, First* by Letitia Aldridge. Ms. Baldrige is best known for her etiquette expertise, time in the Kennedy White House, and public relations proficiency, but *A Lady, First* chronicled her years of working for two Ambassadors at the U.S. Embassies in Paris and Rome. She was the Executive Assistant to Ambassador and Mrs. David Bruce in Paris from 1948 to 1951, then stationed in Rome from 1953 to 1956 to work for Clare Booth Luce and Henry R. Luce. Her stories and anecdotes about both international cities at that time inspired me to dream bigger than I ever would have on my own. Now nearly 60 years after her tales of Parisian life and working at the American Embassy, I entered the same address where much was similar (the grand entrance, the view of Place de la Concorde, the continually evolving relationship between France and America) and much was different (the political climate, the leading priorities, the currency). Not that my short stint and intern status compared to her years of international service, but I felt like I was at least on the outskirts of that same dance floor, watching safely from the sidelines and knowing a bit about the main moves. After reading the book, I thought her life in international relations was so glamorous and avant-garde. And an amazing demonstration of what could happen when you went out into the world with a dream.

Another workweek whizzed by. I spent each day learning, observing, doing, asking, and rushing to keep up with meetings, deadlines, and current global events. There were regular weekly meetings as well as bigger bi-weekly gatherings, and I could tell which days were more important than other days by the quality of ties, suits, and shiny shoes that filled the corridors. I knew the security guards by name now and we had brisk little chats every morning and every evening about their kids, the business of the day, and of course, the weather. Weather might seem like a boring conversation topic to most, but I actually appreciated it; it was an instant commonality to converse about regardless of rank, status, or appearances. A reliable equalizer.

My ego flared up at times when I was referred to in a condescending manner by a few people, but I learned to let it go. I was starting over in a new professional area, and part of the package meant starting at the bottom to learn the most. If my status was viewed as *lowly* that only reflected my temporary ranking, but not my intelligence, knowledge, or professionalism. I resolved to demonstrate my maturity and competence through my communication standards, posture, and actions, and not through reactions or words. After my times in Monterey, Greenville, and Portland, I was very well versed in starting over and jumping into new situations; the transition phase from brand new to being established had value. Plus, I had observed in my career how people who were so intent on always proving *something* eventually shot themselves in the foot because their perspective was too limited and they were overly concerned with other people's opinions. All I needed to do was show up and be excellent. And a cute outfit never hurt.

After living in Paris as a foreigner and having numerous international friends, it was also really nice to be in the daily company of other Americans. I felt a sense of "home connection" and knew I could reference American culture freely and easily without extensive explanations. Plus, I was excited to see familiar catalogs and magazines sitting on desks: *Lands' End, L.L. Bean, J.Crew, Glamour, O* magazine! Having an APO address allowed the familiarities of home to come across the ocean at no additional charge. I was so out of touch with American life that I devoured every magazine lying around. I had no idea what new movies were coming out, which television shows were popular, or what top songs were dominating the airwaves. And what's a Pussycat Doll? Is that a new toy for Christmas? I hoped it was for ages 18 and older.

I showed up to the Embassy every day looking to work and learn as much as I could, but I was silently struggling with the heartache and grief around my lost Kitty. A missing animal might sound trivial to some people, but my animals were my heart and when they were not okay, I was not okay. I had to professionally carry on as best as possible and learned to turn the heartache off until 5:01 p.m.

On the second Saturday that Kitty was gone, my friend Lynn and I spent the day searching the town together. My scaredy-cat would be hiding somewhere discreet instead of venturing out into chaos and activity, and I didn't think she would go too far. Lynn and I searched near the apartment, then ventured farther out to increase our inspection territory. We climbed up side fences to peer into hidden backyards and poked our heads inside closed garden gates and chateau entryways. When anyone asked or inquired about our actions, we showed them a flyer and they immediately responded with encouraging words. The French love animals immensely and understand how furry friends are family members, too. We ran out of flyers to hand out, but carried on the search until we were both exhausted and hungry.

I returned home to feed Kit Ten dinner, trying to appreciate my time with her and not take her presence for granted. But there were two dinner plates on the floor and only one had been used for a week and a half. I hoped Kitty wasn't starving to death. Or hurt. Or worse.

By Sunday afternoon, after ten days of no Kitty sightings, I sat on the futon exhausted. A constant sadness over her being gone had not left my body and now it took me by surprise. I didn't realize how much this situation was wearing on me. I felt so drained. Discouraged. Defeated. Animals run away every day and I could only do so much to find her. But regardless of this logic, I couldn't give up; I couldn't stop searching for her. I couldn't go to sleep at night without knowing I at least *tried* that day to find her and bring her home. Even if my efforts were to no avail and to no meows, I at least slept a little better each night knowing I tried.

Sadness suddenly overtook me. I began praying aloud for more help and more support right now. I needed more assistance. More support. More *something* because my daily efforts were taking their toll. And I didn't want to continually impose this search on anyone else. Turhan was doing a lot to help when he could and my friends were generously helping when they were available, but it was my own sheer determination and feeling of responsibility that was driving me to do everything I could. I needed more help, more support, but I didn't know from who or how to get it.

I dried my eyes, then grabbed a handful of dried cat food and made my way out of the house with a fiery new resolve. I brought Kitty to Paris to be with me and then she had the audacity to run away? That cat owed me money for her plane ticket! Money doesn't grow on trees and cats don't fly on planes! She owed me for this trip! I stomped down the street to the chateau on the corner, determined to find her based on this new motivation.

"Kitty, plane rides aren't free!" I peered through a black iron wrought fence into a giant yard. There were tons of bushes on this property and since it was just down the street, I knew she would love to live—

"*Excusez-moi… Mademoiselle?*"

—in a place that had so much grass, sun, and hiding opportunities. She might be on this property—

"*Mademoiselle?*"

—and moving farther back to the depths of the bushes, closer to the house—

"*Mademoiselle?*"

I whirled around away from the fence, finally comprehending that someone may be speaking to me.

An older couple was standing a few feet away. He was tall with dark hair, soft eyes, and wide shoulders; she had short grey hair, warm brown eyes and was holding her shirt collar closed with one hand, a packet of cat food in the other hand. He was holding one of my flyers.

Monsieur took a step forward. "*Bonjour, Mademoiselle. Vous recherchez pour votre chat perdu?*" Hello Mademoiselle. You are looking for your lost cat?

"*Uh… Oui, Monsieur, Madame. C'est vrai, mon petit chat est perdu.*" Yes, Monsieur, Madame. It's true, my little cat is lost.

"*Nous avons vu votre flyer que le chat a été perdu. Ma femme a effectué une recherche pour chats perdus depuis plus de 30 ans. Peut-être que nous pouvons vous aider, si vous avez besoin d'aide ?*" We saw your flyer that a cat was lost. My wife has searched for lost cats for more than 30 years. Maybe we can assist you, if you need help?

I stood stunned, speechless. These strangers were here… to help me? On a Sunday afternoon they came to find me… and to offer their assistance for finding my lost cat? When only moments ago I was crying and asking for more support and help…

They were my answered prayers standing right in front of me.

And I had completely forgotten my manners. I quickly composed myself to make formal introductions between Marie, Jacques, and myself. I shared with them the details of my search thus far, where I had been looking for Kitty every night, and that I had received a few phone calls from my flyers, but they have turned out to be the wrong cat. Marie and Jacques discussed the situation amongst themselves, looking up and down the same streets I roamed every night. They began to assess where she may have run off to based on traffic noises, hiding places, and food sources. I tried to understand everything they were saying, but my French wasn't as good as I would have liked it to be. And I was just too stunned that these complete strangers cared so much about my little lost American cat.

I showed them where I lived, just a block from where we are standing, and pointed out the street-level garden Kitty exited from. We exchanged email addresses to stay in touch over the next few days as new comrades on a joint mission. I called Turhan right away to tell him about this unexpected generosity from strangers.

"Wow, what nice people." He was as stunned as I was.

"I know. French people love animals. This is probably the perfect country to lose an animal in. I can't imagine this kind of assistance at home. Everyone is too busy with their own lives to even stop and read a flyer."

"So Kitty will come home now because more people are looking for her and she'll be more famous."

"I hope so. It's so weird to only have one cat instead of two." As I said this, Kit Ten rolled over onto her back. She probably loved all of the attention, actually.

Turhan offered to come over the middle of the week to help search again. I hung up and fell asleep quickly.

The next day at work, I emailed Marie and Jacques to thank them for their time and offer of assistance. They responded within a few hours with an offer to update my flyer with more information and a better picture of Kitty; a color picture, in fact. I sent back the best image I could find and asked how much I can give them for the cost of color copies. I didn't receive a response.

I was walking home from the metro station that evening, ready to take my high heels off *right now*, when I saw a bright image on the first telephone poll I passed. It was a piece of paper with a little orange, brown, and white cat staring at me with big eyes and perky ears. My heart swelled at the image of Kitty; the new flyer was eye-catching and prominent. I stopped to review it as other people walked by and glanced at it, too. They exchanged small talk about "*le chat perdu Kitty*" the lost cat Kitty until their voices trailed off up the street.

I walked up the street and saw more, more, more white flyers on telephone poles, public boards, even in shop windows. The flyers were in more places than I would have thought to put them. I strolled through the village square and looked around at all of the visual dots of white paper. Kitty was everywhere.

I didn't have their phone number, unfortunately, so I emailed Marie and Jacques right away with my excitement about their flyers. I told them I would be out looking for Kitty this evening at dusk and that their work had made me feel so appreciative and inspired. I was probably coming across as an overemotional American, but I didn't care. My gratitude for their energy was huge.

I strolled the streets and whispered "Kitty... Kitty," for the thirteenth night in a row. Marie showed up further down the street. She had cat food in her hand and was holding her collar again, as if to keep her throat safe from the wind.

"*Bonsoir, Madame. Merci beaucoup pour les flyers. Ils sont incroyable. Les colours sont parfait...*" Good evening, Madame. Thank you so much for the flyers. They are incredible. The colors are perfect...

"*Je vous en prie, Mademoiselle. Jacques a fait les flyers toute suite et nous avons apprécié leur mise en place autour de la ville.*" You're welcome, Mademoiselle. Jacques made the flyers right away and we enjoyed putting them up around town.

I nodded my head in appreciation and shared that it was very kind of her to take the time, especially as I worked full-time during the day and felt tired at night. Every little bit helped. She nodded with understanding. We looked around the neighborhood for a little while before parting ways.

Two nights later, she joined me again as we prowled the area and tried to think like a small cat, afraid of the world. Marie told me that today she went to shop owners and restaurateurs in the neighborhood and spoke with them personally about the missing cat. She told them that the cat could be near the garbage looking for food or hiding in a back alley corner. She said to please call her if they saw anything. More flyers were in store windows than ever before. Not only did it help to have her ideas and support, but it helped that she was French. If I went to each shop owner with my bumbling French they would most likely be annoyed and not want anything to do with a lost American cat. But with Marie and Jacques as my allies, they could relate and communicate in ways I could not and it was priceless. They were my earth angels.

Dusk skies turned to darker navy skies as we wandered the silent side streets looking for a cat that may not want to be found. We passed an office undergoing construction and two men were folding up a ladder. One stepped outside to smoke a cigarette. Marie paused to show him a flyer.

He held his cigarette in one hand and a flyer in the other. He brought the cigarette up for a puff, squinted his eyes, and then pointed with his right hand.

"*Le chat irait cette direction.*" The cat would go this direction.

Marie and I both followed his hand's guidance.

Marie responded, "*Peut-être, oui. Mais il ya beaucoup d'endroits pour se cacher dans cette direction.*" Perhaps, yes. But there are many places to hide in this direction.

Construction Worker already had his logic thought out. He explained that *this direction* was away from the main streets, it had many gardens to explore, and there were a few back entrances to restaurants for food. It would be cat heaven.

Marie nodded in agreement. Then they discussed possible routes a cat would take depending on the time of day and which day of the week the cat was moving around. Tuesdays and Saturdays were market days so the cat was probably not very active those days if she was a scared animal.

I attempted to listen to their discussion. Mostly I was just amazed at how much time and thought they were putting into which way my cat would have ran away and which days of the week she would be out looking for food. The logistics, as well as the pros and cons of each direction, were all analyzed and evaluated. This conversation never would have happened back home. It was just one more reason why I loved France.

We parted ways with the Construction Worker after almost ten minutes. He gave us a gruff, "*Bonsoir et bon chance, Madame et Mademoiselle*" Good evening and good luck Madame and Mademoiselle, as he stubbed out his cigarette.

Before leaving for the night, Marie provided reassuring words that we were doing all we could and we should not give up hope. I walked back home realizing how much Marie and Jacques were my angels.

By the weekend, the flyers around town were curled at the edges and some were removed due to illegal posting. Marie and Jacques said they received a few more phone calls, but nothing valuable. Until Sunday afternoon when Marie called me urgently.

"*Molly, nous avons peut-être trouvé Kitty! Nous avons reçu un appel téléphonique d'un homme qui a vu un flyer et a vu un chat dans sa cour! Nous arrivons plus avec le chat maintenant. Dans la voiture!*" Molly, we may have found Kitty! We received a phone call from a man who saw a flyer and saw a cat in his backyard! We are coming over with the cat now. In the car!"

Her voice was excited and speaking fast, and I understood the main points: May have found Kitty, coming over in a car now!

I rushed outside when I saw their car pull up in front of the garden. A man was in the backseat holding an orange, brown, and white cat to his chest as my heart started beating faster. It could be her! It could really be her!

They opened the back door so I could see the cat and my shoulders sank as my smile faded. No one said anything as I shook my head no.

Marie and Jacques apologized profusely and with embarrassment for disturbing me with false hope. I explained it was no disruption at all; I completely appreciated their attempt at finding my lost cat. The car pulled away with another person's found cat.

And it was that evening that I finally did what I probably should have done earlier. I completely surrendered to the situation. I finally accepted that this was out of my control. I finally accepted that I had done all I could do. I had to let her go. For the first time in three weeks, I didn't go out looking for her that night. For the first time in three weeks, I accepted the circumstances fully. Kit Ten curled up at my feet as I curled up and felt the loss of my little cat. I silently hoped she was okay and out there having a fun adventure that she loved.

I had no more strength. All I could do was surrender as the wind softly hummed through the open kitchen window. I still wouldn't shut that window, just in case.

LEVITY

I WOKE UP MONDAY MORNING extra tired and worn out, my movements slow and clumsy. I missed the 7:07 a.m. train and had to wait ten minutes for the next one. I stepped on people's feet and bumped into shoulders during the whole ride. I needed another weekend to rest.

Arriving at the office, I shook off the morning blues and transferred into professional mode. The security guards were especially cheerful this morning, which I greatly appreciated, so I offered them a forty-cent cup of coffee as a way for all of us to start the week off well. Then I knocked on Kevin's door and we reviewed the upcoming week's priorities and events together. Our meeting was over when he received a phone call from the manager of his apartment building about replacing an appliance in his government-sponsored home.

It has been very interesting to observe the perks of diplomatic status all around the Embassy. I knew about the benefits of diplomatic immunity in foreign countries where diplomats were given safe passage between countries and were protected from being prosecuted or arrested for violating any local laws. With a diplomatic passport, they avoided going through the headaches of acquiring a long-term visa or dealing with local bureaucracy.

But it was the daily perks and lifestyle benefits that were the most intriguing to me. For example, diplomats had special license plates on their cars that allowed them to park anywhere on city streets and they were not required to pay a parking ticket. American cars were shipped with their owners to each post so the vehicle earned some serious frequent flier miles. Housing was provided upon arrival, complete with American outlets for American appliances, and there was care and security given to living quarters. All possessions and pieces of furniture were packed up and shipped around the globe. Acclimation services were available for every possible need, and only a phone call away, such as resources for learning the local culture, assistance for living needs, personal language lessons, recommendations for best restaurants and attractions, and an expansive social calendar filled with numerous events and activities to meet new friends and other Americans.

Members of the Foreign Service arrived in first class luxury compared to my cargo arrival. I could easily dream about their conveniences, and yet they had no idea the struggles, obstacles, paperwork, lines, planning, exploring or emotional trials required of landing in Paris all by oneself. Even though we were all Americans, I was most certainly on the other side of the window looking in on an easier life of international travel. I appreciated even more that I could share my experiences with Turhan.

At the end of the day, I met him for dinner at our favorite Vietnamese restaurant in the eleventh *arrondissement*. After mindfully surrendering to Kitty's departure, I could at least try to get back to living a normal life. I decided to send her love every day. Before falling to sleep, I imagined a beautiful gold cord that stretched from my heart to her heart, wherever she may be. I saw this cord as a beautiful light that guided her easily and stayed with her always. She would always be safe and loved, no matter where she roamed. This visual brought me comfort and a level of peace that I would always feel connected to her. Plus, it helped me sleep better. Until I was startled awake early one morning due to loud chaos.

The kitchen window was left open every night with the hopes that Kitty would return the same way she exited, but there were a few times I wondered if leaving the window open would invite another cat inside. At 4:03 a.m., I awoke to the sound of hissing and a deep internal growl. I hazily sat up and saw two shadows run through the room. Kit Ten's tail and spine were puffed up in the moonlight like a huge growling poofball chasing something around the room...

Oh shit! Another cat got into the apartment through the open window and Kit Ten was protectively trying to chase her away!

I grabbed my glasses and stumbled out of bed to follow the action. The shadows ran back into the kitchen. Kit Ten had the other cat cornered as I reached to turn on a light and —

"KITTY!" I screamed entirely too loud for this time of the morning. The cat on the flyers all over town was now licking her empty dinner plate enthusiastically right in front of me.

"Kitty!" My eyes filled with tears as I dropped to the floor and touched her little body; she was only skin and bones. I immediately poured dry cat food onto her plate and continued to touch her in stunned disbelief and shock. She was there. In front of me. In the kitchen. Alive. Eating. Home. And before doing anything else, I stood up and slammed the kitchen window shut.

I petted Kitty passionately as she inhaled food she hadn't eaten for over three weeks. She started to purr while she ate. She must smell strangely different after being outside for so long; of course Kit Ten didn't recognize her. Kit Ten settled down in front of her plate as well, thankful for the early morning treats, and we all sat on the kitchen floor as a family. Kitty ate and ate and ate as I inspected her little frame. She didn't have any scratches or blood anywhere, luckily, but I decided to take her to the vet just in case. I removed her plate after five minutes so she didn't make herself sick.

She rubbed up against my side. "Kitty, I'm so happy you're home... I can't believe you came back after being gone for over three weeks..." I sniffled tears of joy.

"Meooow." She rubbed against my leg.

"We missed you, I'm so happy you're home."

"Meow." Kit Ten started to growl again as she smelled her long-lost sibling.

"I need to get some sleep now. You can have more food before I leave for work."

"Meooow."

She slurped up water noisily for over a minute.

I fell back to sleep for a few hours with both bodies curled up against my legs. I made myself wait until seven o'clock before texting everyone I knew three simple words: Kitty is HOME. The happy responses poured in on my phone all the way to work. I was the only one on the metro smiling at every stop. I glided into work feeling lighter than I had in weeks.

I emailed Marie and Jacques with the incredible details, and invited them to come over and meet her tonight after work. They were so happy to hear the good news and accepted my invitation, but they thought it was best to stop by later in the week. Kitty needed to relax and be safe at home for a few days.

The rest of the day sailed by, and when five o'clock finally arrived, I rushed home. As I walked up the main street, new flyers were on every telephone pole and in the shop windows: "*Retrouvé!*" Found! Below Kitty's picture was a message to the town:

Nous vous remercions pour vos appels téléphoniques et des informations sur ce chat disparu. Nous sommes heureux de dire qu'elle a été trouvée et est en bonne santé et heureux à la maison. Nous vous remercions pour votre soutien!

We thank you for your phone calls and information about this missing cat. We are happy to say she has been found and is healthy and happy at home. Thank you for your support!

Marie and Jacques received phone calls of happiness and congratulations from a few people after posting this message. It was amazing to experience how much people cared about animals. France was the perfect place to lose an animal because there was amazing support and understanding for them as valuable family members. My apartment building houses quite a few little furry friends and people regularly stop to talk to the animals as they talk to their owners. And sometimes talking with the dog is more enjoyable than talking to the person.

With Kitty home, safe and secure, I returned to my normal habit of staying at Turhan's apartment a few times during the week in the eleventh *arrondissement*. We regularly explored restaurants and bistros in his neighborhood since every kind of food one could possibly crave, chew, and devour existed in the city. In addition to the Michelin-starred French favorites and internationally recognized hot spots, there was cuisine from all over Europe and beyond: Italian, Greek, Japanese, Lebanese, Spanish, and all kinds of Mediterranean selections. But in this buffet of culinary choices there was still one noticeable void, and I told Turhan we had a new mission to accomplish: we must find a true, authentic Mexican food.

In my travels throughout the city, I spied a few places that *appeared* to offer authentic Mexican entrees, such as a chicken burrito here or a few tacos there. But upon closer inspection, the ingredients did not add up, just like the place Trisha and I had dined at: no proper beans, no rice, no salsa and the tortillas were always some type of crepe thing with no corn ingredients at all. So the search for quality rice, beans and tortilla chips continued, and I knew in my heart of hearts that there must be a decent Mexican restaurant in this big, amazing city. God would not create such a beautiful place as Paris, France and then take away delicious Mexican food. He would not do that to us.

With a *frijoles* famine in my life, I found myself thinking about the one place I never thought I would dream about on this continent. The one place I never thought would be important. The one place I never anticipated missing while I lived in Paris. I was officially dreaming of Taco Bell. A simple bean burrito for ninety-nine cents. A soft taco supreme. A chicken fajita with grill marks. Right this very moment, I could be holding in my hands an orange piece of paper that wrapped around each item, keeping it warm, soft and accessible. And then I'd unwrap my burrito while it was still melting, or a crisp taco shell that—

Oh. I glanced left and then right. Am I drooling on the metro? Was I chewing while staring out the window? I hoped my jaw was not trying to bite into a taco. I pretend to wipe salsa from my chin and glanced up above the doors to count the stops until I arrived at Turhan's apartment. My obsession was too unbelievable to share with anyone who knew what Taco Bell was, and it certainly wasn't worth explaining to my international friends. They would laugh loudly and say, "You are dreaming of the equivalent of a Mexican McDonald's?" I was just starting to move beyond all of the McDonald's jokes and stereotypes they loved to tease me about as a representative of America, and I certainly did not need to offer this new fast food material.

Then one day after work, Turhan returned to his apartment where I was hanging out and announced he just saw a Mexican restaurant on his way back from an errand. I stared at him in disbelief. Is it possible that a Mexican restaurant could be hiding right under our noses here in the eleventh *arrondissement*? Could it really be this close? But I knew not to get too excited yet. I'd been fooled before and had learned enough in my twenty-nine years to have healthy skepticism. I asked with obvious doubt, "What does the place look like?" Appearance would be the first test of a true Mexican establishment.

"It was very colorful with these little lights hanging everywhere... and some type of striped carpets on the wall... very bright... weird music playing..." His voice faded. "It was kinda odd, really..." He now pondered the sight he just saw with a confused look.

My eyes got big and wide. "Were the striped carpets on the walls like small rugs? Kinda shaggy? Like they'd been in the dryer too many times?"

"Yeah..."

"And were the little colorful lights hanging randomly from the ceiling, with no order? "

"Yeah…"

I hold my breath with anticipation, then ask, "And were there piñatas?"

"Piñatas? Like paper animals for children filled with stuff?"

"Yesss…"

"Oh yeah, I think I saw a few of those…"

I jumped up from the couch! "You saw piñatas? Seriously? Really?!" Clapping my hands with excitement!

"Yeah, I saw those piñata things and shaggy rugs and it's a really colorful place… with some fluorescent beer signs on the walls…"

At that moment, the heavens opened and mariachi music filled the air. *Olé!* A Mexican restaurant was found in Paris! *Olé!* Beans and rice and corn tortillas for everyone! *Olé!*

I celebrated with the Macarena dance and put on my coat. He'd understand my excitement once we arrived. We headed out the door before noticing it was way too early for eating dinner in Paris. I couldn't walk fast enough and I couldn't stop talking about what I was going to order: "A chicken, bean, and cheese burrito with rice on the side. And guacamole. And chips and salsa. And a margarita on the rocks. And I don't need anything to be wrapped in an orange piece of paper to enjoy it, I swear!" I held up my right palm. He had no idea what the orange piece of paper was about nor why his girlfriend was suddenly a Mexican jumping bean.

We found the restaurant on a side street and it was exactly how he described it. Striped shaggy rugs that could double as ponchos; colorful little lights strung erratically across the ceiling from front to back as if a fiesta would start at any moment; *piñatas* hung in corners and sat on display surfaces; and *mariachi* music filled the air as we stepped through the double doors. We had arrived. I released a big exhale. There was no need to get on bended knee before entering the establishment. The year and a half I spent in *carnitas* celibacy was now officially ending.

We slid into a booth near the window and Turhan looked around at the scenery with obvious confusion. It was clear he didn't understand why *this* was the place I had been seeking for a good meal. It was tacky, overdone, and lacked any type of confidence, like it was trying too hard to be something real. His expression was a mixture of confusion, doubt and intrigue. He asked one question that said it all: "Why?"

"Why what?" I responded, skimming the menu with no focus. "Honey, this is *exciting*. We are *here*. Let's not rush ANYthing." I patted the top of his hand. His furrowed brow and confused smirk communicated his amusement of All That Was Tacky. I focused on my hunger and aalllll the ordering possibilities. My pulse quickened when I saw "beans," "cheese," "corn tortilla" and "burrito" in the same description line. Should I get some meals to go, too?

The chips and salsa arrived promptly. We ordered margaritas on the rocks. My body started to relax. It was possible we had just found the Mexican Holy Grail in Paris.

After sipping his margarita, Turhan looked around at all of the random decorations and asked again, "Why?" It was still his only word since we entered. I attempted to explain why Mexican food was a special novelty to me.

"Finding a place that makes *real* Mexican food in Paris is like finding a restaurant in Turkey that makes *real* American food."

"But McDonald's is everywhere," he responded with no delay. Hilarious. I gave him a notable glare across the table. He winked in return.

Just like in the States, our food arrived on hot plates that were not to be touched. Just like in the States, I touched the plate, burned my finger slightly and remembered I wasn't supposed to do that. But yummm... the burrito was actually really good. The corn tortillas were made from real corn, not fake crepe tortillas. The chicken, bean and cheese were excellent. There was a side of real guacamole. And the salsa even had chili peppers in it. *Olé!* Turhan ate his whole plate of enchiladas, then finished off my remaining burrito.

After our plates were removed, I silently noticed one thing lacking in the meal. I didn't want to make a deal about it... I didn't want to acknowledge it out loud... don't call up the Michelin authorities... It's okay, all will be fine... but there was no rice. No rice anywhere. No rice in the burrito or on the plate, none to be found. Rice is a staple ingredient in Mexican food. How can rice be overlooked in a Mexican restaurant in a Mexican dish? Maybe this place wasn't as real as the Mexican *piñatas* and ponchos it showcased.

Turhan shook his head as we exited All That Was Tacky and the *mariachi* music faded behind the closing doors. His lack of words and amused expression still communicated his thoughts clearly. I offered another insight for him to consider. "Think of this as an introduction!"

"An introduction to what?"

"An introduction to Mexican food that can only get better from now on!" Smile. "Mexican food loves salsa dancing, by the way. The two of you will eventually be best friends." He smiled at this thought, then grabbed my hand and twirled me with a salsa move as we danced down the Parisian boulevard back to his apartment.

I had made myself at home in his place, staking my claim in the bathroom with shampoo, a toothbrush and emergency makeup. A shelf in the closet had some extra clothes and socks, and my purse and jewelry always went in the same place in the living room. Since my apartment did not have a washing machine and his did, I brought a suitcase of dirty clothes over to his apartment every weekend to wash and air dry all of my goods. On Saturdays, socks, underwear, shirts, pants and skirts were scattered all over the living room couch and kitchen as every chair back and hanging area became a drying rack. Everything was always completely dry by the time I returned to my apartment Sunday evening.

When Turhan stayed at my place during the week, we had to be more attentive to the train schedule because it only came every ten minutes. The metro comes every few minutes in the city, but outside the city limits, we had to plan our timely transportation needs more diligently. We gave ourselves two trains to catch—either the 7:07 a.m. or the 7:17 a.m.—so I knew we had to leave by 7:13 a.m. at the very, very, very latest to be on our last option. We couldn't afford to miss the 7:17 a.m. train and make both of us late to our desks.

One September morning, we had a harder time than normal getting out the door due to a variety of little factors. By 7:14 a.m., as the apartment door shut behind me, we were officially at risk of missing our train and there was only one thing to do: run. As a woman who wears high heels, running was not an easy or elegant activity. But I had a meeting with the Ambassador that morning and there was no way I could be late. It was time to pull out all stops and just go for it.

We were over halfway to the station when I heard the train starting to approach. I tried to pick up my pace, but with a heavy computer bag and these (super cute) shoes, I was not able to run. Luckily, the road to the train station was downhill so I attempted to quicken my speed with the help of gravity. As I was moving along, I heard from my right side an uneven sound approaching from behind: clooop-clop, clooop-clop, clooop-clop. Then the sound was next to me. Then the sound was in front of me. Then the sound was passing me: a man with a limp had just flown by! My best effort was being beat by someone with a limp?! Turhan was jogging ahead, and looked back and laughed when he saw who had passed me.

"Come on, honey!" He yelled. "Pretend you have a limp!" Then I started laughing at myself, which only slowed me down more.

The train was braking at the platform as we approached the front doors of the station. It only stopped for five seconds, so there was no time to waste. Turhan was a few paces ahead of me and plowed through the ticket turnstile with the intention of holding the train door open for both of us, creating a slight delay. But he ended up hitting his leg on the turnstiles and now found himself limping to the train platform. I click-click-clicked my way through the turnstile as Turhan held open the train door, Superman-style. The buzzing sound went off as the doors started closing. With less than a second before they slammed shut, I jumped with pointed toes into the train and landed in his arms, panting and laughing in my dress and heels. My feet were sore. He had a limp leg. We were both out of breath. And it was only 7:17 a.m. in the morning.

We tried to regain our composure and share a water bottle, but couldn't stop laughing at the whole ordeal and the sound of the guy with a limp passing me from out of nowhere: his clooop-clop, clooop-clop, clooop-clop paired with my click-clock click-clock click-clock down the middle of the street. Our fellow French commuters stared at our morning laughter and deep breathing. Ahhh yes, what a way to start the morning: exercise, deep breathing, and laughter. The whole ordeal was exhausting and we vowed never to leave late for the train again. Hopefully. As we rode into the city, I rested my head on his shoulder while he read *The Economist*. We kissed goodbye at the Auber train station and began our separate workdays in different parts of Paris.

Fall crept into Paris and the trees turned wonderful vibrant shades of gold, squash, and scarlet. I loved how the air became crisper and scarves were a daily requirement once again. And a highly anticipated annual event occurred the first weekend of October called *Nuit Blanche*. *Nuit Blanche*, White Night, was a spectacular evening when most of Paris's notable and impressive attractions stayed open late into the night for light shows, light spectacles, parties, and light displays strategically highlighting architecture and special places in the city. When the fall weather cooperated, it was an incredible way to see Paris and take in some unexpected festivities.

During the day, Turhan and I ate a late Saturday brunch,

grabbed some groceries at Franprix, and went shopping on Rue de Rivoli for a new pair of casual shoes he wanted. During the early evening, we met a group of friends for drinks and dinner, then the seven of us walked around the city, following the crowds of people who swayed through the city's bright nocturnal lights. We discovered hidden attractions and navigated groups of people standing in the street, hanging out on bridges, ebbing in and out of museums, and took pictures of rare light sights.

Our group spent over three hours wandering around and now it was nearly 2 a.m. on the Ponts des Arts. I was tired. Turhan's feet hurt in his new shoes. We couldn't think of anywhere else worth walking to as we stood along the side of the bridge, the Louvre looming overhead. The group conversation faded from my ears while they sorted out which metro station each person needed to go to. I looked over the railing at the flowing Seine as my mind tiredly thought about what I needed to do tomorrow. I was suddenly jolted back to the present when, from out of nowhere and with no context to any conversation, a friend in our group confidently and loudly asked, "Turhan, are you going to propose to Molly?"

I froze. My breathing stopped. My stomach sank into the Seine. *Did I hear that correctly?* I didn't know where to focus my eyes. Who asked that kind of a big question in a group setting while I was standing right...

And then his voice said confidently and without hesitation, "Yes."

The water flowed below as I stood paralyzed on the bridge. I turned my head to the left to make sure my body was still working. I had never felt so caught-off-guard in my whole life.

Our friend turned to me and smiled big. "Lucky girl..."

I stared at her with no expression, frozen with disbelief. I looked back down at the murky Seine. My mind didn't know where to go: to the question, to the timing of it, to the feeling of intrusion over such a personal issue... or to his answer. We hadn't talked about this direction for our relationship at all, so I didn't know what to do with this revelation. I couldn't look at him yet. The Seine splashed up against the bridge pillars, the side embankments, the bottoms of docked boats. I watched the water's movement as I stood stationary in its wake. The Louvre reflected grandly off the waves.

Minutes later, as the conversations ended, I felt Turhan grab my hand and the group disbanded. I was roiling, moving, emotional; the river. He was focused, confident, sturdy as always; the riverbanks.

We headed east back to his apartment, walking quietly and holding hands in the dark as his new shoes created a bigger blister with each block. I broke the silence.

"*Nuit Blanche* was a fun night. I wish I had experienced it last year."

"It would be even better if the metro were still working. My feet would like that." He walked confidently, trying to hide any pain.

I nodded quietly. The moon faded in and out amongst the clouds covering us. I leaned in closer to his shoulder as a soft rain began to fall. Did tonight really happen? Was that question-and-answer session real? Although it was the last thing I expected to hear, I might actually be floating effortlessly like the Seine now.

THE FALL DAYS WERE BECOMING shorter as Paris moved through a 24-hour progression of light gray, gray, dark gray, and blackness by 6 p.m. I regularly stopped by the bakery across from the train station on my way home from work and grabbed *un pain de sesame* to nibble on for the last few minutes before my key went in the front door. The streets bustled with people in all directions who were ending their workday and beginning their evening routines. There was something to savor in these times of transition that took us from one priority to the next.

My cats had adapted to their new living quarters fairly well in the past few months. I came home from work to find the two of them curled up tightly in the most random places: crammed into a paper bin in my desk, on a shelf under the bathroom sink, on top of a stack of towels in the cupboard, or sharing a highly coveted chair in front of the heater. Fuzzy faces in all places. They managed to regularly find new spaces to dominate during the day, then snuggled up next to me in the evenings. Kitty looked up at the kitchen window from time to time, and when I caught her glancing up there, I yelled a firm "NO!" She scurried off in complete denial. After a pause, I heard a slight meow come from the bathtub.

As I cooked my *pave de canard aux trios poivres* and seasoned the bright *haricots verts,* I thought about Turhan's answer on the bridge. I allowed myself to *go there* with the future possibilities, but I had so many questions. Would I move into his apartment or would we find a new one? Would we have a wedding here in Paris or elsewhere? What about getting permanent jobs and work visas and all those other dots that needed to be connected? And I still had not initiated a conversation with him about any of this because a part of me wasn't ready to know the answers. Why was I hesitating?

I told Trisha about our night out while we hung out at her place. She nodded with a big smile. "Ohhh, I knew it!"

"See, I told you it was a good idea to get that book on Turkish culture."

"So what would you guys do? Live here, live in Turkey, live in the States? Where would you work?"

I inhaled deeply. "I have no idea, Trish. There are a lot of questions, and it's funny because I feel resistance about them. Like I don't want to figure it out or talk about it yet."

"Yeah, that's cool. You'll figure it out." I decided to join her in her positivity and leave it at that.

The weeks flew by as I managed school, work, living at my place, and staying at Turhan's a few nights a week. I felt a new lightness in the rhythm of my daily life. There was a lot of movement right now, but it was exciting and invigorating more than overwhelming. I was doing more work for the Ambassador and absorbing as much information as I could every day. I had been given more important duties to accomplish and was now familiar with the protocol and customs of her office. Meetings always began with everyone standing when she entered the room. She waved in greeting and made her way to the front with an air of feminine authority: graceful, warm, elegant. There were times when I thought she was made for this exact political appointment.

In my short tenure, I learned that an Ambassador never really knew how long they would be appointed to a post. Although diplomatic stability with the host country was an asset for both sides, situations could change due to any number of possibilities and an Ambassador could be called back home on the next phone call. A State Department need or a Presidential request can come at any time, and a new Ambassador could be appointed quickly and swiftly; there were no guarantees for term or timeline. It was a regal and exciting post, but could disappear with the swipe of a passport.

The Ambassador's schedule was full every day with numerous meetings, events, and responsibilities that were booked weeks and months in advance. Social events happened regularly at the Ambassador's Residence with passed appetizers, live music, and an ongoing exchange of business cards and private discussions. Events were typically scheduled right after work so people could stop by before going home for the evening. By eight o'clock, it was expected that the evening would wrap up and everyone would be on their way. If that didn't happen, the family dog was allowed into the party. And the dog was a crotch-sniffer. If a guest hadn't felt like leaving yet, they would probably feel like leaving soon.

The first week of November began normally as I rushed eagerly into the office and out of the chilly Parisian drizzle. I made my morning rounds to check in with Kevin, who could be hard to track down. Then Sue grabbed my attention with a whisper and called me into the Ambassador's lobby. Her short blond hair was newly styled by her favorite coiffure in the sixteenth *arrondissement* and her bright blue eyes didn't miss anything that happened on this floor. She was standing with a few pieces of paper in hand.

"Hello dear, how are you doing?" She removed her glasses off the tip of her nose and put them on the desk.

"Very well, thank you. I'm really enjoying being here." I rested one elbow on the counter. This office was so comfortable for some reason.

"Good, I'm glad to hear that. Come over here, I need to ask you something." She motioned for me to come behind her desk and sit down. I glided around the side and sat tentatively in a chair next to her. Am I supposed to be here? Isn't this area out of bounds?

She glanced at the computer to check the latest incoming email, then asked, "Are you staying busy? How are things with Kevin?"

"Yes, fairly busy. It varies from week to week, as you know, but it's going very well. Kevin has been very informative, although I can't always find him when I need him. But for the most part I feel like I have everything under control." I smiled and re-crossed my legs. Where is this line of questioning leading?

"Good." She nodded her head sincerely. "So I have a question to ask you. Are you familiar with home leave?"

Shook my head. "No, I'm not. What is it?"

"Home leave is something required by the State Department for all Americans serving abroad. We must return to the U.S. for a certain amount of time so we are aware of current events, exposed to our culture, and to ensure we are connecting with home regularly. It's so we aren't away for too long and lose touch with our country and where we came from."

"Ahh, I see." Nodding with understanding.

"Home leave is usually for a month, about thirty days or so, and I have to do mine before the end of this year. So I will be going home in a few weeks and be gone for most of December." She glanced back at the computer as new emails arrived. The Ambassador's chauffeur walked in with some mail from another office. Sue reached for the latest incoming envelopes and sorted them instantly by priority level.

"So, I know you have some things you're doing for Kevin, but after speaking with him, we were thinking you may be a good fit to cover for me while I'm gone." She glanced at me sideways.

Did I hear her correctly? "Really?" Pause. "Is it… Is it okay with the Ambassador… and other people?"

"It was originally the Ambassador's idea. She wanted to use resources that were already on staff as the budget is tight, and she wanted someone who knows what is happening in her office. Plus, it's a fairly slow time of year, in terms of business dealings so there will mostly be social gatherings and holiday events, in addition to the day-to-day affairs. A lot of meetings are being re-scheduled for next year as people travel and go back home. It's manageable. I know you can handle it."

My heart was beating with giddy excitement. "Wow… yes… I would love to cover for you!"

Sue smiled big. "Wonderful. You will get the hang of things easily, I know it. I'll train you before I leave so you'll know how she prefers things to be done and what needs to be completed every night."

I was trying to remain composed as all of this sank in. A dream come true. Not to mention all of the quality time I'll have with this carpet…

Just then the office's double doors opened and the Ambassador strode out with papers in hand.

"Sue, I need this returned to Colin upstairs. I signed it, but I want to make sure he sees my notes. Do we have word on tomorrow's luncheon yet?"

"Yes, four Ambassadors have responded affirmatively and your reservations are set for one o'clock. Do you want the car here by 12:30 p.m.?" Sue asked while the phone began to ring.

"12:30 p.m. is perfect." The Ambassador turned to me as Sue answers the phone. "How do you like sitting behind this desk? Did Sue ask you about taking over for her?"

"Yes, she did and I told her I'd be happy to. I know I can handle it and do a good job for you while she's away. I'm honored. "

"Good. I'm happy you will accept. I think this is a great temporary solution. You have such presence." She flurried her arm and then she walked back into her office as Sue hung up the phone and winked at me. Did the Ambassador just say I have presence?

Because I know I'm not walking around with presents.

Sue stood up. "So, I need to run and get some things done, but why don't you check-in with me tomorrow and we'll go from there? Sound good?"

I pushed back my chair and stood up as she moved to leave her desk. "Wonderful, I'll talk to you tomorrow then."

We exited the office simultaneously. She turned left to the staircase and I turned right to my office. I walked briskly to my desk and grabbed my cell phone to call Turhan with the exciting developments. I needed to focus and get some work done, but I was buzzing with excitement and anticipation. This is definitely a time to celebrate with a forty-cent cup of coffee. I walked to the break room as Turhan picked up on the second ring.

"Oui?" His professional tone of voice was in effect.

"Honey, I have something more exciting to share with you than finding Mexican food in Paris!"

FINDING TOP

KEVIN STRODE CONFIDENTLY INTO THE lobby and up to my desk, resting his elbows on the counter. "I need to schedule an appointment with the Ambassador for this afternoon. Can you put me on her schedule?"

I turned away from my project and logged into the computer. "Let me check. What time would you prefer?"

"Maybe between 2 p.m. and 3 p.m.? My day is pretty open, but after lunch would be best." He glanced around my desk. Papers were strewn everywhere, but I knew which ones were important and where everything was laid out. It was my version of organized chaos. As I glanced at her schedule, Kevin continued, "Look at this. Now I'm coming to *you* and asking for assistance. A lot has changed in a few months, huh?"

I nodded and typed in his name for an appointment. "Yes, it has. I just put you on her schedule for a fifteen minute appointment at 2:30 p.m."

He leaned over the desk a bit more, his blonde hair neatly coiffed. "I guess you owe this whole opportunity to me since *I* introduced you to the possibility of working at the Embassy in the first place, huh? And *I* gave approval for you to do this job for the Ambassador, so luckily you were good to me earlier." He smiled big. "Without me, you would only be in graduate school right now."

This man was never around the office, he had no idea what I had been working on for the past few months, and now he walked in to claim credit for everything. I respected him as a colleague in a higher-ranking role, but I could still have a little fun. I glanced over my glasses at him and raised my eyebrows as he started to walk away.

"Oh Kevin, one more thing," I said loudly.

He stopped and turned around.

"I am really busy today with a project I need to finish up for the Ambassador before her holiday party. I was wondering, since you just told me your day is pretty open, do you think you can straighten up my desk while I step out for a moment?" I stared at him with a deadpan expression. The Ambassador was at her desk and the office doors were open, so she was possibly hearing my request for his help.

He glanced at the open doors and adjusted his suit buttons as he slowly walked back towards me.

"Ash. What?"

"Well, it would really be more about supporting the Ambassador than me since it's her project. And you wouldn't be too busy for her priorities right now, right?"

"Mum—"

"Great! Thank you *so* much. Just don't touch any of those things on the left side and try to keep this looking good. I'll be back soon!" I breezed by him and out into the hallway to grab a sip of water. *The Universe is balancing itself at this moment in time.*

"On second thought—" I glided back in as he moved back and forth on his legs, not sure if he should go or stay or if the Ambassador was listening. "Never mind. It may be too confusing to sort out at this point. Here"

I reached into my purse and pulled out forty cents. "Have a cup of coffee on me." Smile. "Don't worry, my graduate school budget can afford it. See you at 2:30 p.m."

I turned back to my work. He took the change and strode confidently out the lobby. If he could dish it out, he could take it. And he certainly had no problem taking my forty cents.

Working for the Ambassador meant non-stop learning, maneuvering, organizing, and prioritizing. The holiday season may mean less professional responsibilities, but there were an increasing amount of visitations and social events springing up every day. She was constantly receiving appointments and invitations that required a response with decorum and protocol so as not to disappoint or offend the other party when conflicting obligations arose. Her daily calendar was packed with meetings and pressing issues, and she often required additional information before certain events and speaking engagements. I tried to be a step ahead of her needs whenever possible. Or at least just keep pace.

One of my favorite duties was greeting and welcoming visiting Ambassadors. After they passed through security, I met them in the lobby and guided them up to her office efficiently. They were consistently very elegant and congenial people with a presence that was both captivating and overwhelming. After a first awkward conversation with one Ambassador in which I was a bit distracted, I learned to review any neutral topical events happening in their country an hour before I greeted them. I gauged their comfort level and followed their lead, engaging in small talk while walking together and waiting in the lobby. And I was always proud of myself for resisting the urge to invite them to take their shoes off and enjoy the carpet while they were here.

The Ambassador hosted her annual Christmas party at the Ambassadorial Residence. I had been helping her all week to make last minute arrangements and to ensure everything was covered even though she had a professional event organizer on staff. I double-checked that both Turhan and I were on the invite-only guest list. After seeing all of the preparations and planning that went towards making this event happen, I'd hate to be stuck on the other side of the security gate and miss the festivities.

The holiday party began right after work, so I made sure Turhan knew we couldn't be late to this event; that's tackiness on an international scale. Our names were on the guest list, spelled correctly even, and we passed through high-level security with no delays. The Ambassador stood at the front door as people arrived. She did not miss a single visitor and focused on the personal connection, always the consummate hostess.

As we approached, she greeted me with an enthusiastic "There's my girl! Welcome!" We exchanged *bisous* on each cheek. Turhan was right behind me, large and looming, and she greeted him with the customary kisses as well. Then we eased into the atmosphere with no hesitation, and soon we were inspecting the food, shaking hands, finding my favorite colleagues, and enjoying the lively ambiance.

Diplomats, organizational leaders, State Department Officers, office personnel, and Ambassadors from all over the world arrived and filled up the vast entertaining space. The weather was mild on this mid-December evening so the back patio was open for fresh air and outdoor socializing. Beautiful live music accompanied by a solo singer serenaded the living room and soft dim lighting created a halo effect around the looming Christmas tree. A wonderful spread of appetizers and entrees provided the central places of conversation as people weaved in and out of conversation topics and groups to make strategic connections. Turhan kept whispering in my ear that he was the only male not wearing a tie. I hadn't even noticed. But I suppose if I were the only woman in jeans I would feel out of place, too. He brought up his lack of a neck noose every twenty minutes, and every time I reassured him it was fine, it was fine, it was not a big deal.

"People aren't even looking at us anyways!" I said, looking around. "We're the Nobodies here, isn't that wonderful! I bet the men are envious of YOU." He grunted while looking around to see who was looking at him.

I continued. "Then go upstairs and grab a tie from the Ambassador's husband's closet." Smile.

He grunted again. I offered more solutions since the magic wine was doing a great job. "Walk around and tell everyone this is supposed to be an official 'non-tie event' and they are *out of line*." Smile.

"Start telling people strip poker begins in two minutes and to play you must remove your ties NOW." Smile.

"If anyone notices, just casually say it isn't customary for the holiday stripper to wear a tie at diplomatic events." Smile. He was trying to be serious since this was still a serious issue, but I was wearing him out and he started to smile.

"Unbutton your shirt even more. That's what I came here to see, YEAH!" I yelled a little too loudly and threw my fist in the air. A few people turned their heads. Turhan moved so his back was to them and he was blocking me.

He leaned in and whispered, "These are all good options, I don't know which one to choose. So I will go get us some more champagne and think about it."

I kissed his cheek and responded, "More alcohol is the best solution of all!"

I put my fist in the air again because when you are a Nobody you can get away with that kind of behavior. He walked away playing with the collar of his shirt. A few minutes later, he returned with two glasses of champagne as the Ambassador took the microphone and began to say a few words about the evening.

I leaned over into his ear and whispered, "Where's your tie?"

PARIS GOES ALL OUT TO makes the most of its attractions on the last night of the year. Festivities in all forms and fashions spring up across the city. Sophisticated restaurants offer exquisite dinner menus with the best champagne to toast the evening; elite night clubs promise food, music, drinks and dancing until all hours of the morning; bistros and brasseries have special events and music performances to ring in the first minutes of the New Year; dinner and dancing affairs are held at Michelin restaurants and elite hotels; and of course, the iconic Eiffel Tower attracts thousands to its annual spectacular fireworks display. Reservations fill up weeks in advance to all celebrations and prices are sky high, often double and triple the cost of a normal night. Taxis are hard to find, the metro is not always reliable, and the weather is not promising. But New Year's Eve in Paris is an amazing night.

Considering all of these factors, we were lucky a friend offered to celebrate the old year becoming the New Year with a party at her apartment in the twelfth *arrondissement*. Her place nicely accommodated twenty people (which made it big by Parisian standards) and it had enough space for food, drinks, and dancing. Plus, it was in a great location because Turhan and I could walk back to his place afterwards without relying on a taxi. Regardless of the probability of walking blocks and blocks, I still had to wear my super-cute three-inch pink heels that matched my super-cute pink sateen skirt perfectly. I had to.

Although this night was customarily about the New Year that was arriving in a few hours, I always feel a sense of reflection on December 31st for what the previous year brought. And this year was incredible: Meeting new people from all over the world. Loving my school studies. Meeting Turhan at my birthday party on the Champs-Élysées. Our summer holiday in Corsica. Flying my cats to Paris. Kitty returning home. Working at the Embassy. Enjoying the simple pleasures of Parisian daily life. Hearing he wanted to marry me. And now a joyful celebration of all that was sure to come in the next 365 days.

Before midnight, we danced on the parquet wood floors of an old Parisian apartment and took pictures of the girls, pictures of the guys, pictures of the group, pictures of the good times. We continued to eat, talk, drink, dance. Outside, the rain was fierce, cold and pounding. Inside, the laughter was loud, the music played non-stop, the air was warm, and the smiles were endless. The fun was contagious and the evening only became louder.

This was a good place to be. This was a very good place to be.

There were huge unknowns ahead, but to be in this moment right now, I felt alive. Happiness. Contentment. Ease. I hoped the upcoming year had the spirit, promise, and fun that this night captured. I hoped this momentum continued and this life of my dreams moved ahead perfectly. There were no guarantees, but right here, right now, was good.

Turhan and I kissed in the New Year at midnight and raised glasses of French champagne in a toast with our friends. He twirled me on the dance floor as I managed to keep my champagne glass safe, balanced and well out of harm's way.

Finding Top is the place of true north where a trapeze artist reaches the highest possible point of her soaring attempt. She is at the pinnacle peak of her jump.

It is the point of no wind, no movement, no to-and-fro motion. No hair in her face. No effort in her muscles. No thoughts of what she needs from her body. No distractions coming from the north, south, east, or west. Her body is weightless. She exists in a place of pause and peace.

If her eyes are open, she will have a perspective that she has never seen before. An expanded view of the terrain below, a new appreciation for all she has accomplished, the chance to exhale the old and inhale the new, the ability to look forward and backwards simultaneously.

If her eyes are closed, she will feel a calm sensation in her body and the quietness of the moment. She will sense everything around her with heightened awareness. She will feel her whole being in this position, in this place, at this time. She will appreciate all that is around her at this point of culmination.

Finding Top is a point of victory.
A summit.
A celebration.

Then gravity awakens.
And the downward descent is activated.

GRACE

I LOVED PARIS IN JANUARY. There was a luminescent quality in the winter air as the newness of a fresh year soothed the streets after the hustle and bustle of holiday activities. Gloves, scarves, hats and long coats decorated the sidewalks. A hot *café crème* and warm croissant tasted different this time of year. The semi-annual *les soldes* were underway and encouraged Parisians to leave the warm comforts of home to find irresistible seasonal bargains. Christmas lights and decorations still hung, albeit a little lower, throughout every *arrondissement*. *Les gallettes des rois* (the King's cake) filled up every *patisserie* window as seasonal treats that carried *une fève* (a lucky charm) for one lucky person to find, with the reward being crowned King or Queen for the day. The nights were longer but the warmth of the sun felt bigger. January was a rare blend of anticipation with little expectation as a new trip through the calendar began.

My last days at the Embassy had been easy and swift. I collected contact information and exchanged details with numerous people just in case a job opportunity came up. Due to my work with the Ambassador, I had also formed a relationship with the second-in-command at the Embassy, the Deputy Chief of Mission, and when I shared with him that my time was ending soon, he offered to keep an eye open for any possibilities. Even if the offer was hollow, or I was forgotten in a month, or it was just a nice thing to say in the hallway, I would still follow-up and check-in with them just in case. They assumed I wanted to be paid (yes) and said there was no budge in the budget. Plus, the main hindrance was that I did not have a legal work visa in France and that was not something they could fix or take care of for me, which I knew. My expectations were low, but hope was priceless.

I started the New Year by connecting with almost every person I had met in Paris and inquired about leads, suggestions, or ideas for my job search. I applied for everything I heard about. I asked questions of my professors and school contacts. I set up appointments with friends of friends who may know the right person to reach out to. I hit the ground running because my motivation to maintain this life was stronger than anything else. I spent January writing and researching for my thesis, as well as searching diligently for a job. I could make this happen. I knew it.

The highlight of February was a surprise birthday party for Turhan. I had been planning the event for over a month and it had been a bit nerve wrecking at times because I kept wondering if he knew what I was up to, or if someone would accidentally mention the secret plan, or would it really be a surprise to him? The party was planned for a Saturday night. I told him I had to meet a friend for dinner and he should join us later in the night. I went to the club to meet our friends and then texted him when it was time for his grand entrance. As he walked into the club, a collection of twenty friends yelled, "Happy Birthday!" His shocked expression and non-winking eyes were the marks of genuine astonishment. The party quickly started with a celebratory round of drinks.

The evening was fun and festive, but I had been feeling undertones of discomfort between Turhan and myself for a few weeks now. Like something was off between us. More distance and space. Sometimes silence and awkwardness. Less connection and communication. Less... something. I couldn't put my finger on it exactly. But, I reasoned that relationships expanded and contracted naturally and this was just a phase we were going through. It was normal and a non-issue. My discomfort would pass, I was sure of it. I tried to shake it all off as we danced and drank into the late hours.

Turhan's family came to visit days after his birthday. His mom, dad, and older brother took up most of his time for over a week as he played Parisian host and translator. We agreed that dinner would be a nice way to make introductions, so I arrived at Turhan's apartment one evening ready for an enjoyable time. But it quickly became apparent that tonight would be a struggle on both sides of the dinner table because his family did not speak English and I did not speak Turkish. I knew this beforehand, of course, but I had no idea what the situation would actually be like until it was real. Turhan was relied upon to translate conversation back and forth, and it quickly became exhausting and difficult to keep up with what was being said. As the minutes progressed, talk digressed.

His mom prepared a wonderful home-cooked meal of feta cheese, olives, tomatoes, and bread, and the centerpiece was a delicious meat entrée presented on cooked eggplant slices and lettuce wraps. The whole meal was fresh and filling, but after finishing my plate, I could see that my small stomach disappointed his family; I couldn't keep eating all of the food that was being offered to me. The evening grew increasingly uncomfortable until the only sound at the dinner table was crickets.

Silent smiles. Generous arm gestures toward more food.

Rabbits eating grass in a dew-covered pasture.

Kind eyes. Sideways glances. More polite expressions.

Clouds passing slowly overhead.

The thought bubbles above all of our heads clearly said, "Is this over yet? How do we get out of this?"

More crickets.

Finally, Turhan's brother brought our empty plates to the kitchen, and we all chimed in to help too urgently, like statues finally coming to life. I helped clear the table to demonstrate I was raised properly and valued family meals. At least that's what I hoped carrying three plates at once translated to in Turkish.

I eventually exchanged polite goodbye gestures and slight hugs with each member of his family. His mom smiled warmly. His dad continued to stare at me intently. His brother disappeared into the bedroom.

Turhan walked me out of the apartment and we said goodbye in the hallway. We kissed goodbye, but our lips missed. I left his apartment feeling tired, uncomfortable, and bizarre. Why is nothing connecting right now?

My 30th birthday arrived a few weeks later with the realization of how BIG thirty felt. It was not just the number on a birthday card or a place off in the distance where life would be sorted and settled. It was here, in front of me, and seemed to be a place of life reflection. And did I like everything that was being reflected back to me? Thirty certainly held more questions than answers.

The day's agenda was packed with an early afternoon birthday massage, a coffee in the fifteenth *arrondissement* with my friend Lynn, and then a haircut in the late afternoon before I met Turhan for the birthday highlight. A romantic dinner cruise on the Seine. He surprised me with this idea a few nights ago and thankfully, the cruise ship he found wasn't *too* touristy.

Turhan met me on the pier, a dozen red roses in hand. Then the two-hour dinner cruise sailed up and down the Seine, passing major sites on both sides of the river. The air was clear with only a few clouds as spring was slowly arriving again day by day. The three-course meal and glasses of wine were delicious, but the discomfort between us was still there. Our conversation began to lag halfway into the cruise, and the second half of the meal was spent quietly orchestrating forks, wine glasses, and glances out the window. We were accompanied by the slow setting sun and bright bursts of color at first and then the second hour was in darkness and quiet as the City of Light twinkled all around us, beautiful but not revealing any deeper secrets. Why did our relationship feel off still?

I had become good at pushing down, pushing away, pushing off the growing uncertainty I felt between us. On some level, I couldn't see our future paths matching up, but I also didn't want to see the possibility of parting. *I loved him, I adored him.* How could this not work when we had so much going for us? I kept telling myself things would work out and come together, but it sounded like I was trying to convince myself of something instead of listening to myself for more information. We never talked about getting married or what he had said on the bridge. *Why didn't I want to bring it up?*

The framework around my future in Paris wasn't looking very promising. The main obstacle in my job search was an inability to get a work visa. As an American, I needed to be sponsored by a company to work legally in France. The sponsorship must be initiated and completed by the hiring company and involved tons of paperwork, bureaucracy, time, and fees. On top of that, why would an employer choose me in the first place when a citizen from any of the other 27 European Union countries could be hired on the spot without work visa sponsorship? I had to find either a specific job that was practically created just for me, or take any position that *might* promise to offer me sponsorship after working there for a year. I had heard it could be hard for an American to work in Europe, but I didn't realize what that meant until now.

For months, I had been willing to do anything possible to follow a job lead or connect with a potential employer, but I was not making any progress. I had been applying for jobs, making phone calls, searching, connecting, networking, and trying to think outside the box like never before. I spoke with professors, school contacts, listened to friend's suggestions, and followed the breadcrumbs to friends of friends. My former colleagues at the Embassy had some opportunities, but they were all jobs in Washington, D.C. and that meant going back home, not staying in Europe. No doors were opening. Nothing was flowing. Every direction was a giant stop sign. But I would not let myself rest or overlook anything. I had to keep trying, and I convinced myself it was only a matter of being more inventive and creative in my search.

And then there was what I had learned about the reality of being a Foreign Service Officer. Now that I had some distance from the Embassy, I was able to let the experience settle in a bit more and review all of the information I had collected. Experiencing the day-to-day life was incredibly rewarding and provided a practical understanding of the work, but I had an unexpected realization about the profession: I didn't want the transitory lifestyle at this point in my life. I saw all of the benefits and joys of the job, but when I checked in with my gut more, some elements didn't click for me. It didn't lift up my energy or spirit to move to a new country every four years like I thought it would. Thankfully, the internship was a perfect trial run before investing more time and energy into the intense exam and making further commitments.

Some encouraging news showed up when I had a job interview at the OECD. I had applied for the position a few months ago and received an email to set up an appointment time. As always, I showed up early with eager butterflies in my stomach. The panel of three asked me a variety of topics about my experiences and knowledge, but one of the interviewers was a complete jerk and basically told me I didn't stand a chance against the other candidates they were interviewing. He looked at me and said, "We just thought it would be fun to sit down with people and see who was out there. You seemed like an *interesting* prospect." I walked out feeling humiliated and angry about this complete waste of time.

Then my friend Lynn invited me to an orientation at her work place in the hospitality industry. The train ride was almost ninety minutes each way and I really had no interest in the position or the company, but I felt obligated to give it a chance, just in case. I met with her two supervisors and it became clear to all of us that this position did not match up for either side. I was silently relieved that they made the decision and not me.

I felt the pressure building. I had to make a decision soon

because my landlady needed proper notice, plus I might need to buy a plane ticket to Seattle and figure out arrangements to transport my cats back home. But I wasn't ready to give up, or stop looking, or make a decision. *Just keep trying.* I turned my attention to my thesis paper. *How could I come this far only to have it all disappear now?*

What if I didn't keep trying; was I walking away too early and giving up too soon? Would I miss something? Was I really close and it was just a matter of days or weeks before it all came together? Or, did it mean I was working against what was trying to come into my life from another direction? Was something better   happening behind-the-scenes that I couldn't see? Was I working *against* grace?

I LOVED TO WALK, WALK, walk through Paris at all hours of the day, all days of the week, all seasons of the year. The streets were never the same twice. I followed the main boulevards to new areas of town and then ventured off to favorite, secret places. Sometimes I wandered aimlessly, other times I aimed for a target, and the most important requirement was not being rushed. Today it was cold, wet and windy, so I decided to head to a place that was always welcoming and warm: the Notre Dame Cathedral.

I saw Notre Dame for the first time within a week of arriving in Paris and it immediately took my breath away. The whole structure was awe-inspiring. Like everyone else standing in the *parvis* in front of the church, I took pictures from every angle and distance, trying to capture as much of its mammoth magic on film as possible. I returned numerous times with visiting friends and family to appreciate the history and details. We scaled the top to peer up Quasimodo's bell and to examine the gargoyles decorating the rooftops. We appreciated the landscape of the city from the highest tower and squinted at the farthest possible landscapes in the distance. The views of Paris from this highest vantage point above the flying buttresses were spectacular.

But today, as I eased through the huge wood doors, I wanted to appreciate the interior of the cathedral instead of its external jewels. I discreetly entered into an ancient world where the modern city ceased to exist. Whispers and quiet descended upon my ears. The air was damp and a bit stale from the smell of hundreds of years of very little fresh air ventilation. A lack of light, filtered by stained glass windows, made the entrance feel small and cramped, until the central portico straight ahead revealed the vast main floor, measured by hundreds of benches in neat aisles.

I traditionally walked the perimeter of the church visiting each side altar, but this time I decided to sit on a bench towards the back of the many rows. Surprisingly, there were not a lot of visitors; it was a slow and quiet Wednesday afternoon in April. Daily parades of people would saunter through endlessly from May to September with more elbows to brush against and flag leaders guiding obedient, shuffling crowds. But now it was easy to simply sit and look around at what these walls held. And when I looked up at the dismal beams of light coming through the stain glass windows, I saw more than just faint colors trying to enter the space on a gray day. I saw prayers.

In thin, black, cursive writing, I saw hundreds and thousands of prayers moving, dancing, and gliding through the wide-open spaces and tiny dark crevices that composed the historical cathedral. I saw prayers gently soar up to the highest points and then dip down to the lowest benches. I saw prayers flying through the air as if they are chasing, running, hiding, and playing with each other. I saw prayers bounce off the walls, glide along the vaulted ceilings, move discreetly to a secret corner, and then jump out into the beams of kaleidoscope light, giggling at their own playfulness. I saw prayers soar, breathe, and live, safe in the protection of these ancient walls.

I closed my eyes and felt them swish through my hair, whisper in my ears, and kiss my skin. They twirled around my legs, rubbed against my arms, and then coasted over to the next warm body with comfort and ease. They were inhaled and exhaled with each breathe of each person in every second as they thrived on the heartbeats that entered through the protective doors. They were alive and moving as quiet sources of energy that filled every corner. They were as old and wise as the cathedral's first foundational stones, and as infantile and fresh as the day's opening rays of sunlight. They were everywhere, in everything, and on everyone. Prayers were the reason I came here. We knew each other.

As I sat and watched the silent spectacle, a magical illusion happened as more and more prayers filled the air, and yet no more space was occupied. A continual opening occurred in the atmosphere, allowing every new prayer its own space, its own weight, its own time to stretch. A new prayer never took anything away from the prayers that went before it. There was never a limit to the number of prayers a person could make. There was never ranking or prioritizing. There was always room for every dancing, gliding, soaring prayer. All prayers were welcome here.

In this sacred space, all wishes, thoughts, hopes, and dreams were cherished. Expressions of grief, loss, heartache, and pain were all equally honored and carefully held. I saw prayers of hope mingle and circle around thoughts of despair. Wishes for peace comforted thoughts of anger. Feelings of loss were held by expressions of love. Thoughts of joy danced with feelings of suffering. Every request had a balancing equal that rushed forward to be its answer. An endless space for endless combinations.

With this continual pairing of consoling answers, prayers reminded me that we are all connected through wishes to be granted, needs to be met, feelings to be affirmed, and desires to be heard. Similar qualities we sought in our lives; similar needs we hoped to fulfill as all prayers shared the common quality of being from a human heart. Prayers were uniting and universal, alive. And in every grand cathedral and every small countryside church, the prayer expressed held the same general meaning as it soared and danced in sacred comfort: "God, I am here. I trust you are listening. I need you right now."

I quietly inhaled and exhaled the beauty of these dancing words as they twirled and swirled upon shoulders, altars, sunrays, and shoes. The acrobatic movements reminded me that I was alive right now. There was grace to be found in this time. There was grace in every moment. Grace was here. Grace was now.

Then I stood up with ease, and in my alive skin and with my alive heart, I floated to the back exit.

With the constant opening and closing of these doors, it seemed easy for a prayer to slip out, to be ignored, to disappear. But I felt that even a prayer that might appear to go unnoticed would never be lost because each one was born magnetized to God's ear. I believed this was why cathedral ceilings were so high. And I would never tire of being in the presence of prayers.

GRAVITY

I WAS ATTEMPTING TO WORK on my thesis at Turhan's apartment, but I couldn't focus. The feeling that something was off between us was so strong and my gut was turning, churning, spinning. I stood up and went into the bedroom where he was studying.

"Hey."

"Hey."

"Do you have a minute to talk…"

"Sure." He was reading on the bed and shut the book as he propped himself up on a pillow. I sat on the bed and pushed myself back up against the wall, my fingers looking for something to toy with.

"I wanted to… check in and see how we're doing. I've felt like…" Pause. "Like, there's been distance between us for a while and I can't pinpoint it… so I wanted to know what's been on your mind lately"

He shrugged slightly. "I'm mostly thinking about work and my career a lot right now. I have to figure out what I'm going to do next. I really need to find the right job…" He exhaled deeply.

I nodded, looking down at the striped comforter.

"Are things okay with… us?" I inhaled deeply.

"Yeah… I think so."

"Is it only work stuff that's been on your mind? I've felt lately that you've been… distracted or something? Or maybe it's me?"

Silence. He looked left and right, but never at me. I stared at his face then continued. "Or is it something else?" He still didn't look at me. Apparently his pillowcase was fascinating to look at.

He shrugged. "There are a lot of unknowns right now, for both of us."

"Yep."

It felt like we were both avoiding the elephant in the room. But I'm not The Girl Who Avoids the Elephant; I'm The Girl Who Announces The Elephant. My feelings were strong that this relationship was not in a good place, but I couldn't exactly explain why or figure it out. It was a deeper level gut thing.

He stood up. "Are you getting hungry? We could go to the store to get what we need for dinner tonight."

I stood up from the bed. "Sounds good."

Things were off, and yet it was safe. Everything else in my world felt unstable and unknown at this time, but at least *this* was something known, and I could find some type of stability in *this*. At least I had someone here for me after so many of my friends had left Paris. At least I had *this* to grasp onto as I navigated this uncertain terrain of my current life. At least I had *this* to count on and structure my life around for the time being. At least I had one thing in my world that was good, and enough, until I knew what was next. At least I had something "good enough."

I stuffed the mounting doubt and uncertainty further down into my knee-high boots as we left for the store. Meal planning was an excellent distraction from the fears I didn't want to think about. I'd rather focus on making the chicken parmesan dish I'd been craving for the past few nights.

We pushed through the front door of the building as he reached for my hand and pulled me closer.

GRADUATION WAS A GORGEOUS AFFAIR at the Luxembourg Palace on the grounds of the *Jardin du Luxembourg*. We donned black caps, long gowns, and colorful sashes as degrees were handed out in a ceremony held inside a private auditorium. Parents, professors, friends, and students filled the seats and cheered at the appropriate times. Turhan and I each received a top award for our academic excellence in our programs, and although I was proud of the achievement, it was one more instance where we should have felt united, but we weren't. We took pictures together, but the physical space between our bodies was apparent to me in each shot. Friends offered congratulations and said supportive words, but they had no idea how our relationship was crumbling apart on the inside. I played along with the charade.

The *fête* continued in the palace's grand rooms that looked out over the immaculately groomed gardens. Gold accents and rich embellished decor covered every direction of each room as if Louis XIV, the opulent Sun King, personally approved all decorations, down to the heavy silverware and ivory china plates. We ate like royalty as waiters floated around with unlimited silver trays of *amuse-bouches* and heavy appetizers. Champagne and wine glasses waited to be held on a nearby table next to polished displays of fruits, macaroons, and delectable pieces of cheese on tiny crackers. Every corner of the room gleamed and sparkled, as if promising us our futures could only be successful from this point forward.

Turhan and I left afterwards with a group of friends who were going to a few nearby bars. We walked down the street as if nothing was wrong and everything was right, except we never walked together and we barely spoke.

TURHAN ARRIVED AT MY apartment in the afternoon when the early summer air was clear with sun beaming through every window. Kitty and Kit Ten circled between us with great anticipation of affection. He suggested we go for a walk, but I already had dinner started and the oven was on. I told him I would rather stay here and talk. We were facing each other in the living room, standing. He leaned against the desk with crossed arms; I leaned against a chair with crossed arms. I suddenly felt like an outsider watching the exchange from the safety of the garden:

She asked what he wanted. He explained he had to focus on his career now.

She asked what does that mean exactly and how did she fit in?

He had to think about his professional life more than the relationship. He could not offer anything more.

She stared at the floor and felt her heart start to recede.

He walked over to hug her. She withdrew.

She said it was not enough. She wanted a partner who could make the relationship a priority.

He looked away into dead air. Silent.

She hurt at his change of intention. She yelled at his selfishness. She looked away with trembling lips.

He collapsed onto the couch, hands over face.

She stood devastated. She started to cry.

He sat in silence on the couch, staring down at the floor.

She wiped her tears away and left the room to check on the food, simmering along with her feelings.

The timer in the kitchen went off. Time was up.

She finally realized this was why she hadn't trusted him. His intentions had changed. That was the feeling she was fighting because she couldn't believe it. Didn't want to believe it.

Dead air filled the apartment with silent aromas.

She stood at the stove breathing deeply, the dish now salted with her tears.

Then she entered the living room with no meal in her hands.

She said to him in a steady voice that it was probably best if he left now. She was not able to sit through a dinner with him. She didn't believe they had anything more to share.

He slowly stood up and grabbed his bag. She didn't look in his eyes. He didn't look in hers.

The door shut behind him.

She stared at the door with a hand over her heart, trying to hold all of the pieces together.

An unfamiliar void displaced the air, her breath became labored and irregular.

Her heart was broken after she believed it could only grow.

She felt pieces of her heart slowly tumble to the floor.

Then she fell to the couch crying.

Wishing for what wasn't meant to be.

THE NET

I DOVE INTO SCHOOLWORK as a welcomed distraction to keep from looking at my broken heart in the mirror. My master's thesis was due in a month and it could easily take up all hours of the day. I had no problem with that. A few good friends were still in Paris so I finally made myself step away from the computer long enough to socialize. And although going out and having fun seemed logical, I didn't have a lot of energy for it because I didn't want to see Turhan, or hear about him, or even know about him through other people. We had many of the same overlapping friends and enough in common after dating for over a year that socializing actually filled me with a quiet dread. I preferred to maintain a barrier with my own space, distance, time. The city became a lot smaller when there was only one person I wanted to avoid completely. The millions of people walking around, behind, and in front of me became transparent when I was trying not to see that *one face* in the crowd.

Reality finally set in and I had to throw up my surrender flag. I gave my landlord notice that I would be moving out. I purchased my return airplane ticket home. I hunted down a way to send the cats back to Seattle easily and efficiently since I didn't want to stress about them traveling with me again. Luckily, I found a great service that would take care of everything from when I dropped them off at the airport to when they arrived in the U.S and passed through customs. The cats were scheduled to leave on a flight the day before I did, and fortunately, there was now a daily direct flight from Paris to Seattle that didn't exist when I flew them here over a year ago.

Trisha had been living in Germany for the past few months and was coming to Paris to work on her thesis research. She would be staying with me, so I met her at the train station with big hugs; we made our way back to my apartment talking non-stop. I told her through email that Turhan and I had broken up, but now she could see what that really looked like in my eyes. She started to ask if I wanted to talk more about it, and I just shook my head no. Not ready.

We both had plenty of work to do, so we set up our laptops on the dining room table facing each other with the backs of our screens touching. A fresh cup of coffee sat next to our mouse pads and our hands were dancing away on the keyboards until I hit a big roadblock in my thoughts and couldn't move. She glanced up.

"Just say it."

"It still doesn't feel real. I've been in a daze…"

"Have you talked to him?"

"I sent him an email to ask for copies of some pictures and told him about my plans, that I was leaving."

"And?"

"He called and asked how I was. We talked for a bit." My eyes started tearing up. "He was encouraging and matter-of-fact, as always… it was nice to hear his voice after two weeks."

"Did he say more about his plans, or anything related to your last talk together, or…" Her voice trailed off.

Kitty jumped up onto my lap. "There wasn't more to say, it's not like his priorities changed. He's focused on his work stuff and doesn't see that a relationship could share that same space. And although I *get it* logically and all, it hurts. What changed for him? He couldn't even answer that question when I asked him. Which is why I also didn't feel like I could trust him… like he was withholding from me…?" Big exhale. "I just loved him and wanted to believe the best…"

We sat in silence. We looked outside at the garden. Kitty meowed on my lap.

"And it just… it feels like a level of loss that's bigger than the relationship. It's the loss over the future possibilities, the dreams, the "everything" of staying in Paris. I was buying into a bigger *something* that wasn't happening and now… it's really over."

Big exhale.

Trisha petted Kit Ten. "Yeah, I could feel that things were different between you two."

"Right…"

Trisha put Kit Ten down and stood up. "Come on, we need some fresh air. Let's go for a walk and get out of here."

I stood up too, stuffing tissue in my pockets. "I want to talk about you now and never talk about me again."

We pushed through the apartment building's front doors, arm in arm. The bright summer light hit us hard as we walked over to the park. Trisha finally spilled the beans that she and Miron were starting to hang out more and had been dating since they were both in Germany now. A huge smile spread across her face.

"Tell me more, tell me everything!" I said, squeezing her arm tighter and allowing the sun to drench my face.

MY LAST WEEKEND IN PARIS was during the national Bastille Day celebration. Bastille Day is the French national holiday of independence, celebrating the storming of the Bastille prison that moved the country from rule by the royal government to rule by the people. The Bastille fortress was overtaken by French citizens, and a document called the *Declaration of the Rights of Man and of the Citizen* was put into effect to rule the country. General Lafayette, a French Revolutionary leader, presented the draft of this document to the government. He previously served in the American Revolutionary War under George Washington, and after the Bastille prison was overthrown, the key to the west door of the prison was sent to President Washington as a symbol of liberty. I remembered hearing this story and seeing the key to the Bastille prison at Mount Vernon when I flew to Washington, D.C. by myself in fifth grade to visit my dad. A full circle moment.

Trisha and I took to the streets with the thousands of Parisians who were making the most of the hot summer holiday. We wandered toward the Eiffel Tower where the biggest celebration was going to take place at dusk. No cars were allowed on the side streets, so we blended in with the stream of pedestrians and their easy flow. The night was fresh and warm with excitement. The sun wisely chose to set directly behind the Eiffel Tower, making for a spectacular contrast of black steel and soft pales.

There was at least an hour until the evening festivities began so we grabbed an outdoor table on Rue Saint Dominique to enjoy a few beers. From our sidewalk table, groups, couples, families and individuals of all ages headed toward the beacon of light on the Seine. We slouched into our chairs and talked about our favorite highlights and funny stories of the past few years, disbelieving how fast time had flown by and all that had happened and changed. It was perfect to be toasting beer with her at this little bistro on our last Saturday night together in Paris. We were new women now. As the passing crowds became bigger and denser, we finished our last sips of Stella Artois and slid in with the currents of people.

The Parc du Champ de Mars on the fourteenth of July was a sight I had never seen before. A concert stage was assembled on the far end of the park in front of Ecole Militaire. Free concerts had been going on all afternoon by some of the biggest acts in the country. Lights, speakers, and audio equipment surrounded the space as thousands of people crammed into every inch of the park to witness the great fireworks spectacular. As we filled in to a rare empty space, our new neighbors sang favorite French songs at the top of their lungs.

The sun finally glided down over the horizon line around 10:30 p.m. and the most amazing show on the Eiffel Tower began. Music blared from every loudspeaker surrounding the park as colorful super sparklers blasted from the black steel sculpture. In time with the beat, fireworks exploded with beautiful synchronicity and the night air was filled with color, lyrics, tunes and flashes. People cheered with excitement amid ooh's and aww's moving through the trees and up into the dark navy sky. The thirty-minute celebration climbed to brighter and bigger heights as the dramatic music created a greater anticipation about what would happen next. And with the final bang, the grass, trees, heads of the crowd, and waves of the Seine were overcome with applause and appreciative enthusiasm. The Eiffel Tower slowly descended into darkness, a final bow behind the curtain of night.

Time to go home.

THE CHOREOGRAPHY REQUIRED TO OFFICIALLY depart my home in Paris and get to the airport included renting a car, moving to a hotel for two nights with two cats, clearing out of the apartment, transporting five huge pieces of luggage in two separate trips, and all the various errands and tasks that come up unexpectedly while moving. Somewhere in that chaos, I remembered to stop and breathe.

The day before my flight, Trisha and I drove to the airport twice. The first time we dropped off the cats at their travel service's office. It was a hard temporary parting, but also a relief that someone else was taking care of them and one less thing on my mind. The second trip to the airport was to drop off two pieces of luggage that would not fit in the small car with the other pieces after realizing we couldn't fit all of my baggage into the car at once. And to be fair, I was not simply traveling with clothes, shoes, and a hairdryer, I was travelling with *everything I owned* stuffed into five mammoth pieces of luggage that I affectionately referred to as Crazy-Bags. These Crazy-Bags were my personal U-Haul truck filled with all the possessions I had in the world. And to top it off, my ensemble of bags didn't look like any type of matching luggage set. They looked like the missing baggage department. (Crazy-Bags from The Misfit Collection, imported exclusively from Misfit Island.) The lightest bag weighed sixty pounds, the biggest one was almost three feet tall, another was professionally saran-wrapped shut, one looked normal until you attempted to move it, and the heaviest bag took both Trisha and I to lift it. My Crazy-Bags required two airport carts stacked almost five feet tall. Thankfully, I didn't have to cart around two cats as well.

Trisha and I pushed the carts through the airport laughing at the ridiculous sight. But unfortunately, the Crazy-Bags were a real concern and not just a laughing matter because I didn't know if I would even be able to take all of these pieces on the flight. In the past week, I had made numerous calls for cargo quotes as a back-up plan, but every quote I heard was absurd and the lowest amount was $1200 bucks for three bags. After more comparison-shopping, I called the airline again and it was determined that checking all of the bags onto my flight and paying their individual fees was the best option. So even if I could, for some miraculous reason, get all five bags onto this flight, it would be expensive. $700 bucks at the current exchange rate. Is my stuff even worth that much?

For the past 24 hours, I had prayed, prayed, prayed for a better solution with these bags. I had no idea what that solution would be and it had become too stressful to figure out. As we were standing in line to at the ticket counter, I finally gave up the situation and the stress. I gave it ALL up. I said a silent prayer that this was going to work out perfectly and I didn't have to worry about it. It was already taken care of. I trusted I would make it home safely and easily. *It would be fine.* I leaned over and told Trisha I was not going to worry about this anymore. It will be whatever it will be. *I surrender.*

It was less than an hour before the flight and there were only two agents at the ticket counter, one male and one female. I had flown this route with this airline before and the French male ticket agent looked familiar. I remembered he was a nice guy—friendly, helpful, informative—and exactly what I needed. As the line slowly budged forward, more female agents started to appear. But I knew I had to get in front of the Male Man because if I had any hope of finding a Crazy-Bags solution, it would be through him. He could be the hero helping a damsel in distress.

After half an hour in line, we were finally next up and I was intently staring at the Male Man, willing him to finish quickly. I was staring obviously and rudely, and did not care. There were now seven female ticket agents, but only he would do.

And then it happened. He became available at exactly the same time as a female agent, and with no delay, Trisha and I moved the carts awkwardly and directly to him. As I handed over my passport, Trisha started unloading the Crazy-Bags from the carts onto the baggage scale as discreetly as possible, like moving plastic bags while a baby sleeps. Male Man smiled kindly, moved some papers around, typed on the computer, and started printing luggage tags.

"All of these bags? For just you?" He said with a smile and French accent.

"Yes, all mine. Everything I own in the world!" Hand on my heart. "My most valuable possessions! Will you take good care of them for me?"

He laughed and kept accepting bags and bags and more bags over the counter, putting a tag on each one. The heaviest bag he lifted over the top of the counter all by himself as Trisha and I cheered him on for his strength. He smiled and winked. After confirming my seat on the first flight and handing over my ticket, he declared me checked in.

"*Bon voyage a Seattle! Bonne journee, Mademoiselle!*" He nodded his head with certainty.

"*Merci beaucoup, Monsieur! Bonne journée a vous aussi!*" I replied

Trisha giggled as we turned away. "He was making pretty-eyes at you…"

As we stepped away from the counter, I grabbed her foreman. Staring at her intently, I whispered, "Trish, he didn't charge me for ANY of the bags…"

Her jaw dropped a little. She silently mouthed, "Whooaaaa…"

Both of our eyes were big and not blinking. "Quick, keep walking…"

We shuffled away from the ticket area like bandits, afraid someone was going to notice we just escaped. I held my breath for what felt like a full minute, then looked back behind us and released a huge exhale after we turned the corner. Maybe more good things were ahead?

We quietly proceeded to the security checkpoint, knowing a hard goodbye was coming and not looking each other in the eye. We exchanged multiple hugs and kind words, trying not to cry or say the awful "goodbye" word. We agreed my flight would be fast and her drive to Germany would be easy. And this was not a "goodbye;" it was just a "see ya later!" and "see ya soon!" She was my first hello in Paris and was now my last goodbye at the airport. My voice caught in my throat as we parted, then I turned to the next corridor of my journey.

My first flight from Paris to Copenhagen was short, followed by a longer direct flight to Seattle. This was probably my last trans-Atlantic flight for a while so I hoped it was comfortable in some way. Maybe a little extra legroom or two pillows?

In Copenhagen, I had to check in at the ticket counter again for my seat assignment. Apparently, Male Man couldn't check me in for this international flight, so I had to go to the back of a very, very long line. I overheard that everyone on the flight had to stand in this line, so all I hoped for was an aisle seat. And maybe an empty seat next to me. And warm food. And three good movies to pass the time.

I reached the ticket counter, handed over my Frequent Flyer Card, and made my simple request for an aisle seat, if there was one to spare. The ticket agent was busy, distracted, and didn't really look up. I waited and waited and waited. She finally handed me my papers and sent me walking to the next long line, which led into the boarding area. As I stood in this line, I finally looked at my ticket and felt a pang of frustration: 15A. A window seat. Ugh. I hated having to ask a chair neighbor if I could be let out to use the bathroom or stretch my legs. I glanced back, and the ticket line was too long to re-enter and request a seat change at this late time. I said a silent resolve and prepared myself for ten long hours of sitting, cramping and re-crossing my legs. Ugh.

I slowly moved forward with the dancing tempo of the ticket check-in process—ticket, beep, pass, next; ticket, beep, pass, next. But unfortunately, as I cleared the final ticket checkpoint, the computer beeped back at me and disrupted the dancing flow. The agent looked at me with slight annoyance, like I just stepped on his toes during the tango. He turned to his screen, punched some keys, looked at me again like I was an alien, and then handed me a new piece of paper. He grudged, "Have a nice flight," and the dance began its next round.

As boarding began, we all waited patiently for the back of the plane to load up, followed by the middle rows. Finally, the "rest of the rows" were allowed to enter, and as I showed my piece of paper to the gate agent, she looked at my ticket and pointed me to the left hand gate instead of the right hand gate. I could use that door if I preferred, she offered. Oh, that's nice of her. I can beat some people to my row and stake my claim in the overhead compartment.

But as I entered the plane and started to count the rows, I noticed something crazy had happened: I was holding a ticket for seat 6B, which I thought was the first row of Cattle Class, but it was actually the last row of Luxury Living. Somehow, some way, at some time in the day, I was unknowingly upgraded to First Class. With a discounted student ticket. For the first time ever, I did not need to pass behind the blue separation curtain. I stared at my seat and my ticket, hoping neither would vanish into thin air, and immediately switched into survival mode. Shoulders back. Toss the hair. Straight posture. Be cool. Act like I belonged here. Act like this was what I expected. Of course I was supposed to sit here. Seat 6B was actually my preferred place on *every* international flight. Where was my champagne?

I sat down calmly like a grown woman does after stowing her bag overhead. And even though I had to go to the bathroom really, really bad, I didn't dare get up. I was convinced that if I got up, the mistake would be revealed and I would return to find a Mr. Patterson with an English accent sitting in this seat. And he would know that I was not supposed to be here because I only paid $700 dollars for a round-trip student ticket, not $6,000 for a prime seat. Plus, I had already committed a crime by stuffing the plane with five Crazy-Bags that I didn't pay extra for and I was sure I would be promptly moved to a middle seat in the last row of Cattle Class where there was no choice of food or beverage: Hard fish and watered-down Diet Sprite were the only items served in that row.

Nope, not gonna move. Not gonna risk it. Not going *anywhere* until all passengers were loaded, seated, and we're safely in the air. Remember to breathe. Mentally practice holding a champagne glass. Think sophisticated First Class thoughts.

As I sat clutching both arms of the seat in my best Captain Kirk impersonation, I wondered who upgraded me to this seat. Was it Male Man? Did he upgrade my ticket when I checked in because I had so many bags and only a First Class passenger can travel with unpaid extra luggage? Was it the ticket agent in Copenhagen who needed to give my economy seat to one of the many families in line? Was it necessary to fill up First Class in order to sell a Cattle Class ticket? Was it a complete mix-up with another passenger that could not be remedied? Hmmm. Guess I'll never know. Guess it doesn't matter at this point. Guess my champagne will be here soon.

The minutes passed and a Mr. Patterson and his accent did not show up, so I started to peruse all of the amenities that were now at my Luxury Living disposal. One must be aware of all the conveniences and responsibilities that exist in this world. Electronic controls, entertainment options, cushions, pillows, and the elaborate menu all required my immediate attention. I discreetly played with my chair to see if I could operate it properly as I had never had a fully reclining chair at 35,000 feet. Need to make sure I can handle it while balancing my champagne glass on the side table. Certain skills were required to sit here among the elite, so I must make sure I was prepared. That flight attendant better be pouring my champ-

"Welcome aboard, Ms. McCord. We're happy you're flying with us today. Would you care for a glass of champagne?"

"Yes, please, that would be great," I said nonchalantly, "Thank you." Smile.

Apparently I had forgotten that I was resigning myself to a window seat only twenty minutes ago. Apparently it didn't take me long to upgrade all of my expectations of flying. Apparently I adapt to change easily.

As she generously poured the bubbly and set down a personal bowl of nuts and olives, she also handed me a little present. Hoch, I loved unexpected gifts. But don't offer her a hug in return. Just be cool. Drink the champagne and think more sophisticated thoughts. I smiled politely in return like a grown woman does, and held the present for a minute while she passed the same thing to my chair neighbor. I glanced at his packet to size it up. These are monogrammed, right?

I opened my little present and decided First Class was the only way I would travel and live from now on. Period. No going back. This is the life, the real life for me. *I belong here.* These are My People. And my little present was a Gift From Above. I was just blessed with lip-gloss, lotion, facial cleanser, a toothbrush, socks, breath mints, and my very own real headphones. The Best Survival Pack Ever. They really cared about people in this section of the plane, I could feel it. And then I realized I was the only one clutching the pouch to my heart, so I acted like I had a small cough and then reached for my champagne glass. That is what you do in First Class. Always reach for the champagne next.

My chair neighbor and I exchanged pleasantries, but neither of us attempted to be Instant Friends, such a relief. People in the Classy Cabin really get it and I appreciated that. This is the land of real silver, ivory cloth napkins, mini salt and peppershakers, cashmere blankets, and time devoted to resting. We're busy and important people. Don't ruin the integrity of the Classy Cabin by trying to force small talk or become Instant Friendships. That was sooooo "the other side of the curtain."

The plane took off easily, and I finally released my grip on the chair. It was officially mine, all mine, for the next ten hours. I was gonna do everything I could possibly do in this chair. Enjoy refills of everything, order the best items on the menu, drink the Italian red wine, select the chocolate mousse for dessert. I'd watch every movie and recline my chair to the farthest point back, and lift the foot section as high as it would go so I was completely horizontal. The flight was in the air for over thirty minutes when I finally remembered I had to go to the bathroom.

Now normally, the bathroom was a predictable experience. How many ways can a trip to the bathroom change? But in the Classy Cabin, it was a whole new experience because of the two big, wide windows with the most amazing views of Planet Earth. As I locked the door behind me, I momentarily forgot why I was in there because the scenery below was so mesmerizing. Glaciers, ice walls, and pale blue water covered the ground. The terrain was almost too gorgeous to describe. With my face glued to the twelve by twelve inch opening, I craned my neck to see as much as possible from every angle. The earth had never been clearer, more pristine, or more perfect as it was from this vantage point; awe-inspiring, beyond words. And I didn't want to be known as the person in my new First Class peer group who went to the bathroom for twenty minutes or longer at a time. I decided to come back to visit this view as often as possible during the next ten hours. Maybe I'd even bring my personal cashmere blanket to make it cozier.

As my champagne slowly disappeared (well, after the second refill), a special tray and lovely linens presented themselves in front of me. *Oooh, how pretty.* I really did appreciate fine dining. It was too bad my student budget didn't allow more room for that over the past two years. I really had to suffer through some rough times of eating a baguette I bought the day before, or not having fresh Morbier cheese at my disposal. Life in Paris can be so trying at times, especially when all you want is a simple Michelin-starred meal and then –

"Which item would you enjoy for our dinner service this evening, Ms. McCord? We have three main courses to choose from, in addition to the salad course, a cheese plate, and a dessert item." The flight attendant smiled happily after her presentation.

After careful consideration, I replied, "The chicken entrée will be suitable for me this evening, thank you."

My chair neighbor ordered the gross-seafood-whatever-thing dish. Ew. We're definitely not Instant Friends now.

"And what wine would you like to accompany your main entrée?" She reviewed the options and ended with another content smile.

"I'd prefer the Italian Angelo Gaja, please."

"I'll have the same," said my chair neighbor.

Copycat.

The first course was a delectable salad that arrived cold and crisp, just how I liked it. The bread was warm and gooey-soft, just how I liked it. The butter was cold, not frozen, just how I liked it. It was so wonderful to have mind readers operating in the kitchen who knew just what people liked.

The main course came on a big plate with a new set of utensils and a fresh glass of wine. While taking a bite and enjoying my personal entertainment options, I glanced over at my neighbor's plate. His food stunk. I considered saying, "I'm sorry, but your gross-seafood-whatever-thing is smelling on my side of the chair. Could you stop that, please? Thanks." Smile.

Instead, I moved *my* personal salt and pepper shakers farther to the right so he wouldn't bump them, or worse yet, try to reach for them. Using another passenger's personal seasonings was not First Class etiquette, after all. When he glanced my way, I smiled politely to show I was not thinking any crazy thoughts.

The chocolate mousse was delectably whipped, which was to be expected at a restaurant, but even more impressive on an airplane. How did they make it poof so nicely at this altitude? Again, the work of those geniuses in the First Class kitchen. Gotta love 'em.

The meal was finished and I felt so content. All of that free champagne sure makes a First Class traveler tired, though. Time to check out the controls for the chair. But maybe I'll wait until they moved my plates and utensils. Where is that flight atten —

"Are you finished, Ms. McCord? May I take your items?" She

smiled kindly.

"Yes, please. Thank you, that was lovely." I smiled to show her I was not crazy. I helped my neighbor pass over his tray items since First Class travelers knew when to help each other out as necessary. Then he got up to leave his window seat and I didn't even have to move. Love that.

The entertainment options were extensive and the movie selection was huge. All of the features were on-demand so I could rewind any words I missed, or pause the movie when I made my hourly trip to the bathroom viewing station. I settled on a movie that wouldn't be too hard to follow in case I fell asleep. I reclined farther, farther, farther down in my horizontal chair and wrapped the blanket around my shoulders. My feet were sticking straight out, shoes off. My head was weighing down the pillow, earplugs in place. I was a cocoon in flight.

But despite all of the amenities around me, my mind was never far from what I had just left behind 35,000 feet below. These little luxuries were delightful, but I knew these things were all a temporary distraction from what was deep beneath my cashmere blanket: sadness, loss, heartache, the official transition away from the place I wanted to live. Everything else was just temporary grief relief.

I contrasted this, my last flight from Paris, with my very first flight to Paris. My arrival was full of anxiety, excitement, and adrenaline about the city. Over two years later, my departure sent me packing with all I had experienced, learned, discovered, celebrated, loved, and lost in the beautiful City of Lights. Paris and I were breaking up after more than two years together of sharing our secrets and developing our relationship to the fullest. Paris had stayed consistently the same, yet I had greatly changed. I was a different person now, barely recognizing who I was before my time in Europe. I was new. I was different. I was re-birthed. I was not the same woman who left America over two years ago. And I felt such a strong love and admiration for the woman who chose an amazing adventure for herself with no clue about what was ahead. No idea who she would meet, where she would live, how she would grow, what she would experience, or where she would travel. A woman who didn't fly 6,000 miles away on an airplane; she flew away on faith, trust, and hope, searching for something. More.

Now everything would be new and different again as I tried to figure out what to do next with my life. I had no inspirations, no hunches to follow. I felt like an empty, blank slate, carved out and vacant. Only big questions, no known answers.

And after trying to push it away, I finally allowed myself to think about seeing Turhan for the last time yesterday. It already felt like an eternity ago.

For my final night in Paris, Trisha and I talked about who was still around in the city and who might be able to come to dinner with us at a Japanese restaurant in the 4th. I instantly felt the urge to invite Turhan. Regardless of what was said and not said, regardless of what it was and what it wasn't, I wanted to see him again before I left. I knew it would probably be hard, but I also thought I might regret it if I didn't ask him to come because I didn't think I would ever see him again. Ever. Our lives were now separate and going in different directions around the globe. I sent him a text with the details and asked if he was interested. He responded instantly that he would come.

The meal was mellow and enjoyable as jokes and laughter filled the table between the six of us. Trisha sat next to me and Turhan sat in front of me, but his eyes felt too personal, too intimate. The street view was much safer to take in.

After dinner, we all talked for a few minutes in the street until I felt my eyes filling with heartache. I leaned over and whispered to Trisha that I needed to go. *Now.* She nodded yes. Turhan and I exchanged final *bisous* on the sidewalk. Spending fifteen full months with this person now came down to two kisses on the cheek. We parted how we arrived: as distant foreigners.

Trisha and I walked away from the small group as the sky grew darker and cloudier. It was supposed to be a hot summer day in July, but during the five-minute stroll to the car, the rain started to come down faster, harder, wetter. The teardrops from the sky caught up to my eyes. Even surrounded by pounding rain I knew I would see the sun again. But I didn't think I would see Turhan again, or this life, or this dream.

Then the pilot announced our landing into Seattle as I curled the blanket around me tightly. The ten hours flew by too quickly. Let's go back to Paris. Let's sit in this moment between destinations for a bit longer. Let's hold onto this beautiful glass newly filled with lovely champagne. Why rush to unload all of those pieces of luggage and Crazy-Bags? It's not like customs is going to be fast and—

"Ms. McCord, I can take that blanket and pillow from you now." Her smile was kind, but her hands were quick. She took the soft items away and I was suddenly exposed and cold. What a harsh landing back into reality. *Ride over.* And why aren't the pillows and blankets included as gifts with the flight? Airlines were really so cheap these days. Maybe they should make people pay extra for luggage or... never mind.

The plane taxied to the gate and the fasten seat belt sign chimed off.

Back home. Back on the ground. Back to square one.

With no idea about the force of things to come.

THE GROUND

AFTER HOURS OF EXHAUSTED SLEEP, I woke up in a new bed, new room, new home with no idea where I was. It was silent and dark; no sounds or shadows of disturbance circulated. I sat up halfway in bed to clear my foggy head, and came face to face with a few Crazy-Bags sitting in the corner of the room.

I remembered where I was. And where I was not.

I fell back onto the pillow and crawled deeper into the duvet. My body was weighed down by my heavy heart sinking further into the mattress. Two cats were curled up next to my feet, consistent companions of comfort. We all decided to stay in bed until… later.

At some point in the day, I finally got up to leave the comfort of blankets and reacquainted myself with "home." I was living with my mom for the time being until I got a job and found my own place. The first few days were spent moving around, doing things, going places, taking up space. I went out, I stayed in. I did this, I did that. I made my best attempt at adapting, adjusting to "being here," and moving forward. But the emotions under my skin told a much different story.

My uncertain life path began to haunt me regularly. I questioned the workings of everything and yet found no comfort in anything. Every question started with "why" and no answer justified, satisfied, explained enough. No parts of myself were connecting with my new environment either. And I also, unexpectedly, had culture shock in my home country.

When I moved to Paris, I was open and expecting to make changes in my daily life. I knew things would be different and I was ready to adapt. I was willing to alter how I experienced my day, and incredibly motivated to make the most of the differences. So in the past few years, I had developed a new standard of Normal Life.

Now, Normal Life had changed again, and I was learning to live in my country all over. Everything was so much louder, bigger, faster here. My senses were overloaded and overwhelmed. People talked on cell phones, everywhere, every place, every time. *Ring, ring, ring, HELLO.* Loud conversations continually started and ended in all places. I was accustomed to using the phone mostly to arrange to meet up with people, with all talking and sharing done in person. The phone was only a tool, not the basis of the relationship. But here it was a lifeline and I wanted to cover my ears and keep out all of the intrusions.

I noticed the size of products and the amount of food on every plate with new eyes. I stared down at my order of lasagna at a restaurant. This single dinner entrée equaled three meals in France. My weight began to increase just from looking at the plate in front of me. Huge glasses of sugary drinks were at every table. Was there always so much soda available and I just didn't see it before?

I noticed the continual consumerism on every street corner, shop, newspaper. Buy, shop, purchase, consume—the messages were everywhere. The weekly circulars in the Sunday newspaper encouraged constant buying with persuasive sales, discounts, promotions, flexible financing. I stared at all of the "stuff" that appeared tempting, seductive, inviting in every store. In less than two minutes, I was convinced I really did need new bedding "this week only" even though I woke up this morning really loving the duvet I had. I noticed thrift stores like I had never noticed them before. I remember finding one thrift store in Paris when a friend was moving and we needed a place that would accept donations. We were surprised to find one because second hand stores were not common in Europe; people did not continually purchase the newest and latest items, and then turnover boxes of newly disposable possessions. *So much stuff everywhere.*

Also affecting my culture shock was the pace of daily life. The speed of cars, fast walking, constant movement, non-stop energy was everywhere. I had unknowingly gained a slower pace in my former daily life and now felt bombarded with momentum from every angle. On the freeway I understood the need for speed, but in the supermarket I could get seriously hurt. Where was everyone rushing off to all the time? Why was life so non-stop busy? *Like being busy equaled being important.*

And speaking of the supermarket, *what was that place?* I grew up with aisles and aisles of products to peruse, but I saw it so differently now as I had become used to smaller stores, shorter aisles, less products, fewer options. Now I stared down the long aisle of cereals and felt a bit scared of the fluorescent colors jumping out from both sides. Were there really that many cereals in existence two years ago? I swore this section had doubled in offerings. Walking cautiously around the football field of food, I realized I needed a strategy to deal with this place. I couldn't do it aimlessly; there was too much to figure out and decide and I'd be here for hours. I no longer had brand loyalty so every item was a new choice. There must be a better way to cope with all of the options bombarding me so I could get in and out without being so distracted. What I needed had not changed, but dang those product displays were good. I would never eat three boxes of crackers, but it was like the pricing was set up so you felt stupid if you didn't take advantage of three boxes for four dollars. Emotional marketing was persuasive. I glanced down another aisle and squinted, disbelieving how long it was.

After surveying the scene, one thing became remarkably clear. The perimeter of the store was where all of the fresh food was located: fruit, vegetables, meat, seafood, milk, eggs, yogurt, cheese, whole grain bread. *Stop staring at the bakery case.* Don't forget beer and wine. If I ate mostly selections from along the edges, the food would be fresher, seasonal, and "just in from the farm" with less added ingredients or preservatives that needed to be frozen, boxed, wrapped, canned. Everything would taste better, be healthier, and was probably cheaper because there was no packaging and branding. This would be my own makeshift French market under one roof. And it would save me from cartoon figures attacking my ankles in the cereal aisle.

The next big piece of culture shock I came face-to-face with was the wall of magazines about celebrities at the checkout counter. Celebrities and famous people everywhere, everywhere, everywhere. Oh man, please just go away. Half of these people I had never heard of and didn't know a thing about, yet their life was right in front of me. I couldn't get away from their lives unless I stared at the person's head in front of me. In France, there were maybe three magazines at the checkout counter: a weekly TV guide, a cooking and recipe magazine, and one tabloid publication. Here, it was so easy to pick up a copy and quietly browse the glossy pages, look at the unreal lifestyles, scrutinize the pictures, digest the unrealistic images, believe the harsh headlines. Maybe I just needed a quicker checkout line so I didn't have time to look.

I stood outside the supermarket and noticed another dominant theme. I could do anything with very minimal effort. Drive-through options existed for food, banking, pharmaceuticals, gas, and all I had to do was swipe a card. Cars, cards, and convenience everywhere. Everything was fast and efficient, yet there was very little room for human interactions and relationship building. Stay in your car, pay at a machine, be on your way. I could go through a whole day without saying hello to another person.

Even sitting on the couch I had culture shock. What are all of these reality TV shows? I had only been gone for a little over two years and there were four times as many shows about "reality." What was *Dancing With the Stars*? Who was this blond girl featured everywhere? HEY. I went to high school with that guy who was the Bachelor! I couldn't keep up with all of the shows, the people, the talents, the plots, the situations to get out of, the past winners/losers/failed applicants. There sure were a lot more ways to publicly judge people and to "compare and despair" between my life and theirs. I clicked the television off.

And amidst all of these culture shocks moments, I couldn't get over the unexpected confusion because I grew up in this country. This is what I had known and how I had lived for decades. So how could it all be so foreign to me? Why does it feel like I am an outsider visiting for the first time? Looking at each of these culture shock revelations separately did not seem to be a big deal. They were manageable and mild and I would adjust. But collectively, I noticed one dominant theme: they had the ability to keep me passive. A passive watcher of other people's lives, "reality," or glossy existences. A passive spender susceptible to buying something just because it was advertised. A passive consumer of food on a plate just because it was in front of me and the "typical size of all our meals." Passive to expect life to arrive in front of me via magazines, television, other people's choices as depicted on all of those celebrity entertainment shows. Passive as an observer *of* life instead of active as a participant *in* life. But at least I spoke the language fluently here.

Besides the culture shock and trying to figure out what was next, I was carrying inside a deep grief that I kept to myself, clutched tightly to my heart. I functioned just fine in the normal world, but it was in my own private underworld where the truth and heartache flourished. I had no energy to create a new dream out of scratch. In fact, there was so much I *didn't* want to do right now. I didn't want to date. I didn't want to "get out there" and put on a pretty face. I didn't want to meet new people. I didn't want to pretend, or force, or exert, or try even a little. I didn't want to do anything that was in anyway vulnerable. I didn't want to do anything for anyone else; I just wanted to be left alone.

I searched for comfort and words of wisdom in various resources like books, movies, websites, and inspirational speakers. Most books about a relationship ending did not reflect the greater totality of the other elements. Most resources offered a band-aid to cover the wound, but not much depth to heal the real pain. The focus was on "being happy," "staying positive," "cure a broken heart instantly," and "the best ways to start over now." They told me to meet new people, focus on the good stuff in my life, appreciate what I had now, write out my feelings, get out and be active, and of course, that time healed everything and everything happened for a reason.

But I did not want any of that. I was not ready to put on a smiling face and get back on the dance floor. I couldn't just write out my feelings and then they were gone and over as soon as I put the cap back on the pen. I was not able to focus on creating happy thoughts and being positive because that was so... forced and unauthentic. And I was not going to fake it. The books and experts said I needed to get over it and move on, like a microwave fix-all: put all of the ugly stuff together in one pot. Zap it in Happiness for three minutes and let it sit for one minute. After the first bite, you'll be happy and shining new!

I would rather take the risk of being authentic with my feelings, instead of forcing the appearance of happiness and being "cured." I would rather acknowledge the level of grief this was causing me instead of sweeping it all away under the carpet in the name of convenience and "meeting someone new." The anticipated "new person" couldn't do anything for me, anyway; I had to do it for myself.

And I wished there was a way for grieving to be better understood without leading to the appearance or assumption of depression, self-pity, and "feeling sorry for yourself." I would rather allow myself to be in this space of temporary sadness where I could acknowledge my true feelings, be aware of my true needs, and accept my true process. Allowing the authenticity to move me through this time.

The best resource I found for my grief was Elizabeth Kubler-Ross's *On Death and Dying*. She explained to my intellectual side what my emotional side was experiencing, and detailed the five typical stages: Denial and Isolation; Anger; Bargaining; Depression; and Acceptance. Reading about each of these phases triggered something deep and real in me. And be it big or small, conscious or unconscious, Kubler-Ross noted that each person moved through the different phases at different speeds and in their own way. It was common to revert back to some stages or to experience a few stages simultaneously; some stages lasted longer than others. All of this was exactly what I needed to hear and know because I finally felt understood and normalized.

As I read through the pages, I knew my situation was not comparable to the death of a loved one nor the very real difficulties of having a terminally ill loved one facing death. I knew what I was going through was not the worst form of human grief that could be experienced in the world. My experience could be viewed by simple minds as "only a breakup" or a "big disappointment" or "an unfortunate turn of events."

So with time on my hands, I decided to take myself down this road of grief with the intention of working my way through the deeper emotional layers lurking underneath. At this point, what was there to lose?

1. Denial and Isolation

"Denial functions as a buffer, allows the person to collect themselves, and, with time, mobilizes other less radical defenses... Denial is usually a temporary defense and will soon be replaced by partial acceptance." (Kubler-Ross, *On Death and Dying,* pgs. 52-53)

My denial took the shape as reasoning that America was not where I belonged and it was not where I was going to stay. It was temporary. A mere resting place. I would be back in Europe soon living my dream. I was not staying here. This was not real and this was not permanent. My real life was over there waiting for me. I was just going to exist in a fake life for a bit.

Instead of putting energy towards doing anything in this fake reality, I preferred to be by myself. I didn't want to answer questions about Paris, about my life there, about the Eiffel Tower's highest vantage point. I didn't want to be reminded of what I left behind and what I was missing. I didn't want to be told how beautiful the city was or talk about the French language. I didn't want to hear other people's memories or favorite stories.

I accepted a job at my former place of employment because it was an easy path to follow and a known environment. I showed up every day trying to be fresh and inspired, but I knew I was only a temporary employee. I left my desk empty and was apprehensive about planning anything for months in advance. I probably wouldn't still be working here by then, anyways.

I denied that pain existed within me. I denied that the relationship with that guy I was dating mattered to me. Why should it? It was over. Done. Whatever. Avoidance, denial, and isolation all sounded perfect. Pour me a double of each. I'm gonna pull in a few pillows, gather some warm comforts, and hang out in this space for a while. Why deal with hurt when you could just pretend and not think about it?

2. Anger

"When the first stage of denial cannot be maintained any longer, it is replaced by feelings of anger, rage, envy, and resentment... This stage is very difficult to cope with because... the anger is displaced in all directions and projected onto the environment at times almost at random." (Kubler-Ross, *On Death and Dying,* pgs. 63-64)

What the fuck.

What has all of this been about? Why was it MY dream that had to be destroyed? Why was it MY life that had to be dragged through the gutters, ruined in all directions, and left for rats to chew and gnaw on? Why was it ME who had to waste my time on with that guy? What was the point of having a dream, building a dream, creating everything from scratch, and then handed a return flight back to where I came from?

This is messed up.

As the weeks passed, I noticed my anger came and went with no obvious reasons in sight. The anger sat underneath my skin, permeated my mind, and could be triggered by completely unrelated events. I was diffusing it into other areas of life, any area, and yet felt no progress at all. The anger boiled inside as a slow, painful rage. It was not the aggressive, physical kind of anger where I wanted to hit or violently harm someone. I could not take Nyquil and be finished with the emotions in the morning.

This version of anger sat on me, coated my body in a thin layer of defense and protection. It rested invisibly on the surface, and with the slightest scratch, awakened to a full-blown expression. I felt like it was never far away and never turned off. A time bomb protecting the deep hurt and pain of my internal world. A solid barrier that kept me safe from feeling any more pain and allowing me to maintain a strong level of avoidance. Being angry pushed the stuff outwards with little responsibility. Being angry allowed me to have an outlet, but no progress. Being angry distracted and created space away from people. My anger shielded me from the internal hurt and sadness that was very real. I was not ready to look at those wounds.

But if I was not careful and unknowingly let it reside there for long, anger could be my new second skin. I didn't want to stay this way long-term; I didn't want to have an angry heart. I didn't want to keep circling. I wanted to be over this feeling, done, through with it, moving on. But each time I tried to take a shortcut or ignore what was at my core, I found myself back at square one. Or square zero. I had a willingness to move through it, but the only way I could make any progress was when I was brutally honest with myself, faced the fire, and walked through it. Was I ready to do that?

It appeared I would stay in this phase the longest.

3. Bargaining

"If we have been unable to face the sad facts in the first period and have been angry at people and God in the second phase, maybe we can succeed in entering into some sort of an agreement which may postpone (acceptance)... Most bargains are made with God and usually kept a secret..." (Kubler-Ross, *On Death and Dying*, pg. 93)

Dear God,

My first honest words to you would be "What the fuck," but I am trying not to swear as much because I really do not want to be that type of person. I have considered replacing that behavior with kicking strangers randomly for no reason, but that would severely damage my super cute high heels.

So instead of violent words or violent actions, I would like to reach out to you in the name of diplomacy, bargaining and greater understanding. Honestly, I don't understand why all of this happened. I DON'T GET IT. Did I do something awful and this is punishment? Did I NOT do something and this is punishment? Am I NOT supposed to live the life I want? Am I NOT supposed to keep the dreams I find and create for myself? Please tell me what this is all about because I DON'T GET IT.

I am hoping we can arrive at some type of understanding, agreement, or mutual contract about this time and what I need to do. I am willing to do my best to understand and to move forward. But can you promise me that my next attempt at building the life I want won't fall apart? Can you promise me that I will have something to rely on? Can you promise me that I will not be set up only to experience a tear down? Because this is a very real and heartbreaking fear now.

I'm just looking for some reason and understanding right now. A way to believe and trust that what is happening next will be okay. To know that it will be safe, it will be reliable. This is all happening for a reason, right? And it will get better?

Please, just give it to me straight and tell me this: *Was Paris the highlight of my whole life?*

Are you even listening? Do you even care?

Love,
Molly

4. Depression

"…Anger and rage will soon be replaced by a feeling of great loss. This loss may have many facets… An understanding person will have no difficulty in eliciting the cause of the depression and in alleviating some of the unrealistic guilt or shame which often accompanies the depression." (Kubler-Ross, *On Death and Dying*, pgs. 97-98)

And finally, effortlessly, willingly, I courageously released. A lot.

I cried for the loss of the relationship. I cried over the "what ifs" that wouldn't happen and the '"maybe if I had…" regrets that never vanished. I let it all out, and let it all go.

When the release subsided, I found a void regularly surrounded me. All of my energy was given towards letting go of whatever came up, and then I was empty. I didn't know what else to do. I felt no direction. I felt no knowingness. I didn't know what else to do. I didn't know.

5. Acceptance

"Acceptance should not be mistaken for a happy stage. It is almost void of feelings. It is as if the pain has gone, the struggle is over and there comes a time for rest." (Kubler-Ross, *On Death and Dying,* pg.124)

As the months passed, I began to feel my body in new ways since it was the container for this whole process, from brain, to heart, to holding Kleenex, to feet pounding on the ground. My body felt different, and I wasn't sure that was a good thing. Needing some attention and comfort of its own, I turned my energy to consciously taking care of my physical self.

A dear family friend, Leslie, introduced me to an ancient Japanese practice called Jin Shin Jyutsu that works with twenty-six energy points in the body to maintain internal harmony and balance the flow of physical energy. Leslie described the technique to me, but like most alternative healing therapies, it was hard to understand completely until I experienced it for myself. The results were different for everybody. Was it like acupuncture? Reiki? A massage? She explained it was a bit like all ancient healing arts, but without needles, pins, or pressure. I willingly signed-up with nothing to lose.

Without knowing my recent feelings and all of the loss I felt internally, Leslie asked me some questions because the energetic flows she was working with dealt with deep grief and a loss of confidence. *How did she know that based on feeling points in my body?* Amazing. She said we were working to restore harmony in my body by allowing the energy to move through me. During the session, my stomach growled a lot, but I wasn't hungry at all. The hour flew by and I stood up feeling different. My hips were looser and my breathing was deeper. It was almost 8 p.m. at night and the only thing I wanted to do was sleep.

"You may feel some changes and effects within the next twenty-four hours, so be aware of your body tomorrow. You'll probably sleep well tonight."

"Thank you. It will be interesting to see what happens."

She gave me a gentle knowing look. "If you can stay home tomorrow that might be best until you know how this type of energy work will affect you."

I nodded okay and felt very ready to hit the pillow. I slept deeply and soundly that night, and awoke eagerly the next morning, bouncing down the stairs to start the day anew. I felt great, light. I felt clear and strong and fluid. Maybe all I needed was a good energetic jumpstart and now my body was back in tune! I couldn't stop twisting, stretching and feeling this new looseness in my skin. My body hadn't felt this great in months!

But by four o'clock, while standing in the kitchen unloading the dishwasher, something hit me. Hard. Like an unexpected tsunami creeping up behind me, silently approaching from out of nowhere, I was suddenly overcome with intense, deep sadness. I put the last plate away in the cupboard as my body changed from feeling free to feeling paralyzed. My stomach dropped to the floor. My breathing quickened. My body was emotionally purging a hidden heaviness I didn't even know I was carrying.

And by five o'clock, it was completely gone. The storm had vanished. The air was clear, my tears were dry, my mind was alert, and my body felt lighter, even lighter than before. I stood up amidst the piles of tissues on the floor and looked around at what hit me. *Where did that come from?* It was the most random experience I had ever felt because it seemed to happen out of nowhere. Until I remembered yesterday's Jin Shin Jyutsu session. Whatever "that was," it allowed me to release the deeper, hidden levels I was unknowingly carrying. Although the release process was exhausting and confusing, I now felt an incredible improvement in my spirit, like my body started to finally release all it was carrying and containing for me. This ancient Japanese practice connected my body's physical needs with my spiritual and emotional process. After a big glass of water, I called Leslie to make another appointment. I wanted more clearing. I was not afraid of whatever tears or release might come up next.

Also recommended to me was the ancient Chinese practice of Medical Qigong. I was satisfied with Jin Shin Jyutsu and continued to have sessions with Leslie, but the beauty of these different Eastern practices was that they complemented and worked together to assist with energy flow and healing the body on all levels. If one type worked so well, why not give another a shot?

The Qigong session began in a similar way as I lay on a massage table fully clothed. The practitioner, Johanna, worked with my body's energetic flow through her hands and I didn't really understand it; I just decided to trust. As she progressed around the table, I did what I do best: closed my eyes and relaxed since I had no idea what to expect. But I made sure not to plan anything for tomorrow. The day was open for whatever may need to happen. Kleenex boxes were on standby, if needed.

By the end of the session, I felt incredibly tall. Like I was now 8'2" before putting on my three-inch heels. The ground was farther away. My posture was incredible. My eyes and vision had never felt so clear. I think even my hair was stronger. And I was absolutely, positively, completely starving, like I hadn't eaten a morsel in two days. I consumed a huge amount of protein and decided to do a liver cleanse for the next seven days to release more stagnation. I also made a declaration not to drink any alcohol for a calendar month so my liver would be in tip-top form. No red wine for a month... don't tell any of my French friends about that pledge.

I continued with both ancient practices and felt more comfortable in my skin after each session. The liver cleanse seemed to be effective based on how invigorated I felt afterward. No sip of wine for thirty days was incredibly successful as I started to not even want alcohol at all. My body felt cleaner, stronger, and happier now that it was back to a healthier new point of living. Daily exercise kept the energy moving through me and I was enjoying the high of natural endorphins. And for some strange reason, I now craved vegetables regularly instead of croissants. I never thought I'd see the day.

Slowly, a new definition of what this time was about and what was going on within me emerged. By utilizing and connecting to every element of my being - heart, mind, body, spirit—a grander, holistic understanding of my Self started to take shape. I still didn't know what to do next with my life, but I slowly sensed an underlining hope paving the way. I was still searching for more, but I finally decided to simply trust this work and this time, believing that these changes would pay off and be worth it. I had to believe in that. I had to. Or else what was there to believe in?

"We have discussed so far the different stages that people go through when they are faced with (loss)...These phases will last for different periods of time and will replace each other or exist at times side by side. ...The one thing that usually persists through all these stages is hope." (Kubler-Ross, *On Death and Dying,* pgs. 147-148)

I vowed to simply focus on the small pleasures of daily life that existed all around me. Taking indulgent naps on the weekends. Trying new foods I couldn't pronounce. Discovering new music. Staring at shelves of literary choices in the library. Holding steaming cups of coffee with both hands. Talking aloud to strangers' dogs. Painting and re-decorating rooms that needed fresh life. Staring out windows. Sitting on comfy couches with favorite friends. Watching as nature moved around me. And going for long daily walks through my neighborhood. The route back home felt lighter as my steps were more fluid and newly energized with fresher air in my body. My mind opened up to carry more dreams and less density. *All was well.*

The thick emotions continued to clear day-by-day, week-by-week, and the general trend was towards lightness. Lightness as the long days of winter gave way to spring. Lightness as I slowly released the anger, hurt, sadness, denial. Lightness as my body moved regularly with exercise and meditation. Lightness as my spirit became content with calm and peace. Lightness that lifted me up, up, up to a higher place and an inner place of acceptance. A renewal of hope. A new platform of peace. A knowingness that this time, this experience, this huge life transition was beneficial in some way, somehow. There was *good* occurring in this grief. There was *good* occurring in this process. There was *good* occurring all around me. I claimed the *good* even if I couldn't see it all the time. I believed in the deepest parts of me that this was all meant for my highest and best life path. There was *good* here.

Right?

THE STILLNESS

*W*HEN SHE WAS FLYING IN *the air, a trapeze artist received faint hints that she was not alone.*

She might have heard distant giggling and the soft beating of invisible wings. She may have felt a caressing touch tickle her arms, or the unexplained breeze of soft flapping around her ears. She may have noticed sweet smells of freshness and peace that lingered for a moment, and then gently glided away. She may have felt a wrapping hug of softness envelop her before she fell to sleep.

And when she appeared to be walking with nothing below her, she was unknowingly, always supported by the strength of feathers and the firmness of halos.

A trapeze artist entered a supportive heavenly domain when she was launching, jumping, soaring, moving.

But Angels also knew where to find her when she was in stillness on the ground, too.

AND THEN ONE DAY, OVER a year after my departure from Paris… I Got It.

I got the meaning of all of this.

I Got It.

There was not one hour in one day that I happened to sit down, determined to "just figure it all out." I did not read the wisdom on a website or overhear the reason in a conversation. I did not see a billboard on the freeway with all of the answers as I drove by. Nothing I had been searching for appeared in front of me.

But all of a sudden, the understanding I longed for arrived inside of me easily and completely without effort. Everything I had been feeling and experiencing clicked into place. The scattered pieces now formed a solved puzzle. The fog had lifted, the sky had cleared, and the light shining through the clouds was blinding. Truth blazed brightly through my confusion.

The stillness opened me up to a higher understanding. It was as if the understanding arrived because I was finally able to hear the whispers of truth that always surrounded me. The pause of resting at the deepest point of surrender. The willingness to float in uncertainty without struggle. The ability to accept a time of silence and embrace an eagerness to simply listen. The courage to wander in possibility with no idea where the next direction would lead or when it would be revealed.

Then the doorway of understanding appeared right in front of me, right where I was standing, and flew open with an unexpected gust of Love that knocked me over, gently and playfully. The understanding circled, embraced, and calmly sat on my skin as I allowed it to sink in.

Maybe I was always guided perfectly every step of the way with unseen pushes and gentle nudges. Maybe I was never alone through this process. Maybe I was never alone because the unexpected chills and unexplained stirrings I felt at times hinted at a larger presence. Maybe it was always Divine all along the way and I only noticed the Divine perfection when I dared to stop. The answers were always there, always swirling nearby, always circling my spirit.

They finally fluttered down graciously to arrive within me softly, gingerly, simply. At the right time, the right place, in the right way, the answers found me. And there was no doubting their existence.

Now I understood. Now I had clarity. Now I see.

I Got It.
I Got It.
I Got It.

I exhaled everything I never knew I was holding inside.

And all I felt was the soft touch of feathers holding my shaking shoulders and grateful heart.

THE AWAKENING

I BECAME AWARE OF WORKING with energy, intentions, and manifestation practices for the first time back in 2002 during my initial encounter with the psychic, the woman who later became a valuable spiritual counselor and guiding light. My understandings about the world changed dramatically and unexpectedly in that forty-minute session with her. In hindsight, I saw how that was my first spiritual awakening, and deeper layers of understanding would be revealed when, and if, I was ready.

Talking with God has always been a regular habit of mine, although I prefer to keep the practice private, my own thing, my own sacred connection. I refer to the energy as God, Source, Spirit, All That Is, and the Universe because, to me, those terms are interconnected and bound together seamlessly with immense grace, light, and love. My intuition has opened up leaps and bounds through the years, especially as I exfoliated, released, and listened more often. I deliberately focused on developing my intuition, and as the channels opened up widely and beautifully, more information came streaming in regularly. Clarity and intuitive insights arrived during conversations with friends, taking long walks by myself, or even as out-of-the-blue hits in a crowded room with too many noises.

But one day was particularly different. I felt my soul waking up in a clear, fresh space surrounded by a Divine knowingness. I had cleared away enough of the heavy, dense emotional and ego energies that kept the wisdom out, and without warning, a huge surge of insights came gushing in at once, as if an army of angels finally made themselves known to me. I relaxed into my favorite listening chair, a purring Kitty nestled on my lap, and simply asked, "What do I need to know right now for my highest and best good?"

I felt a soft flutter on my face and a tingle in my spine as the loving, powerful, and wise energy came through.

"It was never about Paris, dear one."

Totally not what I was expecting to hear. I sat absolutely still with wonder.

"It was never about one place on the map and what that location would do for you, or what you would do there. It was never about one relationship or one situation in your life."

"Then what was it about?" Deep breath.

"Expanding into more of your power and knowing your energy more consciously. You did everything you needed to do in Paris. You were incredibly successful in that part of your soul's mission. Everything lined up perfectly. Maybe you need to hear that Paris was an absolute smashing success."

That possibility never even occurred to me. "Then… why was it so hard to let go?"

"Because the grief you felt afterwards was composed of all the energies and all of the feelings you had been carrying around unconsciously and had not fully released yet. You never allowed yourself to feel everything in order to clear all of the energy out. Leaving Paris was a beautiful gift that cracked your heart open even more."

"But why did the transition feel so monumental, like the best part of my life was over?"

"There is never one right way to live your life. There are countless, unlimited ways you can powerfully live this life. You created an expectation of yourself, and an attachment to a specific outcome, based on unconscious energy as if the best part of your life was outside of you. The lesson for you was about how regardless of anything that happened, anywhere in the world, with anyone else, you always get to consciously use your energy to make choices that are best for you. There are always more pieces of you to discover and expand because you are a limitless, eternal, huge energy."

Oh. "So I didn't mess up?"

"You can't mess up. You can only open up to more options."

"So I wasn't supposed to stay in Paris longer?"

"Remaining in Paris was one possibility that could have developed out of thousands of potential options. And then you would have experienced something else that would have potentially opened up your heart more. It is also why you experienced the relationship transition."

"How so? What was the point of my relationship with Turhan?"

"You and Turhan had a soul contract with each other, but this wasn't just about him. Did you recognize the themes in this relationship that have showed up in all of your other romantic relationships?"

Oh gosh. Head spinning. "Yes, I did. I saw how at a certain point I stopped trusting myself." Ugh. "But I also knew to never give up my dreams for a boy, so I get at least one point for that, right?"

"This relationship was a wonderful success for you because of the realizations it brought to you. What if Turhan was never meant to be The One, but he was always meant to be The Two? The soul of Turhan agreed to make unconscious patterns so that you felt catalyzed to make new choices. Regardless of the human interpretations and expectations, he was a perfect experience for you."

Well. I didn't want to give him *that much* credit.

"Your ego doesn't want to give him that much credit, but you needed someone to play a role in which you could see this part of yourself. As you evolve in spiritual mastery, you understand how important your responsibility and ownership of every situation is. A person can only be in your life if you both carry the same energy."

"So you're saying I created an experience that showed me exactly what I needed to know about my own energy? And that was the gift of the soul contract."

"Simply making that statement is an expansion of your consciousness. And you also offered him information that he could choose to use, or not. You were each a potential catalyst for the other. There was only love and soul growth in this relationship, regardless of your human labels and the emotions you worked through. You powerfully created everything you needed to experience in order to evolve. Spiritually, it was an incredible success for you."

"Yeah, well, I wouldn't consciously choose to create all of that stuff." Bleh, bleh, bleh.

"Feelings are not good or bad, dear one. You've just trained yourself to hold those beliefs about them. The secret to working with emotions is right there in the word."

"How so?

"Look at the word differently. E stands for "energy." E-motion is allowing the energy of feelings to flow through you with honesty, grace, and trust in the process. To move through the experience as a form of release and letting go. To move the energy through the body and allow the process to happen authentically and fully. To move and surrender the feelings. Motion is actually the most important part of the word."

Frickin' brilliant.

"Your emotions reveal where to direct and release energy as needed

because the letting go of separation-based feelings returns you to a higher state of Love. Your ultimate power and higher levels of consciousness are found in the ownership of all of your energies and experiences, dear one. You can deny your feelings, and thus deny your power and continue with unconscious actions. Or you can own all of it, love yourself more, and be a conscious creator with all of your energy."

"Well when you put it like that, I'm sold on the concept. Sign me up!"

"You already are signed up because you're alive in beautiful human form. You are here to consciously work with your energy in higher forms. Your journey has been about consciously elevating the energies your soul chose to experience. You've been picking up unconscious pieces of yourself and have been gifted with opportunities to decide what to do next with those energies in the forms of emotions, relationships, physical locations, and significant life transitions. You wanted to powerfully transmute energies to higher expressions in order to match who you are now, what you want now, and how you can be of service to humanity."

"Okay, let me see if I get this. On a soul level, I chose - on purpose - to have certain energies in my life so they could grab my attention, allow me to upgrade them if I choose to, and this connects me to my true power?"

"Correct. There are a number of reasons why a soul chooses certain themes, energies, and life missions. Your energy is imprinted with everything you need to feel and you desired to master. If you were an absolute blank slate, you would not have a reaction or feeling or thought about anything or anyone. Your soul's purest state is Love and you are returning to that by working through the unconscious energies that hold you back and keep you unconsciously circling around in patterns and feelings. Every place you have lived and traveled has created feelings in you, yes?"

"Yes."

"And every person you have been in a relationship with, romantic, familial, friendship, professional, or otherwise, has shown you something about yourself that you didn't see before, and they triggered certain feelings, yes?"

"Yes."

"And every phase of your life, every choice, every action has shown you more about your energy and what you can create, yes?"

"Yes." I'm picking up a theme here.

"You designed an adventure for yourself that would ultimately re-connect you with your personal power and higher levels of consciousness. And you wanted to do that by following your heart's guidance with inspired movements. You wanted to consciously create a Love-based outcome with

those relationships and themes as part of your soul's mission, and you do that by taking ownership of the unconscious energies, releasing the separation-based feelings, and understanding how everything is truly Love."

Head still spinning. "Okay... so... why all of this... right now?"

"There are now higher levels of consciousness on the planet. You have access to more spiritual wisdom and understanding than ever before in human history. You and millions of others are awakening to your true power in ways that you weren't able to do or weren't ready to do previously."

"And yet there are so many different beliefs on the planet... and ways to understand things..."

"That's perfect. Everyone gets to choose exactly what they want in order to feel powerful because there is energy to match everything. Don't worry about what anyone else chooses or believes. Perhaps their choices don't concern you. What empowers you? And can you accept what empowers others? It is not about agreement, dear one. It is about acceptance of the unlimited potentials of energy."

"Yep, acceptance of everyone's free will without expectations of 'we all agree on this same singular concept and now we all sing kumbaya."

"A person can choose any reaction to anything, though it's often the unconscious reactions that guide them until they observe how that energy works in their life. Unconscious energies have the most potential to be transmuted and connected to higher levels of consciousness and personal power."

"Just to be clear, what is consciousness?"

"Consciousness is a connection to higher levels of spiritual perspectives. There are unlimited layers of energy in the Universe and within you. Everything has consciousness because everything is composed of energy. As you increase your personal consciousness, you open up to broader understandings of energy and greater, deeper wisdom about your potentials."

"Why should anyone open up their consciousness?" It is healthy to give a little respectful pushback at times.

"You can make any choice you wish because there is energy to match everything. With the conscious use of energy and a bigger understanding of yourself, you can approach your life in a whole new way that supports your innate power. You see how everything you feel, think, and do offers you insights, and then you can use that conscious knowingness for potentials that empower you, on your own terms, in your own time. With my Love supporting you all along the way. I always show up when you call on me, right?"

Now I'm feeling a little sassy in my listening chair. "Well, there was that one time during the Nordstrom shoe sale when I called on you so I could purchase these *amazingly gorgeous* strappy red heels that were still priced too high, and nothing happened when I called on you. You didn't show up." Ha! Answer that one.

"*Because you, like millions of people, were throwing your energy around unconsciously to avoid your true emotions. And then you would have stressed later about the shoe purchase and would have felt guilty about returning them. I did respond to your request but in a different form. I led you to a coffee shop and made your phone die so you could sit with yourself and breathe.*" Oh yeah. I remembered that. "*And then what happened next?*"

The scenario flashed forward in my head. "And then I went to the car and felt restless, so I drove to a bookstore because it was a perfect place for wandering aimlessly. I reconnected with how books in general made me happy and I thought about maybe making time to write. I walked to the metaphysical section and remembered how much I loved all of the spiritual information I've studied for nearly twenty years and I thought about how I could help people know themselves better with my spiritual studies. And I could focus on opening up with more of my writing, communicating, teaching, sharing." A visual of my notepad from years ago popped into my mind. *Open up more*, three stars.

"*And have those insights helped you more than a new pair of shoes?*"

Oh, how I really wanted to say no just to be defiant. "Yes, absolutely. And just for the record, other ways to get my attention and show you care could include spa gift certificates, random deposits in my bank accounts, more green lights at intersections, and calorie-free croissants...just sayin'."

"*All of that is possible and more because your energy is unlimited. You are a soul, dear one, who is running around on the human playground. There is always another dream out there to create and experience next. And my energy is everywhere to assist with your energy. You cannot escape me, but you can chose how much you want to interact with me. The questions for you now are, what do you want to create next? What new dream is calling to you? And how can you use all you have learned so far in the highest possible way?*"

"Maybe I'll decide to do something else, like make stars in the galaxy, or be a back-up dancer in hip-hop music videos, or invent new styles of high heels."

"*You'll know through your high-vibrational feelings what to do next. You will consciously connect to your power and consciously use energy in its highest form to shine the light of your Soul's essence. Just trust yourself.*"

Hasn't that been the theme all along?" Warm smile.

If only I could bottle up all of these amazing feelings right now and sell them to the world for $99.99 plus shipping and handling. "One more question, please. What is my energetic purpose in all of this?"

"Ah, a very human question. You want a label and definition given to everything. So let me say this: you will know your "occupation" in due time. You will know your soul's energy at the right time in your life. You will re-connect to all of this when you are ready. And it will be amazing."

"OH! I know what it is!" Arms flailing about with excitement. "I chose to be a trapeze artist, right!"

"Yes, dear one. You chose to be a trapeze artist. And as you have realized, there are millions of other trapeze artists out there just like you. They are energetically part of your soul group and you all support one another as you re-awaken to your innate power and follow your dreams with the power of your heart."

Yep, yep, yep! My heart was dancing and beating wildly with this realization. Us trapeze artists, we're everywhere! Just yesterday, I stood next to a woman sharing her latest "absolutely crazy" inspiration for a painting that could be ridiculous, but she was going to go for it anyways just to be completely original. I overheard another lady talking about her new business venture as a holistic nutritionist that felt oh-so-right, but she was terrified about the money not showing up. I walked around a lake behind a group of new moms pushing strollers and doing lunges as one of them announced she did not want to return to an office; she wanted to be an entrepreneur and have a schedule that fit her new priorities. The other female voices all raised an octave with encouragement: "Oh, Denise, you have to! That's wonderful! What courage, good for you!" And I listened as a friend shared her dream of expanding her business more, even though she didn't think she was ready or qualified yet, but she felt an irresistible pull to just go for it. Each time my heart smiled to witness other souls leaping, trusting, laughing, creating, soaring, listening. Yep. That's us. The trapeze artists. My eyes started to get teary with joy.

"Wow, it's so perfect. Everything we can do and create is just amazing. Like we are always supported no matter what crazy notion comes up because the fact that we even have that crazy notion in the first place means we have the energy to support it."

"You are supported in ways beyond measure, dear heart. And it's because of your soul's understanding of the Eternal Truths. You carry these Truths with you always. They are simply waiting for your conscious

activation and this will also happen in a Divine way."

"Eternal Truths? What are those?"

And then a car alarm started to go off loudly in the street. Kitty clawed my knees - "Oowww!" - and jumped off my lap. I opened my eyes to make sure no cars were being stolen; Nope, just the wild winds blowing leaves through an open car window. I tried to quiet myself again, but the Divine connection was gone. A huge hunger took over my body. And then suddenly, a book popped into my mind. I had read it in college as part of my undergraduate studies in Political Science and Women's Studies, and for some reason, had never wanted to get rid of it. I ran to the garage to dig through boxes of books, and found the soft, pliable cover amongst other favorite titles. The book was bent and tattered, with a yellow "used" sticker on the spine from being bought and sold numerous times by college students. It sat softly in my palm, only four inches wide and six inches tall. I flipped through the musty pages and landed on the last page. As I read the passage, I knew it was a Divinely timed message to follow. Momentarily forgetting my hunger, I started to pack a weekend bag and stuck the book in a side pocket.

THE BIGGEST SURRENDER

LONG-DISTANCE HIGHWAY DRIVING HAS a rhythm that allows me to listen. As I drove two hours north up to Resort Semiahmoo on the U.S.-Canadian border, my mind relaxed with each passing mile and a new understanding about everything in my life came into view. *What if every place, every relationship, every feeling, every situation was chosen specifically by my soul to raise my consciousness? What if everything has been a Divine teacher of my energy? And what if regularly surrendering was the opportunity to release one form of energy so a higher energy could come in and move me forward with grace?*

On one hand, it all completely blew my mind and raised many questions that needed answers. But on the other hand, the insights felt empowering and amazingly *right* because they alleviated all other fears. These new possibilities gently guided me to a softer place of peace, love, and trust. I was always right on time, right where I needed to be, right where the next opportunity would arrive so I could connect with a higher level of self-understanding. And that's what Paris did.

The spiritual purpose of Paris was to open me up to how I could really, truly create my life dreams with the powers of guiding intentions, trust, and following through on heart-inspired actions. Paris was the playground where I grew, expanded, and connected beyond anything I'd experienced before. Then, beautiful, wonderful Paris cracked my heart open even wider by allowing me to release every expectation and attachment I had been unconsciously carrying about how my life *should* unfold; I was holding on too tightly to one expectation and unknowingly shutting down other potentials that might be even more appropriate. But my consciousness couldn't see that at the time because I was grasping onto what felt safe, and known, and secure. In a perfect, Divine way, I was gifted with the lesson of letting go of everything outside of myself so I could once again connect more fully with every energy I had been developing internally: solitude, strength, endurance, style, flexibility, heart, and grace. This understanding shifts my perspective around all the places I've lived and traveled, too.

The spiritual purpose of moving to Monterey, California was to understand how to be in my own energy, my own space, my own Self, and all the ways I could handle it. Could I cherish and embrace solitude by allowing inner messages and knowingness to become stronger? Could I trust those whispers and myself better? Solitude became a constant presence regardless of where I went, and it dutifully allowed me to keep going bigger in my own energy without needing a hand to hold or an external conversation to maintain.

Then my joyful cross-country road-trip took me through the heart of the United States and energetically opened up my heart in fuller ways. Not knowing what tomorrow would bring and the ability to move through every unknown day with enthusiasm solidified my need for soaring fun, to get out into the world, and to trust the adventure as it unfolded. My heart was wider and brighter after the messages of Love I felt in Memphis, and that spiritual opening reaffirmed the need to listen and connect to energies that are always present, always supporting the expansion of Love in the world.

That flying high was followed by an energetic low in Greenville that exposed unconscious fears I was carrying. I was thrown into the throes of not fitting in, of being an outsider, of not belonging. The energy depressed me because it unconsciously felt like a separation from God, like I was all alone in the vast Universe with no connection to the eternal love my soul knew as home. Yet this very experience of separation was incredibly Divine because those energies were brought to my conscious awareness so I could really see them. My temporary depression was about spiritual separation and I came to understand how that was completely, utterly false. It's not possible to be separate from Source, but it is possible to feel that way. Just like leaving Paris, North Carolina was a huge heart-opener that brought the most perfect information at that time to my awareness. My power was in deciding what to do with it next.

Starting fresh Portland allowed me to regain my confidence,

reclaim my energy, and get clear about what I wanted in my life. Energetically, Portland served as a fresh start and a reminder that there was always another opportunity to choose again, to try something new, to take what I had learned and move it forward to match the new beat of my heart. Even though I felt stuck in an unsatisfying job, I didn't have to hold back what I really wanted; I just needed to get clear about where to direct my energy next. I remember sitting on the floor on Friday nights, making lists and creating art about relationships, dreams and goals, and how I wanted to spend my life on a daily basis. *All of those lists were coming from my soul as heartfelt guidance.*

Then my trip to Annecy supported the expansion of what I could create with my time, resources, and energy when I courageously followed the power of possibilities. The world is huge and the potentials are endless, so why stay in any scenario that was only minimally satisfying? Traveling to Europe for the first time birthed a new version of Self. Geneva lifted my perspective up to the higher ways I could use my energy on the planet, and this opening connected me to the possibility of going bigger with my intentions and with my levels to trust in order to follow a crazy dream. Because if I didn't choose that for myself, then who would? And if I valued my energy enough, I didn't need anybody else to give me permission, or verify my qualifications, or make sure I was ready and had every damn duck in a row. *I could just go for it.*

And then the biggest leap of all to Paris supported taking everything I had learned and moving it forward.

As the highway miles whizzed by, I saw a new thread connecting all of these significant parts of my life. Each time I was ready for the next opportunity, or job, or relationship, or dream, I was required to surrender and let go of the previous version. Yet I fought valiantly against surrender in numerous unconscious ways. I thought I had to push, control, try, over-think, over-exert, and *keep doing something* in order to make things happen or do it right. I grasped onto what was ready to leave because I was afraid nothing else would show up in its place, or that the next thing would be worse, or less than and a step-back. Why release my grip on what was *good enough* if there were no guarantees? Clearing out the unconscious emotions brought forward something even better, every time.

As my consciousness expanded, I felt deep within my bones that it wasn't even possible to be separate from anything because simply being alive, in this human body is confirmation of connection. And that understanding provides the ability to continuously surrender. Every frickin' time I let go with trust and faith-filled intentions, a more powerful energy took me to the next, best place. Even though I practiced trust in myself, I also had to simultaneously choose to practice trust in Source to take care of me in all ways, to guide me to the next most-appropriate relationships, to show me what I needed to know. My part of the deal was to listen (*stop talking, watching, reading, typing, messaging, posting, tweeting so much*) and be aware of how I am consciously or unconsciously using my energy.

I pulled into the resort's parking lot and again felt starved from all of the energy moving through me. I strolled to the waterside restaurant where the Pacific Ocean was a constant serene presence, flowing just a few feet away from every table. I sat down and a young woman with a bright smile promptly arrived.

"Can I get a drink for you?" She set a menu and drink napkin down.

"Yes, a glass of pinot grigio, please."

"Sure. Let me know if you have any questions about the menu." She pivoted away in the direction of the bar.

Empty tables were everywhere as most people were outside walking the beach. The sun was still high enough to be friendly and inviting. The water was flat for miles. A wine glass was placed on the table, and I ordered a cobb salad and clam chowder. My table had the best view of the Peace Arch on the U.S. and Canadian Border to the north, and Semiahmoo Bay stretched out to the south. The San Juan Islands were distant bumps directly ahead on the horizon. One of those bumps looked to be a seal bobbing for an afternoon catch. He'd love the clam chowder here.

My next life dream was still taking shape and I felt a mixture of quiet anxiety and wobbling fear around being financially supported. I hated to stress about money, but it had a way of determining choices and possibilities either by holding things together, or making them fall apart. Yet if I looked back on every big decision I'd made up to this point, when I felt thrusted forward with the energy of a dream, all the energies that needed to support the dream showed up when I kept my intentions clear, my trust strong, and my actions directed.

One time in Paris, it seemed that all I ever received in the mail were bills, bills, bills. Bills consistently arrived for electricity, phone lines, internet, tuition, and school expenses, as if my mailbox was a giant "Pay Now" magnet. Until one day, sick of receiving the same envelopes and requests for payments, I decided that *money* would arrive in my mailbox. Instead of only sending bills out, I would now receive bills of currency in. I loudly declared, in the words of Napoleon, "*Je le veux!*" I will it!, then slammed the small mailbox shut as my neighbors walked into the lobby and had yet another reason to think of me as a crazy American.

Every day after that, I walked by the mailbox and visualized money arriving somehow, some way, some day. Two to three times a day I saw currency when I looked at that gray box. The bills to be paid still showed up, but I didn't care as much because I knew money was coming. I knew it. I didn't know how, I didn't know when, I just knew it would be there. No doubts at all. Money in the mail, any day now.

A week after this declaration, I received a letter from my brother, Tim, tucked between the electricity bill and my weekly edition of *The Economist*. I had been living in Paris for almost two years at that point and he had never sent me anything, so this was quite a surprise; I didn't even know he had my address. I walked into my apartment and absentmindedly ripped open the off-white envelope to pull out the handwritten letter when all of a sudden... bills started falling to the floor. Dollar bills and euro bills of all denominations spilled down, down, down to the carpet as I held Tim's letter in my hand, shocked.

It turned out my brother had won big in Las Vegas and in his letter he explained the triumphant Texas Hold'em victory. He wanted to share a portion of his winnings with me and wasn't sure if I would appreciate American or European currency, so he sent both types of bills totaling over $250 dollars. I stared dumbfounded at my carpet littered with money. Kitty and Kit Ten came over to sniff out the new paper as I began grabbing the bills in my hand. *My energetic intentions made this situation occur!* Then my logical mind kicked into gear and decided it was merely a coincidence and a case of synchronicity. Just a huge stroke of luck. Merely a chance event that things lined up like this. Except, I don't believe in coincidences because I know in my heart that synchronicity is always Divine. The Universe is much more sophisticated and intelligent than our human minds can even fathom.

As I sat with a near-empty wine glass and completed salad plate, the bill arrived on the table with a message that there was no rush. I reflected on that unexpected financial delight as a reminder of the huge, wide possibilities in the world that I wasn't even aware of yet. Just as I believed in Love and have been In Love, I believed in Faith and wanted to act In Faith; I believed in Trust and wanted to act In

Trust. The choice to let go of doubt and let myself be surprised by what could happen were assertions of acting In Faith and In Trust. Both required the conscious belief that I will always be provided for, *especially* during times when I don't know how, or when, or by whom.

I reviewed the bill totaling $32.46, and without hesitation, wrote in a tip of exactly the same amount for a grand total of $64.92. I choose to be abundance in action starting now. I choose to act In Faith and In Trust knowing there is more than enough of it all. Then I went to my hotel room to change into beachcombing shoes, a light cotton skirt, and a tank top. I grabbed the book I packed and made my way eagerly down to the ocean's edge. The beach was open and naked with gifts from the outgoing tide. Cracked shells, scattering crabs, and smooth rocks adorned each step of the coast. No matter how far I walked or how much I tried to see ahead, I couldn't take it all in; it was an endless expanse of abundance and a continual reveal of plenty. Abundance existed easily and effortlessly in nature in all forms. Thousands of rocks, hundreds of shells, and millions of gallons of ocean water were in this small patch of the earth alone. There was more than enough of everything. There was more than enough in this world to take care of me as I transitioned to my next dream. I'll just pay for everything with rocks.

I sat on a beach log, only a calm wind hitting my cheeks, toes sinking into the sand, and held the soft book in my palm. *The Awakening* by Kate Chopin. The main themes flooded back to me: a woman playing the roles society expected of her as a mother and wife, yet she felt called to expand beyond those responsibilities and duties to embrace the fullness of who she really was. The heroine did this by eventually leaving her life behind and walking out into the ocean, surrendering herself and letting go of the restrictions in her life. Originally published in 1899, it was so controversial at the time of its release that it was the last book the author wrote. After reading it in college, my professor revealed how the suicide was a commentary on the unconscious limitations we experienced as human beings and how the heroine's action was a form of surrender to be more, to experience more, to move to a higher state of awareness about one's place in the universe. She wanted to go beyond what she knew and step into the vastness of possibilities that she was, which existed within and around her.

I stared out at the unending ocean connecting to the forever sky, my skirt occasionally billowing up in the wind, and felt a similar dawning of potentials on the horizon. Emancipation from unconscious patterns, beliefs, thoughts, and actions was underway. An opening to bigger levels of consciousness was occurring as I surrendered limited human perspective, expectations, and attachments, and fully claimed the power of my energy and all I could create here, with my feet on the ground. The waves roiled and the clouds sauntered along as I also saw energetic room for every single person's vastness, abundance, success, and energy. No shoulder-to-shoulder jostling at the counter; no stepping on toes or competing for awards. There was more than enough of everything, everywhere for everyone because we are all connected to everything. We are all in this together. We planned for this great awakening to higher consciousness. We arrived with everything we could possibly need, should we choose it, and we had more than enough.

THE FOLLOWING MORNING, I ROLLED over and reached for my laptop immediately upon waking, even before pushing the red button on the coffee maker. Five minutes before being consciously awake, I had received information I needed to capture and write down before the day's activities washed it all away. In the dream, I remembered saying something like, "Can you tell me now what the Eternal Truths are that you mentioned in one of our previous chats? Nice job choosing the title, by the way."

"You are ready for this knowledge simply because you requested it. The Eternal Truths are simple, dear one:

You are always Divinely loved, but others may challenge this truth by attempting to make you feel worthless, powerless, invaluable, unlovable and dismissive of your voice. Every experience of feeling unaccepted or unloved is part of your soul's growth and is the gift of a soul contract. What will you choose for yourself? What voice will you hear the loudest? What serves your highest and best good? And is lack of Love ever true?

You are always abundant beyond measure, but you will experience lack to allow you the opportunity to connect to the eternal abundance of the Universe again. How can there be any lack in an abundant environment? You can choose abundant thoughts and connect to Universal abundance at any time, and you will be given numerous opportunities to connect to unlimited channels of money, creativity, health, joy, and more. Abundance is natural, but you choose how you want to experience it with your energetic intentions.

You are always safe, but you will experience deep and irrational fears to allow you the opportunity to create a stronger foundation of safety within yourself. Others will provide you with experiences of betrayal, suspicion, deceit, victimhood, and theft so you will have opportunities to consciously build stronger trust within yourself and to walk in greater faith, if you choose. Or you can connect to victim consciousness and see yourself as less than powerful if you want to have that version of the experience.

You are always powerful, but you will buy into the belief that you must own, do, or be certain things to access this power. You will be offered many opportunities to be your true, powerful energy, and it will not be what you expect. Your authentic power doesn't depend on anyone else at all, but you will forget this until you are consciously ready to remember. You will wonder about your career path, creative gifts, intuitive powers, life purpose, and "what to do next" because you will think these are the answers you seek, but only until you reach higher levels of consciousness and all of those questions will shift.

One of the most joyful aspects of these truths is that they are true for everyone who is ready to connect with them."

I remembered my dream-self saying, "Wait, crap, I have to write all of this down!" *Pen, pen, pen.* "Where can I keep this for quick access? I need this information tattooed onto my human body so I don't forget!"

"Dear heart, forgetting all of this is part of the experience. It is required to forget as another way to demonstrate your Soul's power to choose. You will be given many opportunities to remember all of these truths and connect to your beautiful Soul power again. You are more supported and Loved than you could ever imagine. Or why else would you choose this human adventure?"

Then I woke up to the sound of children's voices yelling on the beach. I feverishly typed everything I could remember before the messages escaped and drifted away on top of the waves of the sea.

THE NEXT LAUNCH

Two years later.

"**H**OW ARE YOU FEELING? ARE you ready to become a wife?"

"I'm good, I'm good. I'm really ready."

"You look absolutely stunning. Your hair, make-up, dress, bouquet. Everything is perfection. He is going to be in complete awe of your beauty." Hand on heart.

"Thank you. I hope so." Shy smile, calm eyes, deep breath.

Trisha and I were standing on the top level of a three-story yacht, the light wind blowing around our expensively coiffed hair. I glanced over the railing for another quick, discreet look at the guests stepping onboard for the four-hour affair. The azure blue California sky and blinding sun made the day deliciously warm and comforting. A few seagulls cawed in the distance, but mostly the October air was a sweet mixture of silence, sea breeze, and love.

I turned back to Trisha. "Who would have thought that when we met seven years ago in Paris we'd be standing on a yacht in Newport Beach preparing for a wedding? I'm going to get really emotional if I start thinking about how special this is." Or maybe it was all of the champagne before noon.

"Yeah, me too." Trisha inhaled deeply and touched her hair again. "Quick, change the topic."

"Okay, right. Well, it looks like all of the guests are nearly onboard, so it's almost time to go. And I'm getting more nervous."

We sauntered back into the private cabin reserved for the bridal party. All the ladies were applying finishing touches of make-up as the photographer clicked away, trying to capture as many moments and details as he could. Then suddenly the wedding coordinator poked her brown hair instead the cabin with a big smile. "Ready, ladies? It's time."

I gulped back a final sip of champagne, careful not to spill on my dress, and fluffed my hair one final time. Trisha glanced in the mirror and adjusted her final details.

"Okay." Deep breath. "It's showtime."

We shared a brief hug and then went to take our places for our separate entrances. The photographer snapped, snapped, snapped as we all descended down to the second-level ceremony site, a steady ribbon of bright pink chiffon balancing in nude heels followed by a burst of pure white. We braced ourselves against the stair rails for extra support while holding fresh bouquets and trying to smile effortlessly since the pictures would last longer than the discomfort. Passengers in nearby boats watched and waved at the spectacle. The yacht's second level had floor-to-ceiling glass windows that allowed us to inhale the water views in every direction. Sunlight flooded our shoes, bouquets, smiles as we stood floating between the sky and waves. The wedding coordinator shuffled everyone into place. Then the processional music started.

Each bridesmaid was released in due time to slowly pass every row, holding her bouquet and a steady smile while looking at the altar straight ahead. Then the angel in white made her entrance and touched the groom in navy as a new union was formed. The next twenty minutes were filled with gorgeous singing, loud laughs courtesy of the priest's entertaining remarks, a few tears of happiness, and the reciting of heartfelt words. Then Trisha kissed her new husband, Miron. The glass walls echoed with clapping and hollering, and the cheers spilled overboard into the harbor. Trisha stepped forward to grab their six-month-old son, who was being held in the first row by her mom, and she kissed the baby's tender forehead as mom, bride, and now wife to his dad. She passed the baby over to Miron and they walked back down the aisle as a family; one of those touching moments where both tears and big smiles were equally appropriate.

The recessional music started, and I followed the happy couple back down the aisle with my appointed groomsman until the very last row of chairs. Then I broke into a faster walk in my nude heels to wait for Jay outside on the back deck. Even after two years together, I still felt happy-bumps when I saw his handsome face, just like the first time I saw him at a mutual friend's art show. Ten of us went to dinner together after the show, and Jay and I sat next to each other as plates of egg rolls, grilled eggplants, and noodles were passed around the table. We talked easily and effortlessly, as if we already knew each other's daily life. When introductions around the table were made later in the meal, someone neither of us knew said, "Well, obviously those two have been together for years." Our mutual friend responded with a big grin, "Nope, they just met thirty minutes ago." Jay asked for my phone number before the evening ended, and as my heart skipped a beat, I happily gave him the magic digits since *I don't call boys*.

The yacht was turning around slowly in the harbor as we kissed hello. I leaned in to whisper in his right ear, "I think I was the Drunk Bridesmaid,"

"Yep, probably." He smiled.

"Why do you agree?"

"The boat wasn't moving that much." He laughed.

Huge eyes. "Noooo! It wasn't that obvious."

"No, it wasn't. I'm teasing." Smile.

"Champagne was included in the bridesmaid salon and it's rude to turn down refreshments."

We sauntered around the yacht, soaking up the sun and sea views, then eventually took our seats for the reception meal as the beautiful California day sailed by, carelessly and full.

THE VIEW FROM THE SECOND level of our home is a mesmerizing landscape every morning. Sky-high trees wave fiercely in the winter and softly in the spring; an active wetland hosts croaking frogs, an occasional heron standing on one leg, erratic bunnies, and wandering deer; and plentitudes of peace and quiet surround the daily existence. I watch the eagles soaring above, the cattails blowing delicately in the pond, and feel like I am the furthest possible point away from Paris - and I don't want that previous life at all. In fact, I don't want anything before *now*. *I love this, I love here, I love now.* I've never been happier or more content on a daily basis; an indescribable inner well of joy comes forth with the dawn of each day (or, perhaps more accurately, after coffee is successfully streaming through my veins). Paris, and everything before *now,* has beautifully contributed to this fuller version of my conscious self, which is still only a morsel of the possibilities that stretch ahead far and wide. I'm only thirty-six; pretty sure there's still time on the clock for new dreams, new goals, new adventures, new anything I want to create, even in these stretched-out black yoga pants. Something even better is in the works; I can feel it.

I bounce, bounce, bounce down the stairs to greet a full day, and now there are three furry faces looking for breakfast every morning. Kitty and Kit Ten love their home, and some days, they even kinda-sorta-like their insta-brother, Dito (Dee-to). He is a fourteen-pound black-and-white tuxedo cat that looks like a cross between a panda and a linebacker. Dito and Kitty are the same age and they often chase each other playfully around the house, at least until the hissing starts. And interestingly, Dito only started meowing loudly after Kitty moved in.

After feeding the crazy cats, sitting in my listening chair for a few moments, and taking my morning shower, I now have one more ritual to remember every day: *Don't forget to put that pretty engagement ring on your left hand.*

WITH LIFE ELEVATED TO A new platform, I was ready for the next adventure to arrive. I listened to the whispers, felt the nudges, and allowed the vision to become clearer. The next dream was not exactly in the form I imaged, and it certainly did not arrive on *my* desired timeline, but the direction landed softly, gingerly inside, and it made me giddy to the core. It was a different type of adventure than I had ever embarked on before, yet I believed it could be more authentically fulfilling than anything I've ever done. It requires me to take everything I've learned up to this point and move it forward with higher consciousness. All of my marketing experience, communications expertise, international perspectives, diplomacy skills, spiritual wisdom, and teaching ability were perfectly employed in this new dream as if I had always been on the right path all along, every step of the way.

Familiar butterflies swirled in my stomach as I stood on the new platform. Soft whispers from Solitude filled my ears, reminding me I would always have the answers and know what to do. Flexibility reminded me to go with the energy flows, not against them, and be open to changes as they appeared. Style would guide me to create this dream authentically with my own flair. Strength fortified my core in a bigger, more resolute way than ever before. Endurance ran up and down my spine, providing the support and determination to make it through any rough patches or unexpected lulls. Heart energy vibrated within my veins and solidified my intentions with clarity. And Grace glided along my skin as a constant presence of connection and comfort. Surrendering will be included in the new dream at times, but I'll be ready for it when it arrives because it's become clear that surrender is for the courageous. Trust is for the brave. Faith is for the determined. Those energies, and more, will carry the new adventure forward. My toes clenched about the new potentials.

Yes, we're going out there again, little piggies, and you are most certainly coming along for the ride. All ten relaxed and waved in delight. I think truthfully, they really loved the doting attention, but would never admit it.

I turned my attention outward. Just off in front of me, in the open space that occupied every direction, I saw how the air supporting me was infused with the sizzling energy of millions of other trapeze artists out there leaping, soaring, creating their dreams every day of the week because they are choosing to *go for it.*

Every dream has a lifecycle. Rather, more accurately, every dream has a spiral cycle. As the journey unfolds and lessons are learned, the energy of the dream eventually lifts one up to a higher platform for the next launch, the next manifestation, the next playground. The spiral continues pushing, stretching, guiding one forward to new experiences that may seem just out of reach and too far to grasp, but ultimately that turns out to be a false perspective. The dream is actually waiting for you when you answer the call of your soul.

You don't know what you don't know. I first heard this insight in a women's group and it was a mindbender. *I don't know what I don't know.* Until one reflects back on their path and notices the phases in life where they had no clue what they were getting into, or starting, or only on the verge of discovering, then it becomes clear how we are in a continual spiral of soul exploration. Relentless revelations and undoing unconsciousness. Re-opening to more of "the story," the energies, the possibilities at play. Expanding into more of You and leaving behind the smaller, unconsciously confined version of you.

As Carl Jung stated, *There is no coming to consciousness without pain.* The ego reinforces that there is much to accomplish, achieve, and do in life, so it can be much more desirable to source power from a place of egotistic reward. Yet, similar to an elevator, the ego's level of consciousness can only take one so far and so high because it does not have access to the highest levels of consciousness which exist in the spiritual realms. Ascending to higher levels of soul-knowingness is a conscious choice that requires removing all inner ego barriers. And then who would be so crazy as to reflect on their unconsciousness and then publicly reveal those vulnerabilities with an open heart? The protective ego screams, "In our critical, judgemental world, only an insane fool would expose themselves!"

But the confident, calm soul says, "A modern hero or heroine has no long-term fears about opening up about their journey because ultimately, the learned lessons and acquired wisdom has the power to serve all seekers. There is only more eternal love to create, experience, and share for the advancement of *everyone's* journey."

As one's personal perspective moves from the ego's safe smallness and opens up to the grand spiritual realms, a new era of fearlessness begins. Releasing one completed dream and opening up to the next vision creates an unending cycle of possibilities to experience in one precious life.

Inhale deeply. Everything that is necessary will arrive. All of the details will come together. All will be well. It always has been.

Then a gust of air blew up against my back, as if gently nudging me forward with glee and giggles. I closed my eyes to see beautiful, glistening angel wings fluttering about, daring me to go for it, with the understanding that it was *only* about living from a place of trust. It was *only* about moving authentically in the world. It was *only* about expanding to be better and stronger than before. It was *only* about the push of the heart, the pull of gravity, and the Eternal Truths of being a soul in human form. It was *only* about following where this crazy, precious path could lead with the heady blend of personal power and a higher consciousness. Which was why *this time*, I have my sights set on...

Stop.

Glance over right shoulder.

Quick wink. Big smile.

Well, I don't want to spoil anything yet.

Let the higher levels of Trust begin.

What a trapeze artist may not be aware of until she is old, sore, and permanently sitting is a Very Important Fact about the art of trapeze.

This Very Important Fact is not meant to be kept in the dark.

It is not meant to be information that is intentionally hidden from her.

It is not meant to be undisclosed knowledge that "everyone else knows" and she is unaware of.

And it is not meant to be something that she only discovers after her last swinging attempt.

No, the reason this Very Important Fact is not revealed to her sooner is due to one simple explanation: she must discover it for herself.

Like every other quality and characteristic she has discovered along the way, this fact will have more significance and importance if she comes about it on her own. Just as she focused on developing strength, endurance, flexibility, style, solitude, grace, and heart, a trapeze artist will eventually come across this next valuable piece of information in due time, in perfect order, and in the most Divine way.

So, what could this Very Important Fact be?

{Well, ONLY if you promise not to tell her.}

What a trapeze artist will eventually discover
is that even though she will feel
confused,
uncertain,
tired,
scared,
defeated,
and fearful at times;

She will come to know
that in her life
she is <u>always</u>
jumping,
soaring,
playing,
smiling,
giving,
dancing,
falling,
flipping,
climbing,
healing,

laughing,
loving,

simply and safely,
in the palm of my hand.

DEFINITIONS

Spiritual Awakening: An opening up to yourself as a powerful spiritual being who is connected to the All That Is/God/Spirit/The Universe. Understanding your expansive identity beyond the ego, unconscious programming, and/or limiting self-definitions. Spiritual awakenings elevate you to higher levels of consciousness as you connect with your innate power, soul choices, responsibility, and self-mastery.

Consciousness: Awareness. Mindfulness. Presence. Consciousness is the spiritual understanding that you are a powerful energetic being in a physical body with the ability to intentionally direct your energy, thoughts, emotions and perspectives to higher levels of awareness. Everything has consciousness because everything has energy. Every person is a spark of consciousness who is contributing to global consciousness. *The Modern Heroine's Journey of Consciousness* defines and explores the five types of consciousness on the planet now.

Awakening Consciousness Awakening Consciousness is the understanding that you are a powerful source of energy who is responsible for yourself in all ways. As you connect to Awakening Consciousness, the "bigger picture" of your life becomes evident and you open up to more of your innate gifts, talents, and skills that support your journey as a soul in physical form.

Soul Contract: A binding contractual energy made at a soul level to ensure your soul's growth in this lifetime. The contract is often around an integral life theme (such as owning your power, trusting Self, recognizing Self-worth, etc.). In order to grow through the soul contract lesson, you need someone (or multiple people) to be "the other" in the scenario. Many people have similar soul contract themes in this lifetime around Self-Love and Self-Trust, which is why betrayal, power struggles, disrespect, and other related situations are so prominent on earth at this time. It is also why spiritual awakenings are so significant on the planet because people have had enough of the circular themes and are willing to ask deeper, self-probing questions which lead to Awakening Consciousness.

Additional spiritual definitions provided in The Modern Heroine's Journey of Consciousness, including karma, soul mates, soul agreements, soul groups, and the five types of consciousness on the planet now. Molly also shares modern spiritual wisdom every week on her popular global radio show at **www.BlogTalkRadio.com/MollyMcCord**

Next up! Book Two in
The Awakening Consciousness Series:

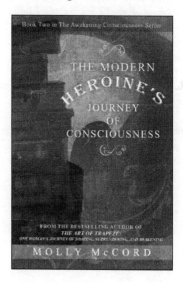

The Modern Heroine's Journey of Consciousness

The second book in The Awakening Consciousness Series is a must-have guide for any spiritual seeker wishing to understand their own spiritual journey on a more conscious level.

Referencing Joseph Campbell's highly influential "The Hero's Journey" alongside her bestselling memoir, *The Art of Trapeze: One Woman's Journey of Soaring, Surrendering and Awakening*, Molly McCord, M.A., brings groundbreaking wisdom to modern experiences of spiritual growth.

The Modern Heroine's Journey of Consciousness offers an original exploration through 11 phases of spiritual growth, from answering the Call of her Soul and Opening Up To A Greater Power, to Surrender, Awakening to Deeper Soul Power, and Mastery of Her Consciousness.

Inspiring, original spiritual concepts include:

- Differences between spirituality and religion
- The five types of consciousness on the planet now
- The Elevator and the Spiral
- Soul Mates, Soul Contracts, Soul Agreements, Soul Groups, Karmic Relationships
- Past life connections to geographic locations
- Surrender and supreme separation from God
- Being conscious in an Unconscious World
- And more "*A-Ha!*" connections and breakthroughs for conscious living

The Modern Heroine's Journey of Consciousness brilliantly explains the gifts at every phase of spiritual growth and reveals how the inner journey is an awakening to more of oneself.

**The adventure continues! Book Three in
The Awakening Consciousness Series**

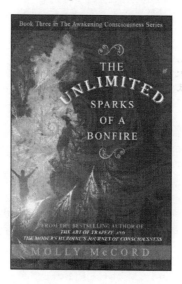

The Unlimited Sparks of a Bonfire

The grand journey of consciousness continues with an exciting travel adventure!

From the frostbite blizzards of Moscow and the warm tropical breezes of Hawaii, to an isolated dry barren desert in Africa, a quiet French village on the outskirts of civilization, and a bustling geisha house in Japan, get ready for an inspiring exploration of soul-shaping experiences!

The Unlimited Sparks of a Bonfire is filled with spiritual connections, passion, emotional depths, and unexpected wisdom to raise your consciousness and connect you more personally with greater Soul discovery.

More books by Molly McCord

Conscious Thoughts: Powerful Affirmations To Connect With Your Soul's Language

This evolutionary guide is a rare combination of modern situations, past life connections, and powerful affirmations that speak to your Soul with high vibrational energy!

Affirmations are conscious thoughts that can be amazingly effective when the root energy is identified. Discover how to heal unconscious patterns, move beyond repetitive lessons, and change your understanding around what is holding you back in life.

Plus, get to the heart of how affirmations work, why they support your spiritual growth, how to use them powerfully, what affirmations do NOT do, and six key tenets for maximum results.

The five short stories with past life connections and healing affirmations include :
- Reclaiming Your Personal Power
- Dealing With Shadow Feminine Energies
- Adult Bullying
- Your Body As Your Ally
- Roadblocks to Creative Expression and a Loving Partnership

Enjoy over 40 original affirmations for Forgiveness, Love, Career, Health, Trust, Creativity, Prosperity, Living Your Best Life, and more!

Conscious Messages:
Spiritual Wisdom and Inspirations for Awakening

A practical, uplifting collection of timeless wisdom about modern spiritual awakening.

From affirming that Where You Are Is Where You Need to Be and owning your personal truth, to cosmic perspectives on emotional energy, being in alignment with your intentions, and expanding beyond limiting belief systems, these 18 channeled messages provide you with simple, direct perspectives about stepping more fully into your soul's light. One to keep on your nightstand for joy, clarity, and empowerment!

WITH GRATITUDE

I HAVE A GROWING TRIBE. It is expansive and eclectic, covering miles and seas, but always close to my heart and dear to my daily joy. The following human members of my tribe have been invaluable in their love, support, friendship, insights, and laughter during this adventure:

To Mom, your encouragement and positive spirit lovingly carry me through life. Thank you for always knowing the best wisdom to share.

To Dad, thank you for providing your encouragement, deep intelligence, and supporting all travel adventures. I have more appreciation than a few sentences can express. Patricia, the first official published author I ever knew who has the tenacity, focus, and brilliance to write forever.

To T & J, my two favorite brothers who are each equipped with enough creative talent to captivate the world. You are wonderful men and I adore you.

To Trisha, thank you for being the perfect soul sister in Paris, and beyond. It was an honor to witness the beginning of your love story, my friend. Our paths will cross again soon on the same continent.

To *tous mes amis de Paris*, thank you for picnics in front of the Eiffel Tower, cheap wine and long conversations, after midnight walks through quiet *arrondissements*, daily *bisous*, dinner gatherings, and all of the travel adventures we packed into two years of one life.

To the spiritually gifted women who have been my beacons on this journey: Michele Morgan, Roz Eriksen, Pam Younghans, and Roe Regan. Divine blessings to each of you for sharing your gifts and ancient wisdom.

And to J, the man who wisely said to me within one of our first conversations, "You have to know the light *and* the dark." How gratifying to connect with a (tall, handsome, single) man who was already *there*. Your hilarious wit, deep intelligence, emotional maturity, and incredible strength continue to fortify me daily. Thank you for being my pot of gold at the end of this first rainbow. Now another rainbow begins with you.

ABOUT THE AUTHOR

MOLLY McCORD, M.A. IS a bestselling author, marketing expert, and modern spiritual teacher with no religious affiliations. Her debut memoir, *The Art of Trapeze: One Woman's Journey of Soaring, Surrendering, and Awakening*, hit #1 in 2 Amazon categories within 3 days.

The Art of Trapeze is the first book in her Awakening Consciousness Series, followed by *The Modern Heroine's Journey of Consciousness*, in which she integrates Joseph Campbell's hero's journey with spiritual growth. Molly released five books in 2013, including her contribution to the bestselling *The Thought That Changed My Life Forever* where she was published alongside such luminaries as Dr. Michael Bernard Beckwith, Dr. Joe Dispenza, and Dr. Bernie Siegel.

Often referred to as a Consciousness Catalyst, Molly's popular website, www.ConsciousCoolChic.com was nominated by Intent.com for Best Spirituality Website in 2011 and her' popular weekly radio show attracted over 70,000 downloads in the first year. She is the Founder and Director of **SpiritualityUniversity.com**.

Molly lives in Seattle, WA with her husband. She is probably laughing at Bill Murray's tweets as you read this.

A CONVERSATION WITH THE AUTHOR

Let's jump right in! What inspired you to write *The Art of Trapeze*?

I'm interested in offering people a deeper way to understand themselves as powerful individuals. *The Art of Trapeze* includes travel, adventure, love, and authenticity, but I also aspire to connect these themes with soul growth and spiritual perspectives to empower anyone who has questions about their purpose. I truly believe everyone is able to powerfully create their dreams—and we are always exactly where we need to be in our journeys.

Inspiration for *The Art of Trapeze* came from the fact that it is important to hear stories of people following their hearts and taking a risk. We all need those messages in our psyches because it brings us back to ourselves and what we can create in our lives. If anything is possible, what do you choose? What do you want your life to include? What calls to your soul and lifts you up?

What were the challenges (research, literary, psychological, logistical) in bringing it to life?

I started writing *The Art of Trapeze* in 2008 and it was 80% complete by 2009—but then I stalled out. I was stuck trying to figure out the last 20% of the story because there was still much more to say and I didn't want to cram it all together. In 2010, I was a semi-finalist in The Next Top Author competition, but even that exposure didn't bring about the solution I was looking for, so I let the book sit on my computer for a few years. I was hard on myself about it at times, but I learned to trust on deeper levels, to love myself through the process of discovery, and to stay committed to my writing ambitions. Then, in

2013, it hit me that the single book I originally planned was really a series. This realization was like a dam breaking open—in a good way!—and my inspiration took off in a whole new direction. I rewrote the whole book in four months, and it was definitely better than the first version. Then the second book, *The Modern Heroine's Journey of Consciousness*, came together easily, and the third book, *The Unlimited Sparks of a Bonfire*, unfolded in an even better way that I could have imagined. In all honesty, *Unlimited Sparks* is probably my favorite book in the series because it holds the deepest messages. But just like with children, maybe I shouldn't claim a favorite!

What was the hardest part of writing this book?

The hardest part was definitely stretching beyond my comfort zone as a writer and digging into more of my authentic self. I believe only confident people can be strong in their vulnerability, and that's where I write from: a place of self-love and strength. Numerous people have emailed me to share how they have had similar experiences and life events, and that's really the hallmark of writing – creating connections with people. As Maya Angelou said, "Human beings are more alike than we are unalike."

Do you ever get writer's block? What do you do?

Being creatively stuck comes with the territory of creation at times. Ultimately, I found writing had to be done on my terms; meaning, my writing schedule needed to meet up with natural inspiration. I've tried what has worked for other writers—write every day, make yourself sit at the computer and type anything, get up early and wait for inspiration to hit, etc.—and those practices never really produced much in the end for me. Instead, writing when I was inspired and "in the flow" brought about the best results and made the work literally effortless. When I am stuck and let the empty page sit and just be, eventually the words and ideas come flooding back in and the story takes off again. You can't get me away from the computer at that point! As writers and creators, we have to be very kind and gentle with ourselves as we authentically create, while also continually re-committing to our passion and showing up to do the work.

What did you learn from writing a memoir?

I believe that when we follow our passion, we continuously learn more about ourselves. Writing *The Art of Trapeze* filled me with incredible joy, temporary restraint, quiet moments of contemplation, and an unstoppable determination. Since it is a memoir, it forced me to become clearer about my messages and writing style and what I was willing to share. And obviously I was willing to share a lot, LOL! I also developed an even greater respect for some of my favorite memoir writers, such as Elizabeth Gilbert, and Cheryl Strayed, and other fellow spiritual seekers who love learning about their soul growth.

What tips do you have for aspiring writers? What have you learned along the way?

Open up and follow your voice! Allow yourself to express what you need to say first, and then go back and edit or revise later. As writers, we have to be open to being surprised by our own unexpected insights. Try not to over-plan the story or characters because you will have new possibilities as the chapters develop. Also, I recommend keeping a journal or note cards handy to jot down ideas and inspirations as they hit you. I've learned that they can quickly disappear and never be found again! I tend to get some of my best ideas while I'm driving, so I will keep paper and pen in the passenger seat, and write down ideas at red lights—not kidding!

Develop a strategy for dealing with your inner critic or self-doubt. Find your writing style and own it. Commit to yourself as a storyteller. Be gentle, kind, and compassionate to yourself as needed. Know that you are here to share what is uniquely yours, whether it is on paper or not, and you must not hold yourself back. You must commit to YOU. Our time on the planet can be spent doing whatever fills us with joy, and it is a great honor to explore and share our creative spirits. As Joseph Campbell said, "Follow your bliss!"—and to that I say, keep writing! The world is always hungry for more stories.

57448467R00181

Made in the USA
Middletown, DE
18 December 2017